21.00
80E

D0407832

PR
2992
.F 3
D 74
Dreher
Domination and defiance

DATE DUE

Laramie County Community College
Instructional Resources Center
Cheyenne, Wyoming 82001

DISCARD

Domination and Defiance

Domination and Defiance

FATHERS AND DAUGHTERS
IN SHAKESPEARE

DIANE ELIZABETH DREHER

THE UNIVERSITY PRESS OF KENTUCKY

DISCARD
LCCC LIBRARY

Copyright © 1986 by The University Press of Kentucky

Scholarly publisher for the Commonwealth, serving Bellarmine College,
Berea College, Centre College of Kentucky, Eastern Kentucky University,
The Filson Club, Georgetown College, Kentucky Historical Society,
Kentucky State University, Morehead State University, Murray State
University, Northern Kentucky University, Transylvania University,
University of Kentucky, University of Louisville, and Western Kentucky
University.

Editorial and Sales Offices: Lexington, Kentucky 40506-0024

LIBRARY OF CONGRESS CATALOGING IN PUBLICATION DATA

Dreher, Diane Elizabeth.
  Domination and defiance.

  Bibliography: p.
  Includes index.
  1. Shakespeare, William, 1564–1616—Characters—
Fathers. 2. Shakespeare, William, 1564–1616—Characters
—Daughters. 3. Fathers and daughters in literature.
I. Title.
PR2992.F3D74 1985   822.3'3   85-13482
ISBN 0-8131-1557-4

To my father, Colonel Frank H. Dreher,
a pioneer in aviation,
who has always challenged me to do my best.

Contents

Acknowledgments
ix

ONE *A Psychological Perspective*
1

TWO *The Renaissance Background*
16

THREE *The Paternal Role in Transition*
40

FOUR *Dominated Daughters*
76

FIVE *Defiant Daughters*
96

SIX *Androgynous Daughters*
115

SEVEN *Redemptive Love and Wisdom*
143

EIGHT *Beyond Domination and Defiance*
164

Notes
171

Bibliographical Note
191

Index
197

Acknowledgments

This study grew out of a 1979 MLA special session, "Domination and Defiance: The Love Between Fathers and Daughters in Shakespeare." To Paul Jorgensen, who introduced the panel and who taught me Shakespeare at UCLA, I owe a large debt of gratitude. I would also like to thank the other panelists, Lynda Boose and Janette Lewis, for their contributions. The many references to Lynda's research in this book are a tribute to her creative scholarship.

I am grateful to the outstanding scholars who have been my mentors in the field of Renaissance literature. Stanley Stewart, Paul Jorgensen, George Guffey, and Earl Miner have taught me by example what it means to be a scholar and a humanist. I would also like to thank Geneva Phillips for encouragement, inspiration, and support.

Many people have contributed their professional perspectives to this interdisciplinary study. Carol Witherell introduced me to developmental psychology. Helen Powell gave helpful advice on early psychologists. Lawrence Stone provided me with a wealth of information on marriage and the family during Shakespeare's time, both in his monumental book, *The Family, Sex, and Marriage in England, 1500–1800*, and at Princeton University during the summer of 1980. Conversations with Judy Dunbar and Fred Tollini, S.J., have deepened my knowledge of Shakespeare. Jan DeVore has given me new perspectives on personal development and holistic health. William Stover has offered helpful insights on politics, culture, and feminism, while John Vasconcellos has provided an inspiring example of holistic politics.

I would like to thank Santa Clara University for summer grants and sabbatical leave. I am grateful for the generous support of the Graves Foundation, which made my extensive background research in England possible. I would also like to thank Holly, John, and Barbara Christensen for opening their home to me in Richmond, Surrey, where I began writing this book.

Through the years, I have worked at several fine libraries. For my primary research, I am grateful to the staff of the British Library, the Firestone Library at Princeton, and the Huntington Library in San Marino, California, my academic retreat since the early days of graduate school. I would like to thank Virginia Renner and Mary Wright of the Huntington staff and my cousin Norma MacCaskey for providing my home away from home whenever I work at the Huntington. Most of my secondary research was done at the Orradre Library at Santa Clara, where Alice Whistler and Fred Isaac offered professional assistance and encouragement.

Preparing this book involved the cooperative support of many people. For typing the original manuscript, I would like to thank Margaret Wagnon; for word-processing assistance, Jo Anna Watt and Lathell North. I would also like to thank Charles T. Phipps, S.J., chairperson of the department of English, for his invaluable support. My colleagues have also been extremely helpful. Fred White introduced me to the mysteries of word processing; Dick Osberg and Mary Ann Aschauer offered valuable advice and encouragement.

Shakespeare's plays look beyond hierarchical competition toward a new, more cooperative paradigm that offers hope to a troubled world. Without the cooperative support of my own extended family of friends, I would not be myself and this book would not have been written. My father, Col. Frank H. Dreher; my mother, Mary Ann Dreher; and my brother, Frank Dreher, gave me my first example of loving family bonds. I am deeply grateful to Norma MacCaskey, Jerry Garrison, Gen and Lyle Farrow, William Sullivan, Jeff Capaccio, Peg McKinstry, Jan DeVore, William Barker, and Cory Wade for all they have shared of themselves. I am grateful to William James Stover, my partner in life, for his love and friendship and for respecting my autonomy, without which creative work is impossible. Finally, I would like to thank my students, for their enthusiasm, their questions, and for continuing to teach me about Shakespeare.

CHAPTER ONE

A Psychological Perspective

The father-daughter relationship figures largely in twenty-one of Shakespeare's plays, from the early *Two Gentlemen of Verona* to his last complete work, *The Tempest*. The father of two daughters himself, Shakespeare explored this relationship throughout his dramatic career; it appears as an integral element in comedies, tragedies, and romances. Shakespeare wrote in an age of transition, as Renaissance discoveries gradually transformed the world from medieval to modern, authoritarian to individual. In his portrayal of the father-daughter bond, he touched on a corresponding personal transition in the lives of parents and children. Repeatedly, his plays depict the father at middle life, reluctant to release his daughter into adulthood and face his own decline, while she stands at the threshold of adult commitment in marriage. The passionate conflicts, fears, and insecurities as each faces a crucial challenge of adulthood cast new light on questions of moral development, male and female sex roles, traditional and progressive social norms. As always, Shakespeare was far ahead of his time, anticipating the theories of Sigmund Freud, Carl Gustav Jung, Erik Erikson, and others on the drama of human development and our enduring quest for love and meaning.

Psychologists are only beginning to understand the deep significance of the father-daughter bond. Much of their research is devoted to mothers and sons, and in a 1979 study the author complains that there is no "substantive literature on fathers and daughters." Yet almost a century ago, Freud recognized the special nature of this relationship, stating that "the earliest affection of the girl-child is lavished on the father" and that the effects of this primal bond endure for life. As another author has recently observed, "at the heart of the father-daughter relationship lies the mystique of perfect love. For her, it is the great love of her independent life. For him, a daughter is, at last, a controllable female, one he can mold to his image of the ideal woman."[1]

Within our own time critics have increased our understanding of the father-daughter bond in Shakespeare. Carolyn Heilbrun discussed its psychological implications in her study of androgyny. Lynda Boose described the archetypal significance of the marriage ritual, which requires the father to release his daughter to another man. Studies of marriage and the family in Shakespeare have opened up a lively debate about Renaissance sex roles. Germaine Greer praised Shakespeare for supplying marriage with a new mythology of love and companionship. Irene Dash demonstrated that Shakespeare's daughters "challenge accepted patterns for women's behavior," defying their fathers "as well as the mores of their society." Juliet Dusinberre also maintained that Shakespeare's women challenge traditional sex roles, that "Shakespeare saw men and women as equal in a world which declared them unequal." Angela Pitt, however, has argued that Shakespeare's comic women "never go beyond the bounds of what an Elizabethan audience would have found acceptable," and tragic women such as Ophelia and Desdemona are destroyed by their deviation.[2]

Two anthologies, *The Woman's Part* and *Representing Shakespeare*, offer provocative new responses to these questions of sexual identity. Coppélia Kahn and David Sundelson examine Shakespeare's treatment of masculine identity from psychoanalytic and political perspectives. Linda Bamber posits opposing assumptions about female chastity in the two genres. Marjorie Garber offers a sensitive examination of adult identity, and Daniel Levinson describes Lear's midlife crisis.[3] No critical study, however, has fully explored the relationship of Shakespeare's fathers and daughters in its historical and developmental context.

My intention is to do just that: to examine this complex relationship by considering both its psychological tensions and the changing concepts of marriage and the family during Shakespeare's time. I will apply these insights to a detailed study of the characters themselves, demonstrating how each father-daughter pair undergoes an inevitable drama of domination and defiance, born of the clashing demands of youth and age, a developmental struggle as certain as the seasons themselves. Facing the specter of old age and death, the fathers must exchange the power of their manhood for a stark realization of the limits of their lives. Theirs is a bitter and stormy transition, a painful inner journey through autumnal decline into the wisdom of old age. Unwilling to face the crisis of middle life, most of Shakespeare's fathers cling desperately to their daughters, demanding that they remain obedient children to confirm their own illusions of masculine potency and control. At the same time, the daughters blossom into passionate young womanhood, their awakening sexual drives creating a powerful antithesis to their fathers' demands. Embracing the challenge of romantic love and adult commitment, most of these daughters cast aside childhood obedience and leave their grieving fathers far behind them. The result is a tempestuous confrontation between the bitter chill of life's winter and the ardor of young love, two conflicting currents that reveal our deepest hopes and fears. Through their archetypal enactment of this most compelling of human struggles, Shakespeare's fathers and daughters reveal to us our eternal drama of identity, of what it means to be a man or a woman in this world, providing us with images of what we have been and the promise of what we may become.

The concept of life as a series of passages, rediscovered in our own time, was not unknown to Shakespeare. Renaissance artists and writers recognized childhood as a stage distinctly separate from adulthood. Theologians portrayed life as a progressive pilgrimage to spiritual maturity. The ages of mankind were numbered from four to seven. Shakespeare gave expression to the latter in Jaques's celebrated speech in *As You Like It*. Recent writers have pointed out the parallel between Renaissance concepts of spiritual growth and present-day theories of psychological development. Piaget's work on cognitive development in early childhood was to some degree anticipated by Thomas Traherne. Jung wrote of Renaissance alchemy as a paradigm of individuation, the progressive development and integration of the self.[4]

Shakespeare depicts the father-daughter relationship in the midst of a difficult double transition. She stands on the brink of adulthood, he faces the crisis of middle life, and their individual drama is enacted against a backdrop of dynamic social change. Although it was commonplace in the Renaissance to describe society as a set of vertical layers and to uphold obedience to the status quo, several forces militated against this, producing an alternative world view that was progressive, dynamic, and developmental. The new discoveries—geographical, scientific, medical, and astronomical—undercut the credibility of the old system, daring people to seek adventure, innovation, even social mobility. Queen Elizabeth herself brilliantly disproved John Knox's contention that women were unfit to rule. She rewarded merit, knighting her principal pirate of the high seas, Sir Francis Drake, and making her master of the horse, Robert Dudley, the powerful Earl of Leicester.

Changes in religion were equally unsettling. The Puritans regarded life as a pilgrimage, emphasizing its developmental quality.[5] The Great Divorce and subsequent changes in the English church broke the hegemony of the prelates over individual souls. No more was religion simply submission to authority and regular reception of the sacraments from a priest one called father, a process that arrested moral development at the level of childhood obedience.[6] The Reformation placed the responsibility for salvation squarely upon the shoulders of the individual. Renaissance Protestants navigated a tortuous path through relativism in a quest for truth and commitment, seeking their own way through prayer, study, and introspection, the process described by John Donne in "Satyre III (On Religion)."

The gradual collapse of absolutism in science and religion together with the humanists' emphasis on reason and free will placed more weight on individual decision. While traditional writers upheld unquestioning obedience to authority, progressive writers described adulthood as a stage of personal responsibility and commitment. Adulthood is the focus of this study, as Shakespeare's fathers and daughters seek new definitions of what it means to be an adult. The daughters emerge from childhood to womanhood and their fathers experience the changing responsibilities of late adulthood. In a developmental crisis that is simultaneously personal and political, each pair undergoes a transition from one stage of life to another. Their relationships are determined by the way each responds to the challenge of change and growth.

Developmental psychologists have provided useful paradigms to explain this difficult passage. Jung conceived of life in four stages: childhood, youth, middle life, and old age. In Jungian terminology, Shakespeare's daughters are undergoing a process of psychic birth, which begins with the awakening sexuality of puberty. This period, with its volatile energies and new loyalties, is no less than a "psychic revolution," which explains the defiance of daughters such as Hermia, Jessica, and Desdemona. These young women are entering the period of youth, which reaches from puberty until thirty-five or forty, the marker of middle life, and the next portentous passage. There stand their fathers, who face the challenge of life in decline, the loss of their physical vigor and potency. They must learn the wisdom of individuation or suffer inconsolable loss and despair. Daniel Levinson, in *The Seasons of a Man's Life*, offers a similar progression: childhood and adolescence, from birth to twenty-two; early adulthood, from seventeen to forty-five; middle adulthood, from forty to sixty-five; and late adulthood, from sixty onward. He posits "a combined biological, psychological, and social basis" for this sequence, noting that Shakespeare wrote *King Lear* and *The Tempest* during his own midlife

[4]

crisis.[7] Erik Erikson divided life into eight stages, with a developmental lesson for each. The first four stages, basic trust, autonomy, initiative, and industry, develop a child's self worth, competence, and faith in life. In stage five, identity, the adolescent develops a dominant ego identity, adjusts to his or her sexuality, and learns fidelity in interaction with peers of the same sex. In stage six, intimacy, the young adult risks commitment in love, work, and friendship, forming lasting romantic bonds. Shakespeare's daughters are entering this stage. Stage seven, generativity, calls upon people at middle life to take part in the care and guidance of the next generation. Shakespeare's fathers are in this stage, looking toward the next. The shorter life span in Shakespeare's time would have eclipsed the time between the two final stages. Stage eight, integrity, is the challenge of late adulthood, when a person faces the end of life and searches for meaning. A maladjusted person faces death with fear and despair. Erikson also emphasized that each of these transitions recalls unresolved conflicts from earlier stages.[8]

For Shakespeare's fathers and daughters, the tensions of transition are multiplied. The daughters must break the emotional strings that tie them to childhood, defying paternal authority to assert emotional independence. Jungian analyst M. Esther Harding saw this as the principal task of young adulthood.[9] Although his traditional contemporaries upheld obedience to father or husband as the primary virtue of womanhood, Shakespeare's dynamic young women quite frequently declare their independence and assert their own wills.

Shakespeare's fathers are shocked and hurt by what they experience as personal rejection. Their developmental needs clash violently with those of their offspring. As the daughters demand more emotional freedom, their fathers express the increased rigidity and self-righteousness of middle life. Insecure and imbalanced, a father at this stage is often unsettled by neurosis. According to Jung, "he cannot part with his youth. He shrinks from the grey thoughts of approaching age, and, feeling the prospect before him unbearable, is always striving to look behind him."[10] In addition, Shakespeare's fathers and daughters are caught in a generational struggle between two conflicting paradigms: the fathers uphold traditional hierarchical order and patriarchal authority, while their daughters affirm the new progressive bonds of individual trust and cooperation. The clash reverberates on many levels: youth and age, female and male, oppressed and oppressor, progressive and traditional. At the heart of it all are two individuals caught in a life transition that threatens their security but offers immeasurable opportunities for personal growth.

Levinson points to the challenges and dangers of this passage: "at best [fathers and daughters] can form mutually satisfactory relationships that include some degree of loving, teaching, learning, supporting, working, and playing together. But this is not easy, and it is more the exception than the rule. If he continues to treat them as if they were small children, they may submit and fail to develop their own autonomy, or they may move away in defiance and contempt."[11]

Shakespeare's plays reflect this challenge. In the romances, a few fathers learn the wisdom of letting go, releasing their daughters into adulthood, but the majority are irascible tyrants, who hold onto their daughters all the more tightly as they squirm to be free of patriarchal domination. Daughters like Ophelia submit, failing to develop autonomy; the vast majority choose defiance, eloping like Desdemona, Hermia, and Jessica, affirming fidelity to romantic love like Imogen, or turning upon their fathers with the unbridled fury of Goneril and Regan. As Shakespeare portrays it, the midlife-adulthood crisis for fathers and daughters is always a stormy passage.

Male Development and the Crisis of Middle Life

Shakespeare's fathers must face the developmental tasks of midlife, giving up their youth while reconciling their inner conflicts in the process that Jung called individuation.[12] Men become more fully aware of mortality as their youthful vigor declines. In order to cope with this affront to their masculinity, they must seek a deeper, fuller sense of selfhood, becoming mentors to younger adults. Personally as well as politically, men do not relinquish power easily. The majority of Shakespeare's fathers face midlife with imperious assertions of their patriarchal prerogatives. Threatened by their daughters' growing independence and their own waning powers, they become domineering tyrants like Cymbeline or busybodies like Polonius. Psychoanalyst Karen Horney noted that "the neurotic striving for power" often appears in the guise of giving advice and managing other people's affairs,[13] all of which Polonius does to excess. Jung observed that "many parents . . . keep their children infantile because they themselves do not wish to grow old and give up their parental authority and power."[14] Daniel Levinson has found in the Faust legend "a classic portrayal of the man at mid-life making a last desperate effort to achieve omnipotence by selling his soul to the Devil." King Lear is caught squarely in this conflict: "He wants to give up power and to keep it.

He is unable to bestow his legacy and blessing upon his daughters because his paternal love is too tarnished by pride and narcissistic self-indulgence."[15]

Men who have reached midlife excessively identified with the traits our culture calls masculine regard any perceived weakness in themselves as feminine. Clinging to their image of masculine power, they deny such weakness in themselves and dominate others in whom they find it, often becoming misogynists or authoritarian personalities.[16] The challenge for these men is to see beyond the persona, their social façade, and to actualize the traits they have repressed. This means coming to terms with their own weakness, what Jung called the shadow, and the unconscious feminine potential within each man. Balancing polarities was very important for Jung. He found within every man an unconscious feminine soul or anima, within every woman a corresponding animus.[17] A primary task of adulthood is to reconcile these unconscious elements. For centuries male poets—Dante, Petrarch, Donne—have written eulogies to the anima, the inspiration that leads them to paradise. The younger man falls in love with this radiant image as Romeo did with Juliet. The older man comes to seek it within himself, developing the capacity for love and empathy that he has heretofore known only in women, gaining greater wholeness, wisdom, and inner peace.

Such is the journey of individuation for the successful man. Prospero comes to terms with both his anima (Miranda), and his shadow (Caliban), releasing his daughter into marriage and acknowledging "this thing of darkness" (V.i.275) as his own.[18] But many at midlife are torn by unresolved conflicts. The animas and the shadows of men who have repressed their emotions and sexuality are contaminated with each other. Women become for them the dangerous and threatening "other," temptresses who betray men with the lure of sexual desire.[19] Violent misogyny erupts in men like Othello and Leontes, an equally violent fear in Pericles, the intensity of their negative emotions equivalent to their own inner insecurity. Neurotic adults at this stage regress to childhood fantasies. Nowhere is this more apparent than in King Lear, whose behavior reflects "an infantile disposition . . . demanding love and immediate reward for his feelings."[20] He identifies with his daughters, whom he has made surrogate mothers. Lear is narcissistic and egocentric. He demands effusive flattery as well as maternal love, and he judges others "according to the admiration or flattery he receives from them."[21]

Lear asks his daughters, "Which of you shall we say doth love us most?" (I.i.52). The love between fathers and daughters in Shakespeare runs the gamut from selfishness to sacrifice. As Horney noted, the word *love* "may cover parasitic expectations on the part of a person who feels too weak or too empty to live his own life. . . . It may cover a desire to exploit the partner, to gain through his success, prestige, and power." In other contexts, it may mean the desire to possess or dominate.[22] All these possibilities characterize the love of fathers and daughters. The younger, weaker daughter may cling for strength to her father or surrogate fathers. A man may bolster his flagging self-esteem by dominating his wife or daughter. Essentially, we can relate to others as persons, respecting their needs, or use them as objects. Lloyd deMause's description of the father-child interaction readily distinguishes empathy from exploitation: "1) He can use the child as a vehicle for projection of the contents of his own unconscious (projective reaction); 2) . . . as a substitute for an adult figure important in his own childhood (reversal reaction); or 3) he can empathize with the child's needs and act to satisfy them (empathic reaction)."[23] For anima-absorbed fathers like Leonato or like the infantile Lear, who dreams of Cordelia's "kind nursery" (I.i.126), the choice is obvious. Only a rare father in Shakespeare chooses the third possibility. Most treat their daughters as objects. To a great extent, as we shall see in the next chapter, their behavior was conditioned by the traditional mores of the time. But Shakespeare's wisdom outdistanced that of his contemporaries. He realized a truth expressed by Erich Fromm, that "without respect for and knowledge of the beloved person, love deteriorates into domination and possessiveness."[24] Possessive paternal love, far from preserving the love of the daughter, produces a recurrent drama of domination and defiance.

Possessive fathers, by far the most common in Shakespeare, are motivated by several factors. They refuse to admit that their daughters have grown up, driven either by a fear of their own approaching old age or by what must be seen as a sadistic urge to dominate. These fathers try to prevent their daughters' marriages or, failing that, match them with men they cannot love. Jung wrote of one such father, who insisted that his daughter marry a deformed, retarded neighbor: "he wanted to marry [her] to this brutish creature . . . to keep her with him and make her his slave forever." This, he felt is "but a crass exaggeration of what is done by thousands of so-called respectable educated . . . fathers who criticize every sign of emotional independence in their children, who fondle their daughters with ill-concealed eroticism and tyrannize over their feelings."[25] Cymbeline's attempt to marry Imogen to the brutish Cloten would put him into this category, along with the familiar *senex iratus* fathers of the comedies.

A mercenary father sees his daughter as a personal possession and determines to marry her at a profit, as do Polonius and Baptista Minola. This unfortunate attitude was subtly reinforced by many traditional handbooks of the Renaissance. Fathers in Shakespeare are often egocentric, perceiving their daughters as parts of themselves, projections of their own animas. A man is naturally reluctant to part with what he regards as an intimate part of himself. Lear agonizes at losing Cordelia, the only person he has ever loved. The problem of egocentricity dominates many comedies and tragedies until its ultimate resolution in the romances.

Fathers in Shakespeare often sound like jealous lovers, their feelings for their daughters intimately tied up with their own sexuality. Psychologist Harry Stack Sullivan pointed out that "if the father's sexual drive is powerful, he may suspect all boys of 'crude sexual motives' and adopt a 'watchdog' attitude toward his daughter's activities."[26] In such a way Polonius suspects Hamlet of crude, animal sexuality. Suzanne Fields adds that "Many men cannot outgrow the madonna-whore image of women. His desperate need to control his daughter, to keep her a virgin, was the only way he could manage not to lust for her himself."[27] This erotic element surfaces as overprotection in fathers throughout the plays. Like Lear, many fathers apparently want their daughters to nurture them, to become surrogate mothers. According to psychoanalyst Helene Deutsch, this is especially true in households in which the wife is dead and most often "with the third daughter, especially if she is also the youngest."[28]

The love between fathers and daughters inevitably calls up the question of incest, when parental love degenerates into perversion. Incest damages our primary bonds of trust, and reduces the parent-child relationship to lust and exploitation. In feminist studies incest has been called the father's initiation of his child into prostitution, a paradigm of female sexual victimization in patriarchal society.[29] Incest is one of the earliest crimes, ranked along with witchcraft and bestiality as an offense that rendered a person unclean. During Shakespeare's time offenders were judged in a trial by ordeal before a priest. Punishments ranged from public whippings to death.[30]

Father-daughter incest appears throughout history. Saint Dympha, who became a patron saint of the mentally ill in the thirteenth century, was a Christian princess and, after her mother's death, the object of her father's lust. She fled, but her father followed and beheaded her.[31] Plutarch's *Lives* recounts the marriage of the Persian emperor Artaxerxes to his own daughter as well as many cases of incest and perversion in the late Roman Empire. The Renaissance was not without its own examples. The notorious Roderigo Borgia,

Pope Alexander VI, committed incest with his daughter Lucretia, who also slept with her brother Cesare in violation of all family bonds. Pope John XXII was reputedly removed from his pontificate for incest, and in Shakespeare's own time (1594) there was the scandalous case of the Cenci. Beatrice Cenci, raped by her father, murdered him with the help of her stepmother and brother and was later beheaded.[32] Such incidents undoubtedly inspired the lurid sensationalism of many Jacobean dramas. Anthropologists Lionel Tiger and Robin Fox called father-daughter incest "the most common of all incestuous encounters," blatant evidence of fathers' desire to dominate their daughters.[33]

Incest represents humanity's primal urges gone awry. It occurs in all classes, all races, among people of both high and low intelligence, and its frequency is astounding.[34] Early in his career, Freud cited father-daughter incest as a frequent cause of hysteria among women. But this theory threatened the foundations of patriarchy and he retracted it, explaining his patients' accounts of incest as fantasies, which became part of his theory of early childhood sexuality. Incest, for Freud, was primarily "a strong inclination in the unconscious" frustrated by an equally strong taboo.[35] Ironically, research has confirmed Freud's earlier findings; father-daughter incest is not a childhood fantasy but an ugly reality.

Statistical profiles made during the 1970s of incestuous fathers and daughters correspond to many of Shakespeare's characters. He depicted only one case of actual incest, that of Antiochus in *Pericles*, but the proclivities are obviously there. Incest generally occurs when daughters enter puberty and their fathers middle life.[36] Mothers are either ill or absent, unavailable for sexual relations with their husbands.[37] Incestuous fathers suffer from weak self-images, although they may be considered successful in their careers. Deprived of adequate mothering in childhood, these men grow up with a sense of deprivation, low self-esteem, and a "smoldering hostility toward women." Still emotionally infantile, they expect to be mothered by their wives, and, failing that, they turn to their daughters.[38] Uncomfortable with their sexuality, men who cannot deal with adult women dominate their daughters, becoming authoritarian "family tyrants." They are jealous and possessive, even before the actual incest begins, seeking to control their daughters' lives and keep them away from young men.[39] From their daughters, they demand all the love and nurturing they have missed. Still a child herself, the daughter becomes "the source of all the father's infantile longings for nurturance and care . . . the idealized childhood bride or sweetheart . . . the all-good, all-giving

[10]

mother."[40] Understandably, most daughters fail to fulfill their fathers' expectations and become victims of their wrath. The emotions that may be unleashed in the father-daughter relationship are intense, primal, volcanic.

This pathological paternal love severely damages the daughter. During the adolescent crisis of identity, the period when she is least sure of herself and needs adult guidance, her father uses her to satisfy his own emotional and sexual needs. When she should be forming bonds of love outside the family, she is arrested in her emotional growth. According to Jung, psychological damage occurs even in father-daughter relationships that are not overtly incestuous.[41] Masters and Johnson call this emotional dependency the father-daughter syndrome or "pseudo incest."[42] Herman and Hirschman conclude that "for every family in which incest is consummated, there are undoubtedly hundreds with essentially similar, if less extreme, psychological dynamics."[43] This pseudo incest grows out of traditional family patterns. Deprived of initiative in patriarchal cultures, women remain children emotionally. Like Cordelia and Ophelia, "grown women . . . return home to serve and care for their fathers or let them interfere in their personal affairs";[44] like Desdemona, they transfer their obedience to father surrogates. Patriarchal norms allow women only two choices in life: domination by father figures or defiance and loss of love. These women learn how to please men, but know nothing about pleasing themselves. Yet such repressed and imbalanced women have become models of traditional femininity.

Whether father-daughter incest or father-daughter syndrome, Shakespeare consistently found patriarchal domination of women unhealthy and condemned it by the logic of his plays. Daughters are liberated by their defiance or suffocate within traditional role expectations that reduce them to objects. Possessive fathers lose their daughters to love or madness, often finding it difficult to differentiate. Only in the romances do fathers find their own feminine principle, the capacity for love and caring, releasing their daughters to adult life.

Female Development and the Crisis of Intimacy

The profound influence that a father has on his daughter's emotional development has been established in our time. "Her father's imprint marks a woman's identity for all time—her sense of self, her work, her love relationships."[45] He is the first man in her life, and as early as the age of six months, a daughter recognizes his body and voice.[46] By his actions and approval, he reinforces her femininity. In varying degrees, he also prepares her for autonomy and competence.[47] The personification of social norms, he is her first judge and authority, and early in life she learns to please her father.

Within traditional societies fathers perpetuate the patriarchal hierarchy, in which men lead and women serve. Psychoanalysts say that the father inhibits the daughter's active drive, transforming her aggressive instincts into masochism. She earns her reward by pleasing others, not by her own active endeavor, and forever after "her sexual love is mingled with the desire to be dominated."[48] Yet fathers can also reinforce their daughters for competence. The intellectual development of daughters has been linked to supportive fathers.[49] Some women, in the absence of male heirs, are raised like sons by their fathers and excel in professional life. Maria Goeppert-Mayer, who won the 1963 Nobel Prize in physics, was the only child of a highly educated family. She went on long hikes with her father, who encouraged her to explore, to take chances, and to shun traditional feminine passivity.[50] Anna Freud became her father's intellectual heir, never marrying but devoting herself to psychoanalysis. Shakespeare's Helena in *All's Well* is such a daughter. Educated by her physician father, she cures the king with her medical skills. But psychological research has revealed the problems faced by such exceptional women: their career achievements often outdistance their success with men. "Women whose fathers treat them as sons . . . often grow up with a distorted perception of the female nature," relating to men "with difficulty because they have missed a crucial stage in their feminine development."[51] Helena's courage and ingenuity, admirable in a man, only repel the immature Bertram she has chosen to love.

Fathers can easily undermine their daughters' mental health. Young women raised with no rights of their own, conditioned only to please their parents, can become severely disturbed, narcissistic neurotics.[52] Research has correlated schizophrenic young women with rigid, authoritarian fathers who refuse to acknowledge their daughters' autonomy.[53] Such is the relationship of Polonius with Ophelia, who, understandably, goes mad. Children may also be driven to unconscious extremes to compensate for parental excess.[54] This is one explanation for the miserly Shylock and his extravagant daughter Jessica.

The father-daughter relationship unconsciously influences a young woman's choice of a husband. Even if she hates her father, she may find herself choosing a mate of similar personality, so strong is her father's imprint.[55]

Daughters deprived of essential interaction with fathers in their formative years have difficulty dealing with men. They are prone to inappropriate behavior, shyness, defensiveness, or excessive assertiveness.[56] Among Shakespeare's fatherless daughters, Beatrice in *Much Ado* and Olivia in *Twelfth Night*, are defensive and hesitant to commit themselves to men. Olivia hides behind her veil and Beatrice creates a brilliant, witty smoke screen to conceal her affection for Benedict.

Some daughters cannot leave their fathers for more adult commitments. Freud attributed this to hysterical fantasies, while Jung called such behavior regressive, referring to "all those young girls who suddenly become hysterically ill the moment they have to decide whether to get engaged or not." The crisis of intimacy, as the young woman stands on the brink of adulthood, requires her to choose between past and future, childhood and adulthood, father and husband. Unequal to the challenge, many young women fall back into childhood in what Jung called "an abnormal and pathological phenomenon [in which] the libido remains . . . glued to the family."[57] Most of Shakespeare's daughters make this transition successfully. A few, such as Ophelia, Hero, and Desdemona, are arrested in their emotional growth, clinging to childhood loyalties or traditional role behavior in which women remain childish and submissive.

Arrested emotional development reveals itself in many ways. Jung described one neurotic young woman who criticized her husband continually for not measuring up to her father.[58] Feminists have observed that even when a woman detaches herself from her father, her behavior often remains that of a child. She chooses a father-surrogate to love and obey.[59] In the traditional marriage of a young woman and an older man, her husband becomes another father, the marriage no transition but transference. Harry Stack Sullivan noted the frequency of marriages in which "the 'ultrafeminine' child-wife of surviving childhood sentiment for the father [is] married to the overmasculine doubter of his potency."[60] The marriage of Desdemona, whose "heart's subdu'd / Even to the very quality of my lord" (I.iii.251-52) and Othello, an older man inwardly wracked by insecurity and self doubts, certainly fits this pattern.

Desdemona's character demonstrates how the traditional feminine role reinforces masochism and neurotic self-effacement. The neurotic has an idealized self-image, composed of "lovable qualities, such as unselfishness, goodness, generosity, humility, saintliness, nobility, sympathy. Helplessness, suffering, and martyrdom are also secondarily glorified." Her life revolves around those she loves, and doing anything for herself is seen as "selfish." She is unable to recognize, let alone act on, her own desires.[61] Extreme masochism renders people helpless and unable to defend themselves. The following description applies to Desdemona as well as legions of battered wives: "the masochistic person feels [she] cannot do anything on [her] own, and expects to receive everything from the partner: love, success, prestige, care, protection. . . . [Her masochism] may exclude from awareness the fact that the partner is not and never will be the appropriate person to fulfill [her] expectations. . . . Usually [she] has the same attitude toward fate in general: [she] feels a helpless toy in the hands of fate."[62] Deprived of healthy self-esteem, idolizing their men, such women lack the assertiveness needed for self-defense. In the face of danger, they remain passive, letting destructive forces take their course and affirming a self-image that glorifies weakness and suffering as the ultimate proof of nobility. Sabotaged by an unhealthy ideal, these women become accomplices in their own destruction.

As we shall see, Shakespeare upheld a far different standard of womanhood. While tragic daughters are often sacrificed to traditional ideals of feminine passivity—Desdemona, Ophelia, and Cordelia failing to make the transition to healthy adulthood—his comic daughters offer an alternative. They reject dependence on fathers or surrogate fathers to affirm the animus, or masculine principle within. The animus is usually repressed by traditional conditioning and projected by a woman upon the man she loves, who becomes her soul's image. In individuation, however, women turn from external authority and become self-reliant, the animus giving them a capacity for reflection, deliberation, and self-knowledge, as well as assertiveness and initiative.[63] Such women become leaders, achievers, problem solvers, like Viola, Rosalind, and Portia, the dynamic women of the comedies. Actualizing the animus frees women from slavish submission to authority, making them examples of "principled independence."[64]

The conflicting tensions in Shakespeare's father-daughter relationships are resolved in comedy, exploded in tragedy, transcended in romance. The comic father is a tyrannical *senex iratus*, a possessive, ranting old man who refuses to let his daughter marry the man she loves, forcing the young lovers to undergo a trial by ordeal. The daughters assert themselves, often in doublet and hose, moving from the filial obedience of dutiful girls to more adult commitments. Tragedy offers a closer view of the discordant elements in this relationship, focusing upon the pain of the fathers as they lose their daughters to other men. Leonato and Shylock in the dark comedies, Brabantio, and ultimately Lear himself embody the agony of fathers tormented by their daughters' rejection or betrayal. In the romances, discord is transformed, tragedy transcended by a newfound harmony in the human family. Daughters are lost, then found, redeeming their fathers in the process. In his last complete play, *The Tempest*, Shakespeare resolves the father's conflict in Prospero, whose personal loss and years of hardship on the island have given him the strength and wisdom to release Miranda to the man she loves. Unlike the other fathers, Prospero sees his daughter's development in a moral vision far wider than the scope of his own ego.

But these are at best generalizations. In order to convey the depth and complexity of this most significant relationship in Shakespeare, I shall examine the fathers and daughters individually, drawing upon developmental psychology and Renaissance moral philosophy.

CHAPTER TWO

The Renaissance Background

During Shakespeare's time, attitudes about women and the family were in transition. Traditional sources defined love as obedience in a woman's relationship with her father or husband, while in progressive discussions companionship in marriage was emphasized, and the wife was called a friend and helpmeet. Although in Shakespeare's plays he upheld order and degree in the political sphere, he presented more progressive views of women and marriage. A consideration of Shakespeare's historical background will help us understand both the condition of women at the time and the profound cultural significance of the father-daughter relationship.

The Traditional View: Hierarchical Obedience

In the traditional Renaissance world order, love and obedience to social superiors constituted obedience to God. Love in this context was not a passion, but a duty. Woman's life was a continuous lesson in submission. She was to conform patiently and silently to the will of her father and, later, to that of her husband, accepting commands, correction, even physical abuse, with sweetness and humility. She demonstrated the ultimate filial obedience by accepting the husband her father selected for her, transferring her allegiance from one father figure to another. Juan Luis Vives, writing in 1524, concluded, "yet the woman is as daughter unto her husbande, and of nature more weaker. And therefore she nedeth his ayde and succour."[1] Fragile, docile, and submissive, the ideal woman would never approach, let alone achieve, psychological adulthood, confronting moral dilemmas and developing her own value system. As we shall see, Shakespeare's lively and independent women of the comedies—Rosalind, Beatrice, and Portia—present a dramatic contrast to this static model of feminine perfection.

Men and women were "like two birds . . . the Cocke flieth abroad to bring in, the Dam sitteth upon the nest to keepe al at home. So God hath made the man to travaile abroade, and the woman to keepe home" wrote Henrie Smith in 1591.[2] Man has traditionally been defined by his career and his place in society; woman, according to whose daughter, wife, or mother she was. There have been, of course, exceptions. Mary Sidney, Countess of Pembroke (sister of Sir Philip Sidney) was an influential patron of the arts. Magdalen Herbert (mother of George Herbert) was an inspiration to many and a friend of John Donne. But would their accomplishments have come to light without the famous men in their lives? In the annals of literary history no female equivalents exist for Ben Jonson and William Shakespeare, talented men who forged their own careers without money or family connections.

Shakespeare spent nearly all his adult life during the reign of the exceptional Elizabeth I, who could not have failed to influence his view of women. She declared herself "married to her people" in defiance of advisors who urged her to marry and produce an heir. Fervently, she proclaimed her public career as her identity and shunned the traditional role of wife. She inherited her throne from her father, but held it for a lifetime with her own strong mind and will. Elizabeth saw herself as a Renaissance prince. Indomitable, indefatigable, endowed with her mother's subtlety and her father's intellect—she was fluent in seven languages, including Latin and Greek—she lived to make England a world power, scoffing at the traditional feminine role, the "strong idea in the world that a woman cannot live unless she is married."[3]

But Elizabeth was an exception to this rule, if not to all the rules. The average Renaissance woman found her vocation in marriage, a life of cooking, cleaning, bearing children, assisting her husband, and managing a busy household. The typical wife would spin, weave, and sew, making all the family clothes. She baked the bread, brewed the family beer, and put away food for the winter: making jellies, conserves, and pickles; curing bacon, hams, and salt meat; storing apples and root vegetables. She managed the family dairy, making butter and cheese, and looked after the poultry, saving feathers for mattresses and pillows. She did the wash, making her own soap and rush candles. In her garden she grew vegetables for the family table, herbs for seasoning and home remedies. Proficient in herbal medicine, she tended the illnesses of husband, children, and servants. Often she supervised servants and apprentices as well as her own children. After instructing the children, hearing their daily prayers, and seeing to her other duties, she did elaborate needlework in her spare time.[4] Her hands were never idle. Gervase Markham admitted that it took a special kind of woman to do all the tasks expected of her: "Our English Houswife must be of chaste thought, stout courage, patient, untyard, watchfull, diligent, witty, pleasant, constant in friendship, full of good Neighbourhood, wise in Discourse, but not frequent therein . . . and generally skillfull in the worthy knowledge which do belong to her vocation."[5]

Although maintaining a household required considerable energy and ingenuity, women were dismissed in conservative handbooks as weak and passive, unable to make their own decisions. William Gouge equated wives with children and servants "because God hath made them all inferiours."[6] Woman's first law was obedience. Like an obedient child, a wife dropped her housework to come at her husband's command. She signed her letters "your faithful and obedient wife" and "your sister to command."[7] Perceived as inferior to men through a combination of biblical tradition, rudimentary biology, and real economic oppression, traditional women spent their entire lives in submission to male authority figures. Thomas Heywood put it succinctly: "Let men obey the Lawes, and women their Husbands."[8]

Contemporary treatises emphasized woman's weakness. John Knox argued that women, naturally weak in both mind and body, were unfit to rule.[9] Thomas Heywood explained that Eve was taken from the left side of Adam because women are the weaker sex, offering some novel gynecological evidence: "as the left side is the weakest, so the woman made from thence, is the weaker vessell. Also all male children are conceived in the right side, and females in the left."[10] The theory of correspondences, that basis of all Renaissance thought, was summoned to justify woman's inferior position. The family was seen as a miniature kingdom, and as civil harmony depended upon obedience to princes and magistrates, so domestic harmony was contingent upon obedience to the presiding paterfamilias. "A familie is a little church, and a little commonwealth" wrote William Gouge, urging wives to submit themselves to their husbands as a model of good government. Referring to anatomy, both Gouge and Thomas Gataker argued that a wife must submit herself as the body submits itself to the head, the seat of all reason and judgment. This brings up the proverbial non sequitur that reason is masculine and the flesh feminine, although all human beings may lay claim to both. "As a head is more excellent than the body, and placed above it, so is an husband to his wife," Gouge affirmed in a familiar commonplace.[11] Correspondences were drawn from government, anatomy, and religion to reinforce the case for male dominance.

One troublesome correspondence equated marriage with the relationship of Christ and his church. Myles Coverdale wrote that "like as the church is in subjection to Christ, so let the wemen be in subjection to their husbands in all things." William Gouge concurred, quoting Ephesians 5.22: "Wives submit yourselves unto your owne husbands, as unto the Lord."[12] The correspondence may have worked in traditional circles, but to more skeptical minds, the suggestion is certainly excessive, paralleling the husband to Jesus Christ.

Questions arise about the extent of such wifely obedience. What would happen, for example, if a noble woman married a man beneath her station, opposing the hierarchy of marriage to the class structure? Or—probably the more common instance—what if a wise and virtuous woman were married to a dissolute man? Was she still expected to obey him? Shakespeare himself twice depicted the latter instance. At the conclusion of *Measure for Measure*, the long-suffering Marianna claims as her husband the degenerate Angelo. *All's Well That Ends Well* concludes with a humiliated Bertram swearing to love Helena "dearly, ever, ever dearly" (V.iii.317) Both men have betrayed their would-be spouses and sought to quench their lust in the arms of other women. Both were tricked into bedding with their wives. These dark comedies leave us with an unsatisfactory, perhaps even bitterly satiric view of marriage when it lacks an equal exchange of love.

But what of Shakespeare's contemporaries? Many apparently saw no problem in such a mismatch. Whether her husband held lower rank or was an outright scoundrel, a wife was expected to obey him. According to William Gouge, in the first instance the marriage relationship overruled the class structure: "In giving her selfe to be his wife, and taking him to be her husband, she advanceth him above her selfe, and subjecteth her selfe to him." In the second, pity the poor woman. "If a man of lewd and beastly conditions, as a drunkard, a glutton, a profane swaggerer, an impious swearer, and blasphemer be maried to a wise, sober, religious Matron. . . . The evill qualitie and disposition of his heart and life, doth not deprive a man of that civill honour which God hath given unto him. Though a husband in regard of evill qualities may carrie the Image of the devill, yet in regard of his place and office he beareth the Image of God."[13]

What was the effect of such oppressive propaganda on women's personalities? In traditional handbooks a woman's personal development is subordinated to her social position. Such books upheld a model of extreme compliance, obedience, and submission to the needs of others, behavior which would be considered a serious neurosis in any adult of today. While in the

Renaissance men were praised for noble deeds and accomplishments—active virtues—women won praise for passivity, behavior for which their male counterparts would be called lazy or cowardly. Modesty and bashfulness, silence and patience were considered admirable qualities in women: all virtues of restraint, not active endeavor. Virginity was seen as one of woman's greatest treasures. But like youth and beauty, it was a physical condition, not an accomplishment. Few men in the Renaissance won praise for virginity.

The traditional marriage came uncomfortably close to idolatry. According to Gouge, a woman was to approach her husband with "an inward wive-like feare." She was to speak only when meet, addressing him with docile submission and reverential awe, "such a subjection as may stand with her subjection to Christ." For Gataker, as well, a woman was expected to fear her husband "like the *feare* that the godly beare unto God . . . desire to do every thing so as may please . . . and give him contentment, and avoid whatsoever may displease him, or minister discontentment unto him."[14] The good wife apparently lived in a continuous state of anxiety, solicitous to please her lord and fearful of his displeasure.

If her husband misbehaved or reproached her unjustly, a wife's only recourse was the patience of Griselda. Gervase Markham maintained that a wife must never become angry with her husband, even if he mistreated her: "she shall shun all violence of rage, passion, and humour, coveting less to direct than to be directed, appearing ever unto him pleasant, amiable, and delightfull." Gataker counseled patience even when "the husband should chance to blame and finde fault without cause." For a wronged wife, Heywood counseled "the onely remedy for injuries is to study how to forget them." She was to remain marble constant, a perfect pattern of patience. "For a wife to beare with the weakenesse and unperfections of her husband, is the true character of a wise and vertuous woman."[15] Such was the behavior of Katharine of Aragon when cast aside by Henry VIII, but her patient suffering failed to win him back. Somehow, a wife's patience was expected to change her husband—perhaps by making him prostrate with guilt by her long-suffering obedience. This was the traditional model. Quiet, chaste, modest, patient, obedient, and often long-suffering, the ideal woman bore her subjugation and misfortunes with stoic grace, never raising her voice or questioning the rules that made her a willing servant to the men in her world.

According to traditional mores, a woman owed her father, and later her husband, a lifetime of obedience. Like Desdemona, she was expected to be "a maiden never bold; / Of spirit so still and quiet, that her motion / Blush'd at herself" (*Othello* I.iii.94–96). But Desdemona and many other daughters in Shakespeare defied this tradition. Their independent spirits are all the more remarkable when contrasted with the dominant values of the time. As daughters, society expected them to be doubly obedient: first as females, then as children.

Within the Renaissance hierarchy, some were born to serve and others to rule. This was apparent in the prevailing class system, under which members of the lower classes looked to the aristocracy for leadership. The entire society was conceived as an interlocking succession of social strata, each level looking up in obedience to the authority above: children to parents, wives to husbands, men to magistrates, and through them up to God. Thomas Gataker envisioned all individuals, "severall persons in their severall estates, as they are inferiours or superiours, tyed by naturall or civil bonds either to other," and Robert Pricke saw all human society united by obedience to parents and superiors: "It upholdeth, and continueth all those estates, degrees, and orders, whereby the societie or fellowship of man is, as it were, by certaine joynts and sinewes, joyned and knit together." Until the Great Divorce in 1533, the English church had been another such pyramid of hierarchical authority, and so it remained when monarch replaced pope as head of the English church, maintaining the order of bishops and priests while unsettling a few minds about religious orthodoxy. The world, we are told repeatedly, was conceived as a great chain of being with all creation in ascending order reaching up to God.[16]

In this vision of hierarchical order, children saw obedience to their parents as part of the divine plan. They were repeatedly reminded of the fifth commandment: "Honor thy Father and thy Mother." Filial obedience had been divinely decreed, and Anglican homilies admonished churchgoers that disobedience was the oldest and most grievous of sins. Born through their parents' flesh, children were considered their parents' property. John Stockwood explained that "children are worthie to be reckoned among the goodes and substance of their fathers" and Thomas Gataker wrote that they "are part of their parents, because they come out of their bowels." The notion of children as property, bourgeois and inhumane as it may seem today, was deeply imbedded in Renaissance thought. Children were their parents' goods, to be used as they saw fit, and owed them lifelong obedience for begetting them: "Children are not free & at their own libertie, but by the lawes both of God and man tied and bound unto the subjection of their fathers."[17]

The equation was often made between children and servants. Both were economically dependent upon their masters, both expected to serve and obey. But for children, the bond was more than economic. They were expected to kneel and ask for their parents' blessing every night, to bear parental discipline with patience and humility, even when they were punished wrongfully.[18] Children were expected to obey unconditionally even if wiser than their parents, something Cordelia cannot do in the first scene of *King Lear*, when her father asks for a ridiculous vow of love. For strict traditionalists, filial obedience was unrelated to individual intelligence or ability; it was part of a hierarchy ordained by God. As Stockwood emphasized: "there are many children found sometimes far to exceed their fathers in wit and in wisedome, yea and in al other giftes both of mind & body, yet is this no good reason that they should take upon them their fathers authoritie. The wife may not therfore be a maister, because she hath more knowledge sometimes then her husband, but she must obey, & the husbande is to rule, because that God hath willed that it should bee so."[19] Tradition exalted obedience beyond reason.

Bartholomew Batty's description of the love children owed their parents would probably have contented even King Lear: "children shall truely love their parentes with all their hearte and minde, they shall give unto them all high dignitie and reverence: they shall so esteeme of them, as that no treasure in the world ought to bee more deare and precious unto them."[20] The conflict at the beginning of *King Lear* is intensified by a paradigm shift in which a highly traditional older generation is challenged by a generation of realists. Lear, Gloucester, and Kent cling to the old hierarchical order, the first two in their assumptions about children's duty and Kent in dutifully following his master throughout the play. The coldly pragmatic Goneril, Regan, and Edmund manipulate their fathers by mouthing traditional clichés and flattery. A different kind of realist, Cordelia alienates Lear by speaking plain truth but later redeems him with her love.

The proper filial attitude, according to traditionalists, was fear mixed with love, a reverential awe. In almost every respect, this parent-child relationship coincides with what modern psychologists have described as an authoritarian family structure, an atmosphere of strict obedience in which children feel for their parents "fear, respect, covert hostility, and dependence, with only the most modest admixture of affection." Such was the experience of Lady Jane Grey: "For when I am in presence either of father or mother, whether I speake, keepe silence, sit, stand, or go, eate, drinke, be merie, or sad, be sowyng, plaiying, dauncing, or doing anie thing els, I must do it, as it were, in such weight, measure, and number, even so perfitelie, as God made the worlde, or else I am so sharplie taunted, so cruellie threatened . . . that I thinke myselfe in hell."[21]

Conditioned by the concepts of original sin and natural depravity, traditional parents endeavored to "break the will" of their children, so "whip the offending Adam" out of them that they might grow up to become civilized members of society. Children were trained like hawks and broken like horses, according to the guidebooks of the time. Shakespeare used such taming metaphors satirically for the courtship in *The Taming of the Shrew*, but many of his contemporaries considered strict discipline of wives and children essential, with beating an important part of their training. Parental discipline was supposed to be administered wisely and moderately, so as not to injure or maim the child. Batty warned parents not to beat their children about the head, a practice which produces "so many deafe, blockishe, foolish, bleere-eyed, and oftentimes madde children." They were to "observe and keepe the golden meane, least that they amaze their children with too much threatening, discourage them with their too sharpe and bitter reproaches: or with their rigor and crueltie to kill and murder them."[22] Yet the many admonitions against excessive beating indicate that abuse of wives and children was a common practice.

Daughters were carefully watched, removed from temptation, and kept busy to avoid the danger of idleness. Parents sought to protect their reputations and keep them from the "feminine" sin of vanity. Handbooks of the time reflect an underlying concern that if daughters were not carefully trained and chaperoned, they might prefer to become something other than perfect Renaissance women.

Batty counseled, "Mothers, take upon you the charge of your daughters . . . looke to them carefully that they may bee kept within the doores, and hidden in some honest labour and exercise." His detailed regimen for daughters provides further evidence of parental anxieties. A young woman was to be kept away from anything that might prompt her to vanity or romance, denied access to imaginative literature and even musical instruments. For fear of vanity she was not to wear jewelry or adorn herself. She was to be kept secluded, even from her parents' social gatherings, lest like some Juliet, her eyes might light upon an Elizabethan Romeo. Like a votaress of chastity, she was left with her Bible, her distaff, and her household chores, always in sight of her parents or some suitable chaperone. Her dependency was reinforced to such a degree that she was virtually helpless without parental guidance. "If it chaunce thee at any time to walke or ryde out of the Towne or Citie, leave not thy daughter at home without a godly governour: for without thee shee knoweth not, neither is she able to live, and when shee shall chaunce to be left alone, let her be afraide," he writes.[33] Today this maiden would be diagnosed as agoraphobic.

Citing the maxim that idleness breeds wantonness, Thomas Gataker recommended for daughters a ceaseless round of household chores. Myles Coverdale, as well, urged parents to keep their daughters busy spinning, weaving, and sewing. Perhaps the repression of women was responsible for much of the extensive and ornate needlework of the sixteenth century: they could at least weave out their fancies in rich tapestries. Coverdale allowed young women music, but limited this to singing metrical arrangements of the Psalms, like those composed by Sir Philip Sidney and his sister Mary, Countess of Pembroke. Otherwise, daughters were to be kept from "all unhonest games and passe tymes," social gatherings, and imaginative literature.[24] They were raised like hothouse flowers until they could be presented, chaste, modest, and obedient, to the men who would rule them as husbands for the rest of their days.

Shakespeare's comedies are replete with fathers like Egeus in *A Midsummer Night's Dream*, determined to match his daughter to the man of his choice despite her equally stubborn protestations to the contrary. His domination and her defiance set up many a dramatic conflict, revealing the depths of the father-daughter bond and the extent of its challenge in marriage. To modern audiences with a romantic view of marriage, these fathers appear perversely dictatorial, forcing their daughters to choose between romantic love and filial obedience. An examination of Renaissance marriage customs, however, clarifies the motives of these apparently overbearing fathers.

According to historians, marriage in the Renaissance was less a personal relationship than "a means of tying together two kinship groups, or obtaining collective economic advantages and securing useful political alliances. Among peasants, artisans, and labourers, it was an economic necessity for partnership and division of labor in the ships or in the fields." For traditional Elizabethans, marriage was naturally arranged by parents and kin rather than by the couple themselves. This practice occasioned little resentment since "personal accommodation to circumstances, necessity, and authority was an ingrained pattern of behaviour."[25]

Parental consent was required in a child's choice of career, religious vocation, or marriage. Parents were expected to provide for their children's future. As John Stockwood pointed out, "it is the dutie of parents to give their daughters in marriage."[26] Many of Shakespeare's fathers—Capulet, Egeus, Baptista, and Leonato—are only performing what they consider their parental duty, although, as we shall see in the next chapter, their motives vary considerably.

Parental authority in marriage was reinforced by religion. Batty argued that parents had a God-given "right and authoritie to place and bestowe their children" and Smith explained, "in the first institution of Mariage; when there was no Father to give consent, then our Heavenly Father gave his consent: God supplied the place of the Father, & brought his Daughter unto her Husband, and ever since, the Father after the same manner, hath offred hys Daughter unto the Husband." Gouge equated parental authority with God's, affirming "that children ought to have their parents consent unto their marriage is without all question evident. For . . . God himselfe hath given us herein a patterne: He first brought the woman to the man (Gen. 2.22) whereby he would shew that he who gave a being to the woman, had a right to dispose her in marriage: which right parents now have."[27] This is precisely the argument Shakespeare gives to Duke Theseus at the beginning of *A Midsummer Night's Dream* when he counsels Hermia to marry the man her father has chosen:

> be advis'd, fair maid:
> To you your father should be as a god;
> One that compos'd your beauties, yea, and one
> To whom you are but as a form in wax.
> [I.i.46-49]

Paternal responsibility was incorporated into the Christian marriage ceremony as the ritual giving of the daughter by her father to the priest who then married her to her husband. The rite is of great antiquity among both pagans and Christians, and the phrase "giving a daughter to wife" occurs often in scripture. The ritual itself states that "the minister shall receive her at her father's . . . hands." This signifies the father's part in resigning her up to God, who through the authority of the priest "now gives her in marriage, and who provides a wife for the man, as he did at first for Adam."[28]

Arranging their children's marriages was a serious parental responsibility. In his translation of Plutarch's *The Education or bringinge up of Children*, Sir Thomas Elyot counseled parents to marry their children as soon as they reached the dangerous age of puberty, as marriage curbs their youthful passions and "is the most sure bridall of youth." Thomas Heywood advised parents to take "great care . . . in disposing of their children," referring to a proverb "that the fathers to mary a son need spend but one day, but in the disposing of one daughter they ought to consider with themselves ten yeers."[29] So Capulet, at the beginning of the play, takes his parental responsibilities seriously but is in no great hurry to marry off his beloved Juliet.

Daughters, as we have seen, presented their parents with special cares and anxieties. It was the parents' duty to see that they were safely married as soon as they reached puberty. Sexual attraction, even among virtuous young people, was considered an unsafe basis for marriage. Romantic love or "love melancholy" was considered madness, making young men and women completely unfit for the serious task of choosing a mate. They were urged to leave the matter to their parents, ignoring their own feelings, which were untrustworthy and potentially sinful. Vives counseled young women, "Neyther forsake thy father and mother, to followe thy lover: nor geve them perpetuall sorowe, to geve thy lover the short pleasure of thy selfe. Neyther wish rather to fare well in thy body, than in thy soule: neyther thy body to be in joye, and thy soule in woe." Similarly, Stockwood advised young people to follow "the direction and good advice of thy father," warning them against "unbrideled & unsettled lusts, making matches according to their own fickle fantasies, and choosing unto themselves yokefellowes after the outward deceivable direction of the eie." Nothing could be more dangerous than to give in to their sexual feelings. Their parents could best choose for them with sober minds and the eye of reason, finding them a fit partner. According to the traditional philosophy of the time, marriage was a means of channeling those otherwise destructive sexual urges and "any reasonably presentable member of the opposite sex" would suffice.[30] The primary considerations were family alliances and economic and personal security.

Marriage, then, was a parental duty, not a child's prerogative. There was, however, some disagreement as to what involvement, if any, the future bride and groom were to have in the planning stages. Some felt that fathers should meet and work out the financial provisions of dowry and jointure and afterwards introduce the future husband and wife, who would obediently comply. So Myles Coverdale affirmed: "Now doth the obedience or disobedience of the children at no tyme declare it selfe more then in contracting of wedlok. Greater honoure canst thou not shew unto thy parentes then whan thou folowest them herin: nether greater dishonoure then whan thou herin resisteth them". Theorists such as Heinrich Bullinger, John Stockwood, and John Budden concurred, Bullinger giving the father complete control over his daughter's marriage, Stockwood affirming that "choise of wives and husbands" is "in the authoritie of their fathers," and Budden maintaining that children "should have nothing to say whatever" in the matter.[31]

Vives described how a young woman should conduct herself when her parents were arranging her marriage. By no means was she to express her preferences or even demonstrate interest, as this was unseemly in a young maiden. "It becometh not a maide to talke, where hir father and mother be in communication about hir marriage: but to leave all that care and charge holly unto them, which love hir as well as hir selfe dothe. And lette hir thinke that hir father and mother wyll provyde no less dylygently for hir, than she wolde for hir selfe: but muche better, by the reason thay both have more experience and wisedome. Moreover it is not comely for a mayde to desyre marriage, and muche lesse to shewe hir selfe to longe therfore." Initially such a dutiful daughter, Juliet demurely tells her mother that marriage "is an honour that I dream not of" (I.iii.65). This, of course, is before she meets Romeo. Hero, in *Much Ado*, is a model daughter throughout the play. In II.i, when her father and uncle arrange her marriage, she says nary a word, but is upstaged by her witty cousin Beatrice, the brilliant foil to Hero's traditional young womanhood.

Vives denied virtuous daughters any words, feelings, or actions concerning their marriage. He did, however, allow them to pray for good husbands.[32] Their parents would do the rest. Children in the Renaissance were routinely matched for life with less of a say than modern children have when their parents buy them clothing or other commodities.

Did most young women accept this arrangement? According to historians, most of them did. It was possible in some circles for a child to reject a parent's choice if there was great discrepancy in age or social station, but to reject "an otherwise eligible suitor" because of personal dislike or preference for another "would be considered perverse and ungrateful by even the most indulgent father," and so most young women simply accepted their fathers' choices and made the best of them.[33]

Some Renaissance writers, however, allowed children a small part in the process of deliberation. While Vives felt it immodest for young women to discuss marriage, both Batty and Stockwood urged children to open their hearts, letting their parents know their preferences—all of this, mind you, with the appropriate humility. "Let children humble them selves before their Parentes, and most lowly and gentely say, (my good father and mother) let mee have, I pray you suche an honest and godly young man or mayde, whom

[27]

I love in the feare of the Lorde, and in the way of wedlocke and lawfull matrimony, if hee or shee shall be thought worthie and meete for your affinitie, kindred, stocke, and Parentage, honest and wise Parents will not deny the thing that is in such wise so honestly & in such humble manner required," counseled Batty. Stockwood gives similar advice.[34] Of course, parents still had the final say and expected their children to obey them.

Most marriages in the sixteenth and early seventeenth centuries were arranged by parents or guardians, with some difference among social classes. Within the aristocracy and landed gentry, marriages were arranged, usually when children were quite young. Among the middle classes, economic interests and parental pressures prevailed, while the poor, with no considerations of lineage and property, could often choose for themselves. But people still married for security and economic partnership even when they selected their own mates.[35]

For children with well-meaning parents and reasonably low expectations, the arrangement apparently worked, although there were many abuses. Not all parents were wise and virtuous like those described by Stockwood and Batty. Children were all too often used in marriages designed to increase their parents' economic or political power: "Contracts by which children were bartered like cattle were still being made . . . up to the end of the sixteenth century."[36] Laurence Stone cites one notorious seventeenth-century example in which Sir Edward Coke forcibly abducted his daughter from her mother, tied her to a bedpost, and had her severely whipped until she consented to marry the mentally unstable brother of the Duke of Buckingham in an attempt to restore her father's lost favor at court.[37] E.E. Stoll refers to "that fine old Jacobean mansion," Aston Hall, near Birmingham, where visitors are still shown the upper chamber in which Sir Thomas Holt shut up his daughter who refused to marry as he wished, until she died there.[38]

There was also the grievous practice of child marriages. Contemporary writers such as Coverdale insisted, "an unnaturall & unhonest thinge is it to mary yonge folkes which have not yet attayned to theyr lawfull & juste yeares." Gouge strongly condemned "the practise of such parents . . . of children, as make matches for them in their child-hood, and move them to consent, and so cause them to be maried: Such marriages are mock-marriages, and meere nullities.[39] Yet with avaricious and unscrupulous parents, the practice continued. In absurd parodies of the marriage ceremony, children were carried to the altar while still babes in arms, required to repeat matrimonial vows which they could hardly pronounce. Phillip Stubbes lamented in 1583 that "little

Infantes in Swadlyng Cloutes, are often Maried by their ambicious Parentes and freendes, when thei knowe neither good nor evill, and this is the origene of muche wickednesse, and directly against the worde of God."[40] Many parents considered their children's marriage an opportunity for economic and social gain. A boy of two was married to an older girl so that his father might get as her dowry "monie to bie a pece of land"; another father married his small son to get money to pay off his debts. The abuses were scandalous. Exchanges of dowry and jointure were used by the respective fathers until their children attained their majority, at which time the marriages would be either ratified or dissolved. Grounds for dissolution included lack of consummation, but some families attempted to get around this by ceremoniously bedding the child bride and groom before witnesses, declaring that they had slept together. Frederick Furnivall lists thirty-one instances of child marriages in the ecclesiastical court of Chester between November 1561 and March 1565/66.[41] If this is a representative sample, the practice was sufficiently widespread in the sixteenth century to raise a response of outrage and indignation. A growing number of progressive voices condemned a social system that regarded its inferiors—women and children—as chattel, allowing greedy and unscrupulous individuals to dominate them.

The Progressive View: The Personal Bond

During Shakespeare's time, the traditional order was challenged by developments in science, religion, politics, and economics. The Elizabethan age was a dynamic moment between two historical epochs, the feudal and the capitalist, with new concepts emerging from the crumbling of the old and the challenge of the new. The great chain of being remained in the background in an atmosphere of increasing confusion and innovation. Traditional writers such as Bartholomew Batty complained "that at this day, there is almost no dutie performed unto Magistrates & Elders, nor any reverence or regard unto Parents."[42] For progressive minds, the time was ripe for discovery and experiment, part of an "all-round emancipation of the individual . . . a community enlivened by free choice and opportunity."[43] Puritans gave children a veto over their parents' choice in marriage, and Renaissance humanists wrote of reason, free will, and individual responsibility. The English theatre, born in these changing times, dramatized the conflict. Generations were often polarized in plays, with parents upholding tradition, and children demanding the self-determination claimed for them by contemporary reformers.

The seeds of controversy had been sown during the Reformation. Writers such as William Gouge upheld tradition, condemning children for disobedience, but in matters of religion argued that they should think for themselves, even disobeying their parents if need be: "if a father command his childe to goe to Masse, to forsweare himselfe, to marry an idolater, to steale, to lie, or to commit any other sinne forbidden by God, the child ought not to obey: those things cannot be done *in the Lord*." So, too, Robert Pricke wrote that "if Parents doe command or enjoyne their children any thing contrarie to the worde of God, expressed in the holy Scripture, they are not to obey them. And there is good reason, for although the authoritie of Parents be great: yet the authoritie of God is greater." Thomas Gataker extended this to wives, stating that in any "opposition between Gods will and mans will . . . God is rather to be obeyed than man."[44] In many such instances, hierarchical obedience was undercut by the Protestant emphasis on conscience and individual responsibility.

This period produced a new kind of woman. Unlike her medieval sisters, she was no longer "a mere chattel."[45] Together with her male counterparts, she enjoyed greater freedom and mobility, benefiting from humanism and the rise in literacy. Humanists emphasized the importance of learning for women as well as for men; regarding the development of rational discernment as a duty under God. In the various guidebooks of the time—Castiglione's *The Courtier*, Erasmus's *Education of a Christian Prince*, Ascham's *The Scholemaster*, and Elyot's *The Governour*—young people were encouraged to improve their minds through a program combining classical learning with practical knowledge. Higher education for women became fashionable under Katharine of Aragon, who carefully supervised the classical education of her daughter, Princess Mary. Katharine herself was one of the most learned women of her time, an example for a generation of brilliant and witty Renaissance women who might have been models for Shakespeare's heroines. Sir Thomas More's daughter Margaret impressed even King Henry with her learning. Lady Jane Grey was devoted to Plato. Mary Sidney, Countess of Pembroke, translated classical tragedies, and Queen Elizabeth herself read a passage of Greek every morning. According to her epitaph, Shakespeare's eldest daughter, Susanna, was "witty above her sex" and "wise to salvation."[46]

Some Renaissance men praised wit and learning in women. Lodowik Lloid observed in 1607, "*Dama* . . . in expounding her fathers darke and obscure questions, might worthiliy claim to be *Pythagoras* daughter. *Caetius* writes of some women . . . which came in apparell like men, to heare *Plato* read philosophy in schooles. Were not the Fathers happy to bring up such daughters, and were not their husbands more happy to marry such wives?"[47] Such a man would have admired Shakespeare's Portia.

English women enjoyed more freedom than their continental sisters. Frederick, Duke of Württemberg, wrote after visiting England in 1602 that "the women have more liberty than perhaps in any other place."[48] One critic believes that Shakespeare drew his heroines from the lively society women of the time, women like Lady Sidney, Lady Rich, and Lady Warwick. Although by the end of Elizabeth's reign, the humanistic fervor had diminished, with most young women turning from the classics to music, dancing, and needlework, women's status had definitely changed. Middle-class and upper-class girls were educated and had begun to think for themselves: "Some of the old rigid notions about the unquestioning obedience of daughters had begun to show signs of relaxation." This gradual emancipation affected women in all levels of society: wives of professional men; country women, their husbands' partners in farming or cottage industry; and noblewomen, who managed large estates in their husbands' absence.[49]

Travelers were apparently fascinated by Elizabethan women. Emanuel Van Meteran observed that English women "were not shut up or kept so strictly as in Spain and some other countries. On the contrary, they had free management of their households and could go out to market to buy what they liked best to eat. They are well dressed . . . fond of taking it easy, and . . . they sit before their doors, decked out in fine clothes, in order to see and be seen by the passers-by." Their independent ways were also mentioned by Thomas Platter: "Now the women-folk of England, who have mostly blue-grey eyes and are fair and pretty, have far more liberty than in other lands, and know just how to make good use of it, for they often stroll out or drive by coach in very gorgeous clothes, and the men must put up with such ways." He concluded that "England is a woman's paradise."[50]

English women loved the colorful fashions and entertainments of the time. Whatever has been said about the reputation of the public theatres, this apparently did not prevent many ladies from attending performances.[51] Their presence undoubtedly influenced Shakespeare's plays. In their desire for independence, many Elizabethan women also wore men's clothing. Phillip Stubbes complained as early as 1583 that some "have dublettes and jerkins as men have . . . yet thei blushe not to weare it: and if thei could as well chaunge their sexe, and put on the kinde of man, as thei can weare apparell assigned only to manne, I thinke thei would as verely become men in deed as now thei degenerate from godlie sober women, in wearing this wanton leude kind of attire."[52] Surely a number of women would have preferred the freedom accorded to men to the life of "godlie sober women." Is there really anything so "leude" and unnatural in a time of transition for an oppressed group to desire equality, liberty, and opportunity? Shakespeare's female characters in doublet and hose reflected more than theatrical convention. There was a wave of feminism in England from the 1580s onward, during which time a number of women "provoked an uproar" by wearing men's clothes and carrying swords. This practice continued into the early seventeenth century, although these early feminists were officially reprimanded by both King James and the bishop of London.[53]

Women's growing assertiveness in marriage produced a varied response from men. William Gouge lamented that "wives for the most part are the most backward in yeelding subjection to their husbands." Citing an assortment of scriptural injunctions for women to be meek and silent, he complained of "the waspish and shrewish disposition of many wives." Most of what he called "aberrations of wives" represents their refusal to conform to the traditional, submissive stereotype:

A conceit that wives are their husbands equals.
Unreverend behavior towards her husband.
Unreverend speech to and of her husband.
A stout standing on her own will.
A peremptorie undertaking to doe things as she list without and against her husbands consent.
An obstinate standing upon her owne will.
Disdaine at reproofe; giving word for word; and waxing worse for being reproved.[54]

Much to the dismay of men like Gouge, some Renaissance women had apparently taken in enough of the new humanism to think and act for themselves. Disgruntled traditionalists lamented what had been lost. But others found changing conditions less a loss than an opportunity. If men and women could no longer live within the traditional structure, then perhaps together they could create something better. Cornelius Agrippa recommended a marriage based not on dominance but on companionship and cooperation, advising men to take a wife "for thy continuall felowship, not to service and bondage. . . . And let her not be subject unto the, but let her be with the in all trust & counsail."[55] In this relationship, the wife was neither chattel nor subject, but her husband's loving partner.

Historians of the sixteenth and seventeenth centuries have recognized new marriage patterns: "a rejection of papal doctrines of the superiority of celibacy as well as of the traditional feudal concept which saw marriage as a property transaction with love as something normally to be found outside marriage."[56] Although still subordinate, woman was given a more significant status in marriage. Puritans opposed traditional marriages in which parents had bartered their children like cattle, emphasizing conjugal love, through which individuals could better love and serve the Lord. While Catholics and High Anglicans had seen marriage as a remedy for concupiscence, Puritans like William Tyndale, Richard Baxter, and later John Milton stressed the importance of companionship, placing it before procreation as the first priority in marriage. Protestant reformers saw marriage as "an honorable and natural society of man and woman, of which children were the proper result but not the prime cause."[57] As we shall see, many of these Puritan attitudes toward marriage are reflected in Shakespeare's plays.

Married love for Puritans was both a blessing and a duty. "A man must love his wife above all the creatures in the world. . . . No neighbour, no kinsman, no friend, no parent, no child should be so near and dear," wrote William Whately. Henrie Smith emphasized compatibility: "So man and wife should be like, because they are a paire of friends. If thou be learned, chuse one that loveth knowledge: if thou be Martiall, chuse one that loveth prowesse: If thou must live by thy labour, chuse one that loveth husbandrie." Smith counseled husbands never to strike or abuse their wives, for conjugal love produces a more enduring bond than coercion. Without love, he believed, there was no marriage: "unlesse there be a joyning of harts, and knitting of affections together, it is not Marriage indeed, but in shew & name."[58]

Puritans found "an honourable sexual dimension" in a married love. Unlike Catholics, they viewed sexuality not as something sinful, but a natural attraction between two souls, intended by God "to bring the man and the woman together and to permit them, in marriage, to express, sustain, and fortify their love."[59] Such love was an integral part of God's plan, sustaining men and women in times of trial. Smith explained that "God coupled two together, that the infinite troubles which lye uppon us in this world, might be eased, with the comfort and helpe one of an other." Cornelius Agrippa advised men to look beyond property and dowry to the love that was God's purpose in marriage: "Thou therefore, who so ever thou arte, that wylt take a wyfe, let love be the cause, not substance of goodes, chose a wyfe, not a garment, let thy wyfe be maryed unto the, not her dowrye. . . . Al covetousness, desyre of honour, envy, and feare sette a parte, with . . . reasonable and chast love, so take thy wyfe, commytted and geven to the for ever by the hand of God."[60]

Protestant reformers attacked forced marriage, child marriage, and marriage for money. Thomas Heywood criticized parents who "will enforce them to marry where themselves like, and not where their children love; the effects of which are commonly discontent and misery." "To force together two persons who have neither liking nor love for each other" would, according to Martin Luther, produce an "eternal hell and lifetime of tragedy."[61] Reformers recognized that love was accountable neither to reason nor to parental authority: "A Father may finde out a fit wife, and thinks such a one a meet match for his Sonne: and her parents may be also of the same minde . . . and yet it may be, when they have done all they can, they cannot fasten their affections. As Faith, so Love cannot be constrained. . . . There are secret lincks of affection, that no reason can be rendred of." Of this mystery, Thomas Gataker concluded, "even a naturall mans dimme eye may easily see & discerne a more speciall providence of God oft carrying things in these cases."[62] Puritans attributed love's mysterious irrationality not to madness, but to God's grace. Along with their belief in predestination, they felt that "from all eternity God inclined the future spouses to that love, in order to lead them to marriage."[63] In this way Puritans believed that marriages were made in heaven.

Marriage for Puritans was not only divinely ordained, it was also a personal contract or covenant, which necessarily exalted the role of wife. Instead of her husband's obedient subject, she was now his willing (although still obedient) partner. The concept of partnership may have developed from the veto power given to young women: "marriage could only be a partnership in Puritan terms if the woman was free to choose a husband and was herself adult enough to be his partner."[64] Women had gained greater autonomy and could marry with adult commitment, moving beyond traditional enforced obedience. Their marriages could not fail to be more personally fulfilling.

Family structure was also changing, with families becoming smaller and more caring. Diaries and letters reveal genuine affection, demonstrating that many parents regarded their children not as property, but as their "comfort" and "delight." These documents indicate a similar change in the marriage bond: "a strong complementary and companionate ethos, side by side with and often overshadowing theoretical adherence to the doctrine of male authority and public female subordination." Family bonds were becoming more personal, and marriage involved greater flexibility and cooperation between husband and wife, often including economic partnership as they worked together in trades or home industries.[65]

Individuals at many levels of society began to exercise choice in marriage. Among the poor, children were sent away as servants or apprentices for economic reasons. As soon as these sons and daughters gained a sufficient degree of economic stability, they were "fairly free to choose a spouse for themselves." Among the aristocracy in households of princes and the upper nobility, young men and women of noble families were often "thrown together away from parental supervision and in a situation of considerable freedom as they performed their duties as courtiers, ladies and gentlemen in waiting, tutors, and governesses." We see an example of this in Shakespeare's *Two Gentlemen of Verona*, as Valentine goes to court in Milan and promptly falls in love with the duke's daughter. In the glittering court of Elizabeth I, more than one of her maids of honor incurred the queen's displeasure for her amorous adventures and clandestine marriage. Even beyond the court, it was possible to marry without parental consent. The high death rate, combined with a later and later marriage age, left many children orphaned and able to marry as they chose. So Petrucchio in *The Taming of the Shrew* sets out after his father's death "to wive it wealthily in Padua" (I.ii.75). Young women, however, were considerably less free than young men, as their brothers often arranged their marriages.[66]

Batty warned that children must avoid "this detestable sinne of disobedience (the which alas at this day is too common) lest they intangle them selves into marriage without the consent of their Parents: for this is not only great disobedience, but rather verie great madnesse." Stockwood, too, lamented "the common practice amongst us at this daie" for young people to marry in secret and "the too usuall bad custome of children marrieng, without the consent and allowance of their parentes."[67] Amid the protests of traditional writers, more and more young people were marrying for love.

Mary Tudor, the younger sister of Henry VIII, married for love in 1515, causing a national scandal. As a child of eleven, she had been bethrothed by her father to Charles of Castile. After her father's death, Henry VIII arranged a politically expedient marriage with King Louis of France. The marriage was celebrated in the fall of 1514. She was eighteen and "by all accounts exquisitely beautiful and graceful." He was a broken down old man who died a few months later. The widowed Mary was left in France with a small retinue that included Charles Brandon, Duke of Suffolk, a man she had loved for years. The couple married secretly and returned to England to face the king's displeasure. Although they lived in forced retirement, the fairy tale marriage of the beautiful princess to the man she loved captured the public imagination.[68]

Later in the century two poets left records of their love matches. Edmund Spenser recorded his courtship of Elizabeth Boyle in *The Amoretti*, celebrating married love in the *Epithalamion*, *Prothalamion*, and throughout *The Faerie Queene*. John Donne eloped with Ann More at the turn of the century, much to the chagrin of her powerful family, who separated the lovers and threw him in jail, whence he sent his friends the terse missive: "John Donne, Ann Donne, Undone." The couple were finally reunited. She bore him a dozen children, and he wrote such neoplatonic accounts of love as "The Canonization" and "A Valediction: Forbidding Mourning." By the end of the sixteenth century, marriage for love had become an inspiration for many in life and literature.

Marriage Laws in the Renaissance

Not only did traditional and progressive views clash on questions of women's roles, marriage, and the family, further confusion was created by the marriage laws themselves, which were also in transition. In the sixteenth and early seventeenth centuries two contradictory conceptions of marriage coexisted, anything but peacefully. The older, pre-Christian conception of marriage as a civil contract endured alongside the more recent Anglo-Catholic conception of marriage as a sacrament in the church. Marriage in the Middle Ages had been a private contract between two families, arranging the dowry (money or property given by the father of the bride) and jointure (money provided for the bride by the groom's family in the event of death or desertion). For those without property, marriage was a private contract between two individuals: spousals or vows made before witnesses. Of these spousals there were two kinds: One was a spousal *per verba de futuro*, an oral promise to marry in the future: "I *will* take thee to wife." This was a betrothal vow or engagement unless consummated (which presumably implied present consent, thus constituting a legally binding marriage). The other was a spousal *per verba de praesenti*, an exchange of vows in the present tense: "I *do* take thee to wife." If such vows were exchanged before witnesses, they were an irrevocable contract. With only a few words, a couple could be legally married.[69] Shakespeare plays with his audience's awareness of spousals *de praesenti* in *As You Like It*, contributing another level of dramatic irony to the mock courtship in IV.i, when Orlando and "Ganymede" recite vows before Celia.

Spousals existed alongside the more elaborate Order of Holy Matrimony within the Anglican church, which gradually became the prevalent form of marriage. For persons of property, the traditional church wedding involved five steps: the legal contract between parents, arranging dowry and jointure; the spousal, or formal betrothal; the public proclamation of the banns in the church; the church wedding; and the consummation. Ecclesiastical courts still recognized a spousal *de praesenti* as a legally binding marriage, and this "handfast" practice continued among the poor. Puritans also considered marriage a private contract rather than a church ritual. Thus, Elizabethan marriage laws afforded many a young couple the opportunity to marry as they chose and thwart their parents' plans. As long as the man was over fifteen and the woman over twelve, their witnessed vows were indissoluble. The church condemned the practice as sinful but legally sanctioned it in the ecclesiastical courts. Even a claim to a precontract was sufficient to annul an existing marriage, and such claims, supported by bribed witnesses, were often used as a means of escape from an arranged marriage.[70]

Love and Marriage: The Dramatic Perspective

This period of dynamic change provided inspiration for a new age of English drama. Representations of love on the stage reflected the changes, questions, and confusion of the times. Modern scholars are themselves in controversy about the relation between life and dramatic art. Juliet Dusinberre sees "the drama from 1590–1625 [as] feminist in sympathy," maintaining that Shakespeare's contemporaries asked the same questions that he did, advocating a change from the traditional views of women and marriage. "Shakespeare's women are not an isolated phenomenon in their self-sufficiency," she argues, but simply more memorable because he was a better artist. Dusinberre relates the feminist sympathies on the stage to a wave of feminism in England from the 1580s onward, seeing Shakespeare as a mirror of his time.[71]

For Lawrence Stone, the portrayal of love in Elizabethan drama was contrary to prevailing practice. He notes "a clear conflict of values between the idealization of love by some poets, playwrights, and the authors of romances on the one hand, and its rejection as a form of imprudent folly and even madness by all theologians, moralists, authors of manuals of conduct, and parents and adults in general." For Stone the traditional order was still the norm for most Elizabethans, and the tragedies of *Romeo and Juliet* and *Othello* would be perceived as examples of young people who "brought destruction upon themselves by violating the norms of the society in which they lived," in this case filial obedience.[72] The many conflicting views during Shakespeare's time make it almost impossible to generalize. Some Elizabethans undoubtedly agreed with Dusinberre, while others, probably the majority, would have agreed with Stone. As we have seen from the preceding survey of primary sources, traditional and progressive voices together made up the *discordia concors* of the Elizabethan world, the constant interplay of opposition providing much of its dynamism.

Chilton Latham Powell sees a gradual evolution in the drama. Early morality plays such as *Juventas Pater Uxor* and *The Disobedient Child* upheld the doctrine of filial obedience, showing a bridegroom who chooses for himself punished with a shrewish wife. Later comedies were more progressive. The daughter in Lyly's *Midas* is given the power to veto her father's choice. In comedies from the mid sixteenth century on, parents are no longer the moral norm, but the reactionary and often ridiculous obstacles for young lovers to overcome. Powell cites Houghton's *Englishman for my Money*, in which three sisters outwit their father, who wants to marry them to foreign suitors; Dekker's *The Shoemakers' Holiday*, in which Lacy disguises himself and marries Rose, despite the objections of both families; Drayton's *Merry Devil of Edmonton*, in which a cruel father puts his daughter in a nunnery in order to foil her persistent lover, who elopes with her disguised as a priest; and other plays of this nature, including many of Shakespeare's.[73]

Shakespeare's depiction of young love was progressive, his portrayal of marriage influenced by the Puritans and humanist reformers of his time. Marriage in his plays renews society in the comic mythos; it is a romantic commitment, and the most significant of human bonds. For Shakespeare, "the new voluntary ties" of the comedies replace the traditional bonds of the history plays.[74] In the comedies and romantic tragedies, love emerges as a force of inspiration and renewal for individuals and the enduring bond that comprises human society. Time and again, he presents young men and women who marry for love, rejecting the traditional arrangements of their parents. The moral vision in Shakespeare's plays is not ironclad obedience to the *ancien régime* but a new moral order based upon free will, choice, and commitment, a personal bond of love and trust between two individuals that becomes an inspiration to their world.

[38]

Shakespeare's young lovers fall in love at first sight, and this love inevitably leads to marriage. They are affected by a mysterious forced epitomized by the magic in *A Midsummer Night's Dream*, which creates harmony out of discord and brings lovers together in a manner which passes all human understanding. His portrayal of love is not unlike the Puritan belief in divine intervention. It argues "something of great constancy; / But, howsoever, strange and admirable" (V.i.26-27).

In his memorable portrayals of friendship as well, Shakespeare celebrated the significance of the personal bond that gives meaning and constancy to this mutable world. Consistently, he upheld fidelity, trust, and commitment, and consistently, too, he berated those who broke their faith. V.G. Kiernan answered those who see Shakespeare as a spokesperson for traditional order, arguing that he upheld not the hierarchy but this personal bond of trust and commitment, without which our lives would be as savage as any beast's.[75]

Shakespeare portrayed the human family in transition and the ensuing conflict between old and new. In his parents, particularly the fathers, we have the traditional assumptions about authority, prejudice, privilege for some and domination for others, and the demand for unconditional obedience from women and children. Theirs is a society based more upon power than love. In Shakespeare's young lovers, we have an alternative: a relationship of commitment and trust, love and loyalty. This more humanistic view values individuals regardless of rank. Parents and children, men and women, masters and servants—all are accorded due respect. Nowhere is this more apparent than in *As You Like It*, a play in which the bondage of domination and authority—tyrannical brothers who rule with power and violence—gives way to the bonds of love and friendship. This is affirmed by the Duke Senior and his followers, Rosalind and Celia, the faithful servant Adam who teaches his young master a lesson in loyalty, the reconciled brothers Oliver and Orlando, and the young lovers themselves. This new manner of relating requires honesty and trust, giving of oneself, not arbitrarily taking from another. It demands of its young lovers a trial by ordeal, in which they demonstrate their ability to risk and hazard all they have, the courage to commit themselves and share intimately with one another. This is the bond upheld in Shakespeare's comedies, tragedies, and romances: a new paradigm for human relationships, which continues to challenge, inspire, and educate.

CHAPTER THREE

The Paternal Role in Transition

When confronted by their daughters' marriages, Brabantio, Egeus, Capulet, and their Renaissance counterparts faced a difficult double transition, fraught with social and psychological conflict. The evolution from feudalism to capitalism during the early Renaissance shifted the center of authority upward from feudal lord to monarch and downward to individual patriarchs who ruled over their nuclear families with a power that made the father "a legalized petty tyrant within the home."[1] As we have seen, however, progressive forces supporting personal choice and commitment in marriage gradually appropriated for the individual the father's once exclusive prerogative. The conflict between traditional and progressive social forces only intensified the personal conflict of parents and children.

Marriage has always been a crucial moment of transition, a rite of passage. Traditionally, it leads young women from childhood to adulthood, representing a no less difficult transition for parents from middle life to old age, with its final demands of retirement, reflection, and integration. Family relationships undergo considerable stress as individuals must accept new roles and a new distribution of power and authority.

At the very moment their children emerge from adolescence, risking adult commitment, their parents feel the tensions of their own transition. It is time for them to release parental responsibility and face the final stage of life along with the inevitability of death. Their authority and power, which have given meaning to their lives, are progressively stripped away. As their children rush into the next stage with enthusiasm, most parents meet this change with understandable resistance, looking ahead with anxiety and backward with regret and loss.

The Paternal Role in Transition

To resolve these tensions within the family, societies have ritualized marriage, enclosed it within a chrysalis of ceremony and sanctity, calling upon familiar traditions and divine intervention to make this difficult transition. Anthropologists have noted intercultural similarities in ceremonies of birth, marriage, and death, rituals that help us face these mysterious changes from the familiar to the unknown. The high level of anxiety in modern industrial societies has undoubtedly increased with the erosion of such rites, leaving individuals on their own to deal with the challenges of time, change, and mutability. Solace might still be found in the theater, for as rites of passage are divided into rites of separation, transition, and incorporation, so the movement in Shakespeare's plays takes the audience through these same three stages.[2] Separation, transition, and incorporation occur on the societal level in the comedies. Society is initially separated into two polarities: the young lovers and the oppressive older generation. The green world functions as an arena of transition, and the lessons affirmed through the trial by ordeal incorporate the once divided society into a comic synthesis. In the major tragedies, this threefold pattern takes place on the individual level. The hero experiences alienation, separation, and inner conflict because of an assault on his or her belief system. In *Hamlet*, *Othello*, and *King Lear*, final *anagnorisis* or tragic recognition brings integration and incorporation within the psyche of the protagonist.

I will discuss the challenges of youth in later chapters. For now, let us consider the fathers' response to this transition. As they enter the anxiety-ridden final stage of their lives, their daughters abandon them for the adventure of awakening love. This tension occurs in all Shakespeare's father-daughter relationships. Well might the fathers, many of whom are widowers, feel deserted, responding with anger and resentment, hurt and frustration as their daughters leave them alone to deal with the specter of old age and death.

Their isolation is part of a process that brings the individual full circle, according to present-day theories of human development.[3] People move gradually through life from the ego absorption of infancy into increasing competence and physical independence, while forming stronger bonds of caring and commitment, reaching out to family, peers, and the outside world in work and service. Upon entering the final stage, however, they find life uncomfortably simplified. Competence, independence, and responsibilities ebb away, leaving them alone to find a sense of purpose in the challenge of individuation. Shakespeare's fathers face this sobering and much overlooked requirement of adulthood: to look within and define themselves to themselves. This is something no one else can do for them, a difficult inner journey each person must inevitably make alone.

Without a sense of meaning, without ego integrity, an older person is tormented by time and loss. With integration come wisdom and inspiration: without it, only anxiety, frustration, and despair. The final passage of integrity can be postponed in desperate assertions of potency and pathetic imitations of youth, but it cannot ultimately be denied. As Shakespeare's fathers release their daughters, they release their loving and obedient subjects, confirmations of their masculine power and authority. In addition to the tangible loss of persons they love, the fathers are losing parts of themselves as they look down the dark tunnel of time to the inevitability of their own mortality. The betrothal of their daughters brings on this developmental crisis. But a crisis can also be a crossroads, an opportunity for growth. Any stressful situation is a catalyst, drawing out a person's inner strength or weakness; so this crisis develops the characters of Shakespeare's fathers.

In response to his daughter's love for another man, many a father of the Renaissance stubbornly asserted his own power. In 1589 John Stockwood severely criticized fathers for tyrannizing their children: "beware that they turne not their fatherlie jurisdiction and government into a tyrannical sowernesse and waywardnesse, letting their will goe for a lawe and their pleasure for a reason. . . . The parentes do sometimes abuse their power and authoritie, and will compel their children to marie with those, whom they love not," but, he maintained, "this is not fatherlie power, but a tyrannie."[4] Numerous writers of the time criticized forced marriage and related abuses of paternal authority, indicating that there was extensive paternal domination.

Shakespeare's fathers in the comedies and tragedies react to their daughters' emerging sexuality and love for other men with pain and consternation. The threat of losing their daughters troubles them deeply. Brabantio, learning of Desdemona's elopement, is stricken with grief. "O unhappy girl!" he exclaims, "With the Moor, say'st thou? Who would be a father! . . . O, she deceives me / Past thought!" (*Othello* I.i.164-67). Leonato, believing that his daughter has dishonored him, tells his brother:

> give not me counsel;
> Nor let no comforter delight mine ear
> But such a one whose wrongs do suit with mine.
> Bring me a father that so lov'd his child,

[42]

Whose joy of her is overwhelm'd like mine,
And bid him speak of patience.

[Much Ado V.i.5-10]

As one scholar has pointed out, "so intense . . . is the emotional investment
of Shakespeare's fathers in their daughters' love that the thwarting of the
fathers' expectations often brings forth imprecations and diatribes of surpass-
ing bitterness."[5]

History and legend are replete with fathers reluctant to release their
daughters in marriage. Fairy tales and folk legends tell of arduous trials imposed on prospective suitors, often with dire penalties. Princes were forced
to slay dragons, climb glass mountains, make their way through forests of
briers, and answer complex riddles. They had to complete impossible tasks
to marry the fair princesses. In classical legend, the suitors who could not
outrun Atalanta were put to death by her father. In actual history, Charlemagne would not allow his daughters to marry but kept them and their increasing brood of illegitimate children at court with him.[6] The dynamics of
incest and pseudo incest are discussed in an earlier chapter. Paternal possessiveness and sexual jealousy have been noted by many psychologists, one of
whom calls this neurosis "the Lear complex."[7]

Shakespeare's plays are filled with anxious and angry fathers who insist
on controlling their daughters' futures, thwarting or arranging their marriages to their own advantage, with anything but an altruistic concern for their
welfare. Beset by jealous anxiety, unwilling to lose their daughters' singular
love and obedience and face the bleak prospect of life in decline, Shakespeare's fathers hold on tightly to their parental prerogatives. When they allow
their daughters to marry, many match them with men they cannot love in a
stubborn attempt to retain their exclusive place in their daughters' affections.[8]
Thus, the paternal preference for Cloten over Posthumus, Burgundy over
France, Demetrius over Lysander, Thurio over Valentine, and a host of other
undesirables.

While all Shakespeare's fathers are threatened by their daughters' romantic attachments to other men, their possessiveness falls into different categories. The *reactionary fathers* want their daughters to remain children and
will not acknowledge their emerging adulthood. The *mercenary fathers* love
their daughters as personal property and resent the loss of this valuable commodity. The *egocentric fathers* are unwilling to surrender their daughters because they perceive them as parts of themselves. The *jealous fathers* want to

[43]

retain all their daughters' love for themselves, bitterly resenting their suitors. Some fathers demonstrate more than one of these aberrations. The chapter will conclude with a discussion of King Lear, who suffers from all of them.

The Reactionary Fathers

Unwilling to release their daughters into adulthood, the reactionary fathers stubbornly refuse to acknowledge that their daughters have grown up. Their behavior stems from a multiplicity of motives. Instead of moving on to the next stage of their lives, they cling tenaciously to their old power and authority. In politics, people seldom give up power willingly. So it is in the politics of the family. These fathers have grown accustomed to their daughters' filial obedience, their dutiful and unquestioning observance of their fathers' will. For years the attention and affection of these sweet, submissive girls have reinforced their fathers' masculine power. Quite simply, the fathers enjoy the role of paterfamilias and do not want to give it up.

Their daughters' growing independence and love for other men constitutes an insufferable blow to the fathers' pride. Instead of seeing their daughters as young women, the fathers perceive them as children, suddenly naughty, disobedient children. Angry and shaken by this abrupt change in their daughters' behavior, these men stridently demand unconditional obedience. As the daughters reach out to the future, their fathers cling stubbornly to the past in a desperate attempt to deny the passage of time that seeks to diminish them, transform them from self-important heads of households into the impotence of old age. Certainly, fear as well as injured pride prompts their reactionary response. Reflecting the closed-image syndrome, these men refuse to acknowledge any changes in their daughters' behavior that would upset their own static view of themselves and their world.[9] Brabantio and Cymbeline are two obvious examples. After her elopement with Othello, which he can hardly believe, much less understand, Brabantio addresses his daughter in the Senate chamber:

> Come hither, gentle mistress:
> Do you perceive in all this noble company
> Where most you owe obedience?
> [I.iii.177-79]

He expects his cherished daughter to relate to him not as the young woman she has become, but as his obedient child. Her answer is a gracious attempt to assuage her father's feelings while announcing her transition into the adult world:

> My noble father,
> I do perceive here a divided duty:
> To you I am bound for life and education;
> My life and education both do learn me
> How to respect you; you are the lord of duty;
> I am hitherto your daughter: but here's my husband,
> And so much duty as my mother show'd
> To you, preferring you before her father,
> So much I challenge that I may profess
> Due to the Moor my lord.   [I.iii.180-89]

In keeping with tradition, Desdemona continues to honor her father while transferring her obedience to her new husband. Coupled with the shock of her elopement, however, her words strike the miserable Brabantio like a slap in the face. Stung by what he can see as only brutal betrayal, he disowns her, giving the newly married couple not a paternal blessing but an ominous curse.

Much of Brabantio's amazement arises because he does not really know his daughter. His only child, she has been his pet, a sweet and dutiful girl who has obediently performed the household tasks. She was the devoted and gentle girl who refused to marry any of her Venetian suitors, remaining at home as her proud father's hostess. She was a "good child," conforming to her father's will. Yet if we look more closely at Othello's description, we see a Desdemona her father has completely ignored. Underneath the sweet and quiet surface is a young soul yearning for adventure. Certainly, she did the household tasks, but as soon as she finished them, she returned to her father's side to listen to Othello's odyssey of battles and strange exotic lands. Apparently, Brabantio has overlooked the haste and enthusiasm with which Desdemona returned to hear Othello's story and the "greedy ear" with which she "devour[ed] up" his "discourse" (I.iii.149-59). Perhaps he considered her attention merely politeness to his favorite guest.

In truth, Othello's "fair warrior" (II.i.183) is a complex being with a strong traditional sense of duty to those she loves but an equally intense longing for adventure. Bored with the tame domestic role accorded to Venetian women, she wished for a life of action, "She wish'd / That heaven had made her such a man" (I.iii.162-63). Failing that, she wished to find such a man and follow him, casting aside her childhood, the comforts of life in Venice, and all "the wealthy curled darlings of our nation" (I.ii.68). Underneath Desdemona's quiet demeanor is a heroic spirit longing for adult commitment. But Brabantio cannot see this; he cannot acknowledge her adulthood. She is for him either a sweet and virtuous girl, bewitched by the unscrupulous Moor or, as the scene ends, the ungrateful reprobate who has betrayed him and broken her poor father's heart.

Cymbeline, like Brabantio, refuses to acknowledge that his daughter has grown up. After her secret marriage to Posthumus Leonatus, a man he had taken into his home, Cymbeline, too, responds with outrage and disbelief. He recoils from what he sees as his daughter's rejection, spurning the man whose virtues he had earlier admired. Cymbeline had intended to wed her to Cloten, the foolish son of his second wife. When Imogen marries for love, Cymbeline refuses to see her as anything but a spiteful, disobedient child:

> O disloyal thing,
> That shouldst repair my youth, thou heap'st
> A year's age on me.   [I.i.131-33]

Like a naughty child, Imogen is punished, locked in her room, her young husband banished. Cymbeline ignores not only his daughter's adulthood, but the very fact of her marriage. He encourages Cloten to court her, making a mockery of the traditional father's role. Not only does he separate her from her husband; he actively endorses bigamy.

These moral issues are only disagreeable details to the angry Cymbeline, who regards Imogen's marriage as the action of a headstrong, disobedient child. In his mind, his daughter cannot have matured into a woman, with new loyalties and commitments; she has merely misbehaved. In a later scene he asks:

> Where is our daughter? She hath not appear'd
> Before the Roman, nor to us hath tender'd
> The duty of the day: she looks us like
> A thing more made of malice than of duty.
> [III.v.30-33]

In reality, Cymbeline behaves with more malice than duty. Besotted with his new queen and prey to her Machiavellian tactics as well as the promptings of his wounded ego, he fails in his duty as a father. His arrangement of Imogen's marriage would be condemned even by traditional standards. Neglecting her welfare, he matches her with a man she cannot love, simply to please his queen. In denying Imogen's marriage to Posthumus, he acts with real malice, encouraging her to violate her marriage vows and commit mortal sin.

When confronted by such paternal failings, Shakespeare's young women are forced to mature. In his paternal role, Cymbeline has been Imogen's moral teacher. When he urges her to commit bigamy, she must actively disobey him to follow a higher moral law, as Protestant theologians have counseled. Like Juliet when abandoned by her parents and hypocritical nurse, Imogen must affirm her inner authority, following the guidance of conscience.

Cymbeline's behavior would be seen by Shakespeare's contemporaries as terribly wrong. Certainly, Imogen's secret marriage was irregular, but once she was married, her bond with Posthumus was to be honored and maintained. A father who interfered was severely condemned. As William Gouge wrote, "the bond of marriage is more ancient, more firme, more neere," than any parent-child relationship. "What wrong then doe such parents unto their children, as keepe them, even after they are maried, so strait under subjection, as they cannot freely performe such duty as they ought to their husband, or their wife?" He added, "Greater is the wrong, and more sinfull is the practice of such as keepe their children from their husbands, or from their wives." William Hay condemned parents who interfered with a betrothal, breaking up a couple "in order that a richer, more noble or more powerful match may be found," finding them guilty of mortal sin.[10] How much more guilty is a spiteful, angry father who seeks to violate his daughter's lawful marriage?

There are two male villains in this play: the corrupt, lascivious Iachimo and the uxorious, selfish Cymbeline. Both assault Imogen's chastity and the sanctity of the marriage bond, but the bond proves stronger than any attempts at sabotage. It is not tradition and hierarchical obedience but personal loyalty, trust, and commitment that Shakespeare upholds as the basis for human relationships. He underscores this in *Cymbeline* by giving the traditional argument for filial obedience to none other than Cloten, whose character undercuts its credibility:

> You sin against
> Obedience, which you owe your father. For
> The contract you pretend with that base wretch,
> One bred of alms and foster'd with cold dishes,
> With scraps o'th' court, it is no contract, none:
> And though it be allow'd in meaner parties—
> Yet who than he more mean?—to knit their souls

[47]

On whom there is no more dependency
But brats and beggary, in self-figured knot;
Yet you are curb'd from that enlargement by
The consequences o'th' crown, and must not soil
The precious note of it with a base slave,
A hilding for a livery, a squire's cloth,
A pantler, not so eminent.   [II.iii.116-29]

Although marriage laws in Shakespeare's time were drawn from conflicting traditions—the spousals and church wedding—there was certainly not one law for aristocrats and another for the common people. Cloten's attack on Imogen's contract is founded on a false premise; equally false is his claim for continued filial obedience since she is now a married woman. But both these arguments and all they represent are transcended by Imogen's fidelity—hence her name, Fidele—to personal commitments over strict hierarchical obedience.

Fathers such as Brabantio, Cymbeline, and Polonius are reactionary, both personally and politically. Unwilling to lose their paternal power, they insist that their adult daughters behave like obedient children. The resultant suffering and confusion demonstrate how wrong their actions are. Shakespeare repeatedly denounced the use of force and coercion in any human relationship. He was writing during the Renaissance, a time in which one was obliged to obey princes and magistrates. But in the more intimate bond of marriage and the family, Shakespeare affirmed time and again in his plays that behaving as a domineering paterfamilias was a cruel and anachronistic way for a father to relate to his children. Arbitrarily arranging their daughters' marriages to suit themselves, Cymbeline, Capulet, Egeus, Baptista, and other autocratic fathers are caricatured or condemned by the logic of the plays. Repeatedly, the old patriarchal order is denied and the way paved for a new social order based on personal trust and commitment.

The Mercenary Fathers

The mercenary fathers prize their daughters as valuable possessions, failing to see them as individuals. Instead of allowing them the freedom to develop into mature women, they cling tightly to their daughters, unwilling to release their treasures to other men.

A careful examination of the language of Shakespeare's plays illustrates the degree to which men perceive women as beautiful objects, precious gems, not living human beings. The imagery of money, jewels, and potential theft is pervasive. In *Two Gentlemen of Verona*, for example, the Duke is as careful with his daughter Silvia as he would be with any valuable jewel. He locks her away in a treasure chest—in this instance a high tower to which he himself keeps the key:

> Knowing that tender youth is soon suggested,
> I nightly lodge her in an upper tow'r,
> The key whereof myself have ever kept,
> And thence she cannot be convey'd away.
> [III.i.34-37]

The tower image, obviously phallic, also suggests hidden incestuous urgings. In *The Merchant of Venice* Portia's father has hidden her picture in a lead casket so that only a discerning suitor may obtain his treasured daughter. Brabantio refers to Desdemona as his "jewel" (I.iii.195), as she is later Othello's "perfect chrysolite" (V.ii.145) and pearl of great price (V.ii.347).[11] Initially, Iago arouses her father with the news that Othello has stolen her away: "What, ho, Brabantio! thieves! thieves! thieves! / Look to your house, your daughter and your bags!" (I.i.79-80). Brabantio later claims he has been robbed: "O thou foul thief, where hast thou stow'd my daughter?" (I.ii.61). In *The Merchant*, Jessica flees with her father's ducats and a casket of jewels, although his parting words were to "lock up my doors" (II.v.29) and remain safely inside. Stricken with anger, grief, and betrayal, Shylock pours out a confused litany of his daughter, his jewels, his ducats—all the precious possessions he has lost (II.viii.15ff.).

It is one thing to describe beautiful women metaphorically as jewels or treasures, but actually to perceive them as objects, even precious objects, makes men love them in a misguided and distorted way. Most of these fathers love their daughters dearly but are insensitive to them as people. Egeus's language in *A Midsummer Night's Dream* reveals the extent to which he perceives his daughter Hermia as a valuable property, transferring title to her as one would a piece of real estate. Hurt and angered by Hermia's love for Lysander, which he feels as personal rejection, Egeus determines to marry her to Demetrius, whom she does not love, again exerting his will over his unruly and disobedient child. His first-person possessive pronouns together with the significant words *right* and *estate* reveal his possessive love. Incensed by Lysander's taunting remark that Demetrius has her father's love, Egeus responds:

> Scornful Lysander! true, he hath *my love*,
> And what is *mine my love* shall render him.
> And she is *mine*, and all *my right* of her
> I do *estate* unto Demetrius.
>   [I.i.95-98, italics mine]

Capulet is another such doting and misguided father. His genuine affection for Juliet at the beginning of the play shifts abruptly in Act III, when he treats her as his property. Capulet first appears as a loving, reactionary father. He does not want her to marry yet, although other ladies in Verona, Juliet's mother included, were already mothers at her age. He would like Juliet to remain at home for two more years before she weds, as he tells the insistent Paris:

> My child is yet a stranger in the world;
> She hath not seen the change of fourteen years;
> Let two more summers wither in their pride,
> Ere we may think her ripe to be a bride.
>   [I.ii.8-11]

Juliet's mother, by contrast, is cold and distant. Matched in youth to an older man, she thinks it time for Juliet to wed and instructs her in the formalities of meeting her suitor.

Capulet would like Juliet to be happy. He agrees to Paris's demands, envisioning a long courtship and requiring Juliet's consent: "But woo her, gentle Paris, get her heart, / My will to her consent is but a part" (I.ii.16-17). Initially reluctant to release his beloved only child, Capulet refers at the feast to the passage of time and his increasing age. He is beginning to acknowledge another stage of life for himself and his daughter but prefers to hold back for now. Yet in Act III he suddenly changes his mind and insists upon marriage without allowing time for courtship, in obvious contradiction to his earlier plan. Even more surprising, he hastily arranges the marriage in two days when he had at first desired to wait two years "ere we may think her ripe to be a bride." Irene Dash has noted how "love and protectiveness of the female child yield to familiar perceptions of woman as property and procreator."[12] Yet his motives are not only procreation and progeny. Tybalt's death transforms Capulet's reactionary hesitation into its opposite by attacking his pride and sense of control. Death makes him conscious of his own mortality, his impotence in the face of the inevitable. In a desperate effort to assert himself, to exercise control over at least one situation and somehow counteract the chaotic absurdity of death, Capulet hastily affirms his paternal authority:

> Sir Paris, I will make a desperate tender
> Of my child's love: I think she will be rul'd
> In all respects by me; nay, more, I doubt it not.
>   [III.iv.12-14]

At this point he forgets his earlier attention to Juliet's feelings, his insistence that Paris "woo her," that "My will to her consent is but a part" (I.ii.16-17). He attempts to marry her in a demonstration of his own power, reminding one of Egeus's statement in *Midsummer*: "I beg the ancient privilege of Athens, / As she is mine, I may dispose of her" (I.i.41-42).

Capulet presents Juliet's marriage to Paris as a fait accompli, refusing to listen when she tearfully begs to "speak a word" (III.v.160). In his outrage and wounded pride, he turns from doting father into petty tyrant. His daughter becomes his livestock, to dispose of as he wills. He threatens her: "go with Paris to Saint Peter's Church / Or I will drag thee on a hurdle thither" (III.v.155-56). If she will not marry Paris: "Graze where you will, you shall not house with me" (190). He tells her:

> And you be *mine*, I'll give you to *my* friend;
> An you be not, hang, beg, starve, die in the streets,
> For by *my* soul, *I'll* ne'er acknowledge thee,
> Nor what is *mine* shall never do thee good:
> Trust to't, bethink you; *I'll* not be forsworn.
>   [III.v.193-97, italics mine]

The preponderance of first-person pronouns in this passage demonstrates his egocentricity, his pride. His fury at losing face before another man foreshadows the prideful fury of Lear when Cordelia refuses to comply with his plans. In each instance the father is concerned with his image: he will not be forsworn. His pride makes him deaf and blind to his daughter's needs.

If some fathers use their daughters to assuage their egos, others are even more reprehensible. Not only do they treat them like property, they are determined to marry them at a profit. Such is the attitude of Silvia's father in *Two Gentlemen*. Valentine complains of "My foolish rival, that her father likes / Only for his possessions are so huge" (II.iv.174-75). Similarly, Baptista

Minola, in *The Taming of the Shrew*, announces that he will sell his younger daughter, Bianca, to the highest bidder:

> 'Tis deeds must win the prize; and he of both
> That can assure my daughter greatest dower
> Shall have my Bianca's love.   [II.i.344-46]

He arranges her marriage without consulting her, violating even traditional practice, in which fathers considered the compatibility of the couple before making a match.[13]

But by far the most reprehensible father is Polonius, who is not only mercenary but a crafty manipulator. He uses everyone, including his own offspring, to aggrandize himself and increase his power. Act II, scene i, reveals much about Polonius's relations with his children. He sends Reynaldo to Paris to spy on his son, and Ophelia rushes dutifully in to report her most recent encounter with Hamlet. This scene demonstrates his blatant disregard for their privacy. He does not respect them as individuals; they are only pawns in his elaborate game of power and intrigue.[14] Polonius is a manipulator who watches, analyzes, and uses people. We find in I.iii that he has intelligence reports about Hamlet's frequent visits with Ophelia:

> 'Tis told me, he hath very oft of late
> Given private time to you; and you yourself
> Have of your audience been most free and bounteous.
> [I.iii.91-93]

When Ophelia says Hamlet has given her many "tenders" of his affection, Polonius seizes upon the word with a gusto that would amuse Freud, demonstrating his crassly economic value system:

> think yourself a baby;
> That you have ta'en these *tenders* for *true pay*,
> Which are not *sterling*. *Tender* yourself *more dearly*;
> Or—not to crack the wind of the poor phrase,
> Running it thus—you'll *tender me a fool*
> [I.iii.105-09, italics mine]

In this vein he continues:

> Set your entreatments *at a higher rate*
> . . . .
> Do not believe his vows; for they are *brokers*,

Not of that dye which their *investments* show,
But mere implorators of unholy suits.
[122, 127-29, italics mine]

Eager to retain her honor and reputation because they reflect upon his own, Polonius removes Ophelia from the danger of seduction by Hamlet. He forbids her to see him again, as an affair would reduce her market value. Hamlet's madness, however, opens up a whole new realm of possibilities. If his madness is indeed love melancholy, one very common cure was marriage. In this case, the marriage of the prince to the woman he loved would put Polonius's grandchildren upon the throne of Denmark. Bursting with ambition, he labors to establish his credibility as a humble subject with the king and queen, subjecting them to elaborate preambles in which he poses as model father, then obedient subject. He pulls out Hamlet's letter and brags of his dutiful child:

I have a *daughter*—have while she is mine—
Who, in her *duty and obedience*, mark,
Hath given me this.
[II.ii.106-08, italics mine]

After reading the letter, he reiterates:

This, *in obedience*, hath *my daughter* shown me,
And more above, hath his solicitings,
As they fell out by time, by means and place,
All given to mine ear.   [124-27, italics mine]

When Claudius asks, "But how hath she / Receiv'd his love?" (127-28), Polonius answers, "What do you think of *me*?" (129, italics mine), then whips up a virtuoso performance to prove himself "faithful and honourable" (130). He explains how he ordered Ophelia to repel Hamlet's advances, not only to preserve her own virtue but also because "Lord Hamlet is a prince, out of thy star" (141). At the same time, he rejoices inwardly that his latest plot will win him not only the gratitude of the king and queen but a royal alliance.

Now that Polonius has ceremoniously presented his hypothesis, it remains only to be proved. For this he also has a plan. He knows that Hamlet "sometimes . . . walks four hours together / Here in the lobby" (159-60). (Why else would Polonius study the habits of the prince unless he planned to manipulate him?) Here Polonius betrays his own crude view of human nature, specifically human sexuality, in which people are little more than animals. In earlier scenes he has suspected Laertes and Hamlet of unbridled lust. Now he intends to use this lust to advantage to win a declaration of love from Hamlet while he and Claudius are hidden within earshot. "At such a time I'll *loose* my daughter to him" (162, italics mine), he says; such is the language used in the coupling of a stud and a mare. He has referred to Hamlet similarly in an earlier scene, telling Ophelia that he might walk "with a larger *tether* . . . / Than may be given you" (I.iii.125, italics mine). A few lines later, Hamlet calls Polonius a "fishmonger," common slang at the time for a pimp or procurer, a dealer in flesh (II.ii.174).[15] He recognizes that Polonius would sell his daughter to advantage with no more regard for her feelings than a farmer for his livestock.

Polonius dies, appropriately, behind an arras, in an act of spying and manipulation. Seeking to establish himself by rising in a corrupt social hierarchy, manipulating other people, Polonius is an amoral authoritarian personality, his value system based entirely on power and profit. Together with Claudius, he represents the corrupt patriarchal value system, part of the rottenness that pervades Denmark, in which people are prized not for themselves, but as means to an end. Both men use their authority only to satisfy their appetites, relying on rank and duty, manipulation, force, and coercion to get what they want. But the play also presents an alternative. Hamlet upholds love, not duty, as the highest social bond (I.ii.254-55), prizing Horatio not for material value, but for his loyal friendship and greatness of soul:

> Give me that man
> That is not passion's slave, and I will wear him
> In my heart's core, ay, in my heart of heart,
> As I do thee. [III.ii.76-79]

Once again Shakespeare portrays the abuse of patriarchal power and the moral alternative, a new basis for human relationships.

The Egocentric Fathers

Like the mercenary fathers, the egocentric fathers dominate their daughters, but for different reasons. While the former treat their children as objects to be sold, traded, or manipulated, the latter perceive their offspring as parts of themselves. In Jungian terms, they suffer from inflated egos, the inability to distinguish between self and other.[16]

The language of many fathers in Shakespeare demonstrates the degree to which they suffer from this blurring of ego boundaries. Leonato, in *Much Ado*, is crushed by Hero's apparent betrayal and loss of chastity, suffering even more deeply because he identifies with her. A widower with an only child, until now he has conceived of that much-loved child as part of himself. The plethora of first person pronouns in the following passage demonstrates the depth of his identification:

> Griev'd *I, I* had but one?
> Chid *I* for that at frugal nature's frame?
> O, one too much by thee! Why had *I* one?
> Why ever wast thou lovely in *my* eyes?
> Why had *I* not with charitable hand
> Took up a beggar's issue at *my* gates,
> Who smirched thus and mir'd with infamy,
> *I* might have said 'No part of it is *mine*;
> This shame derives itself from unknown loins'?
> But *mine* and *mine I* lov'd and *mine I* prais'd
> And *mine* that *I* was proud on, *mine* so much
> That *I myself* was to *myself* not *mine*,
> Valuing of her—why, she, O, she is fall'n
> Into a pit of ink, that the wide sea
> Hath drops too few to wash her clean again.
>   [IV.i.129-43, italics mine]

Devastated by her disgrace, which he feels as his own, he wishes her dead with a suicidal despair that includes them both (IV.i.110, 125-29).

This view of their daughters as extensions of themselves is characteristic of Shakespeare's fathers. They refer repeatedly to their offspring as parts of their own bodies. This explains in part their shock and amazement when their daughters act independently, choosing to leave them for other men. Such defiance is as incredible as it would be for their arms and legs to disobey them. Shylock's material loss is magnified by Jessica's betrayal. Having lost his own flesh and blood, he demands a pound of flesh in revenge. "My own flesh and blood to rebel!" he laments, "I say, my daughter is my flesh and my blood" (III.i.35,40). Lear acknowledges even the hateful Goneril as "my flesh, my blood, my daughter" (II.iv.225). For her rejection and Regan's, he feels first utter amazement, later complicity, for his daughters drew their lives from his loins (226-27). Their fate is his fate, their value system the one he taught them: "nothing will come of nothing" (I.i.92). But Lear must be cast onto the stormy heath before he can see his daughters and subjects as more than extensions of himself. Like an infant, he must detach his ego from his mother (or in his case, his daughters), see himself as he is, moving from dependence through independence to interdependence. His isolation as king and his identification with Cordelia have prevented him from seeing beyond himself, releasing his daughters to adulthood, and pursuing his own spiritual growth.

Even Prospero, certainly the wisest of Shakespeare's fathers, has a moment early in the play when he snaps at Miranda, "What? . . . my foot, my tutor?" (I.ii.468-69). Like his foot, she has been part of him. Having assumed full care of his daughter for the past twelve years, Prospero must now leave the stage of parenthood and generativity,[17] moving on to late adulthood when "every third thought shall be my grave" (V.i.311). His transition is intrinsically bound to Miranda's. He must release her to adulthood as he must free his spirit Ariel. Throughout the play he gradually detaches himself from his cherished child and entrusts her to another man. Various productions of the play focus on Prospero's frustration at releasing Miranda and his anger at his usurping brother. Other productions emphasize his wisdom and balance. But by the end of the play, he has transcended worldly attachments, forgiven his enemies, and prepared to release his daughter, renounce his magic, and move on to the final stage of life.

The Jealous Fathers

The father-daughter relationship in Shakespeare is rendered more complex by the daughters' emerging sexuality. Prior to puberty, these daughters have been sweet and docile young girls, their fathers' love confined to possessiveness and pride in their offspring. With the dawn of sexuality, further complications arise: the fathers' own incestuous feelings for their daughters, and the daughters' awakening desires for other men.[18]

The sudden irrationality of their daughters' sexual passions is most difficult for their fathers to take. They see their daughters' behavior as bizarre, aberrant, insane; they have never acted this way before. Their attraction to some outsider suddenly becomes more compelling, more important than everything they have ever known. Fathers like Egeus, Cymbeline, Capulet, Brabantio, and the duke in *Two Gentlemen*, are stunned by the sudden change in their daughters. This irrational metamorphosis pervades *A Midsummer Night's Dream*, in the symbolism of the magic flower, the transformation wrought by sexual passion: spontaneous, irrational, yes, but undeniable. Girls become women with strange emotions that their fathers cannot accept, emotions that change their lives and leave their grieving fathers far behind them.

Egeus and Brabantio have but one explanation for the startling change in their daughters: surely they have been bewitched. "This man hath bewitch'd the bosom of my child," Egeus says of Lysander, citing the charms he used to deprive her of right reason (and filial obedience):

> Thou, thou, Lysander, thou hast given her rhymes
> And interchang'd love-tokens with my child:
> Thou hast by moonlight at her window sung
> And stol'n the impression of her fantasy
> With bracelets of thy hair, rings, gawds, conceits,
> Knacks, trifles, nosegays, sweetmeats, messengers
> Of strong prevailment in unhardened youth:
> With cunning hast thou filch'd my daughter's heart,
> Turn'd her obedience, which is due to me,
> To stubborn harshness.   [I.i.37-38]

How else can these fathers explain their daughters' irrational behavior and defiance of their will? Brabantio has known Desdemona as "a maiden never bold; / Of spirit so still and quiet, that her motion / Blush'd at herself" (I.iii.94-96). So contrary to nature, to all reason is her elopement he can only conclude that Othello has enchanted her:

> O heaven! How got she out? O treason of the blood!
> Fathers, from hence trust not your daughters' minds
> By what you see them act. Is there not charms
> By which the property of youth and maidhood
> May be abused?   [I.i.169-73]

With this accusation he confronts Othello:

> thou hast practis'd on her with foul charms,
> Abus'd her delicate youth with drugs or minerals
> That weaken motion: I'll have't disputed on;
>   [I.ii.73-75]

He tells the duke that his daughter has been "abus'd, stol'n from me, and corrupted / By spells and medicines bought of mountebanks" (I.iii.60-61).

Brabantio seeks to annul the marriage by citing impediments known in canon law as *impedimentum dirimens, vis et metus,* in which fear, duress, and constraint overruled the will. This included the practice of witchcraft.[19] But Brabantio makes his accusation not only for the sake of annulment. He sincerely believes Desdemona has been bewitched. How else can he accept the sudden passion that has made her reject him for the embraces of this strange and alien man? He continues to believe this until her explanation of her "divided duty" persuades him otherwise.

Egeus, too, is hurt by his daughter's powerful attraction to Lysander, which he can comprehend only as witchcraft. In order to punish Hermia for rejecting him, he orders her to marry Demetrius. Shakespeare makes it clear that Demetrius and Lysander are alike in all respects but one—Lysander has won Hermia's love. But to Egeus this is no small consideration. His resentment at losing his primary place in his daughter's affections makes him insist on marrying her to one she does not love. He will then remain the primary man in her life and reassert his paternal power in this transaction. So it stands at the beginning of *Midsummer* with Egeus the jealous and irate father, an immovable object confronting the irresistible force of sexuality and romantic love.

If these fathers are troubled by their daughters' emergent sexuality, they must also come to terms with their own sexual feelings. Many a father at this stage is uncomfortably aware that he finds his own daughter an attractive woman. He has watched her blossom into young womanhood and is flattered by her beauty and attention. Incest is an undeniable element in this emotional bond. The surprising frequency of father-daughter incest demonstrates the strong sexual tensions inherent in the relationship.[20]

If a father feels like a rejected lover, this would explain the vehemence of his response when he discovers that his daughter has been involved with another man. Juan Luis Vives in 1524 described one father's outrage at his daughter's loss of chastity, the violence of his reaction revealing his jealous outrage that another man had possessed his coveted daughter: "Hippomenes, a greate manne of Athenes, whan he knew his daughter defoyled of one, he shutte hir up in a stable with a wilde horse, kepte meateles, so the horse whan he had suffred greate hunger longe, and because he was of nature fierse, he waxed mad, and all, to tore the yonge woman to fede himselfe with."[21] Incest was not unreported in Shakespeare's England. In 1622 William Gouge condemned parents for excessive and unnatural love of their children:

the excesse is too much doting upon children. . . . Even God himselfe is lightly esteemed, his worship neglected, his word transgressed, all dutie to others omitted, their owne soules forgotten thorow care of children. Is this not mere apish kindnesse? For Apes kill their young ones with hugging. But what may be said of those who are so hellishly enamoured with their children as to commit incest or buggery with them?[22]

While incestuous undercurrents surface in many of these plays, Shakespeare depicts only one case of actual incest. In *Pericles*, the king of Antioch takes his daughter as a lover and drives away unwanted suitors by requiring a trial by ordeal, posing the riddle of his own incest. The story is presented in Gower's prologue to Act I:

> This king unto him took a peer,
> Who died and left a female heir,
> So buxom, blithe, and full of face,
> As heaven had lent her all his grace;
> With whom the father liking took,
> And her to incest did provoke:
> Bad child; worse father! to entice his own
> To evil should be done by none:
> [Prologue.21-28]

Ultimately, this pair is struck down by lightning, a punishment of the gods, but not before Pericles has guessed the horrible truth. He flees and in his wanderings marries Thaisa, daughter of Simonides. Years later, after the death of his wife in childbirth, he meets the young Marina in a distant land. She revives him from his melancholy and he feels a strong attraction for her before learning that she is his lost daughter, born of Thaisa in a storm at sea. The potential for incest is ritualistically introduced, then rejected.[23] Pericles's daughter becomes a regenerating force, the means by which he recovers his health and eventually his lost wife. Like Leontes and Cymbeline, he is reunited with his daughter, regains his paternal identity and becomes once again whole. Such is the daughter's redemptive power in the romances.

The father's attraction to his daughter remains a potentially explosive emotion, however, carefully acknowledged in marriage rituals. Historians note the frequency of bride stealing and even violent mock combat. Among the Welsh and the Irish, capture of a wife and a chase on horseback by the bride's father and brothers have been incorporated symbolically into the wedding festivities.[24] Anglo-Saxons and other Teutonic peoples celebrated marriage as a private transaction in which the bride was sold or transferred from father to bridegroom. The marriage consisted of two parts, which endured as the spousals in Shakespeare's time: the betrothal, or *beweddung* and the nuptial transfer of the bride, or *gifta*, in which the father was compensated in money or cattle for the loss of his daughter. This sum later became the *jointure*, the money paid to the bride as insurance against widowhood, her father providing the dowry or *portion*.[25] The marriage rituals of York, effective from the late twelfth century, incorporated these two ritual exchanges into the church wedding. They were preserved in the marriage ceremony during Shakespeare's time and have endured to our own day.[26]

For centuries, the Christian church has recognized the special bond between father and daughter. The church wedding, like other rites of passage, involves separation, transition, and incorporation. Before a young woman can be joined to another man in matrimony, she must first be separated from her father through the gifta, a ritual release necessary for her transition to the next stage of life.[27] The marriage ceremony requires a father to release his daughter in full public ceremony before she pledges her faith to another man. Renaissance marriage manuals reinforced this transfer of duty from father to husband. William Gouge wrote that "By marriage children are put from their parents. . . . A parents power by the marriage of his childe is passed over to the husband or wife of that childe." Cornelius Agrippa, too, firmly maintained that the marriage bond transcended all other family loyalties: "Let the father geve place, the mother geve place, the chyldren, the brothers and systers, leat al the heape of frendes geve place to the swete benovelence and entier love of man and wife. . . . For the father, mother, chyldren, brethren, systers, kynfolke, be the frendes of nature, and workes of fortune: man and wyfe be the mistery of god."[28]

Nevertheless, many a jealous father in history and literature has withheld his blessing, essential to the ritual transfer, preventing "the daughter's deliverance from family bonds that might otherwise become a kind of bondage." Lynda Boose cites four of Shakespeare's tragedies in which this violated ritual dooms the daughters' marriages. In *Romeo and Juliet*, even the presence of a priest does not compensate for the absence of Capulet. The combination of marriage and funeral rites underscores the fact that the proper marriage ritual has not been carried out.[29] Still her father's child while now Romeo's wife, Juliet in Act III is suspended between childhood and adulthood. She is unable to go with Romeo to Mantua—indeed, no one even suggests this—because she has not been released from her father's house. She seeks to be at once the loyal wife and dutiful daughter, an impossible dilemma that leaves her no recourse but the friar's desperate plan and the sleeping potion—failing that, the "happy dagger."

In *Othello*, Brabantio delivers Desdemona to Othello after the fact in a mockery of the ritual:

> Come hither, Moor:
> I here do give thee that with all my heart
> Which, but thou hast already, with all my heart
> I would keep from thee.   [I.iii.192-95][30]

He leaves them with a poisonous insinuation of her deception, which later returns to haunt Othello.

In *Lear*, we see a father asking his youngest daughter to swear that she loves her father "all" on the very day she is to be promised in marriage to one of her suitors. Recognizing the inherent contradiction, Cordelia cannot lie to obtain her dowry, the most opulent third of the kingdom. She knows that:

> when I shall wed,
> That lord whose hand must take my plight shall carry
> Half my love with him, half my care and duty:
> Sure, I shall never marry like my sisters,
> To love my father all.   [I.i.102-06]

Cordelia cannot lie to win her dowry, and she cannot have Lear's blessing without it. In the course of the play she, like Juliet, is caught somewhere in limbo. Without the ritual transfer, her marriage cannot be fruitful. She returns to England for her father's blessing and dies redeeming what he has lost.

Hamlet offers another distorted marriage ceremony. In the nunnery scene, Ophelia enters with a prayer book. As the play is generally staged, she stands between Hamlet and her father (concealed behind the arras) with the king as a witness.[31] An exchange of vows at this point would constitute a legal marriage. But Polonius has no intention of releasing her. When Hamlet asks "Where's your father?" (III.i.133), Ophelia chooses filial obedience over loyalty to the man she loves. The rites are truncated, Hamlet dismisses her in a rage, and Gertrude later strews her grave and not her bridal bed.

The fathers' jealousy and possessiveness dooms their daughters in the tragedies, but actually works to their advantage in the comedies, functioning as the antithesis necessary to create the comic synthesis and new social order. As Northrop Frye has pointed out, Shakespeare's comedies follow the plot structure of Greek new comedy, in which a young couple's future is threatened by some opposition, usually the young woman's father. The forces of disharmony in comedy are the *alazons*, or blocking characters, who make unreasonable demands. The *senex iratus*, or heavy father, is a familiar *alazon*, among whose ranks we find many fathers in Shakespeare.[32] Unwilling to lose their daughters' love as they have known it, these fathers hold on bitterly, stubbornly, to their parental prerogatives, demanding obedience when their daughters have already shifted their allegiance to romantic love. Their behavior is selfish and angry, their love possessive, tyrannical, and potentially devastating, as it would surely be in a tragic cosmos. These fathers bluster about in self-importance, seeking to dominate their daughters who are no longer children. Fearing to lose them, they have them closely watched or lock them up in a tower at night, as the duke does to Silvia in *Two Gentlemen*. But to no avail. In the comic mythos of renewal, the transformation has already begun, a transformation as inevitable as the cycle of the seasons, and as their daughters blossom, their fathers have already been left behind.

"The course of true love never did run smooth," Lysander laments in *Midsummer* (I.i.134), unaware that the very difficulties the father presents strengthen the love of the young couple. The father's possessive love for his daughter forces the couple to undergo a trial by ordeal, which builds a relationship out of initial infatuation. This is certainly true in *Midsummer*, in which a wiser and humbler Hermia emerges from the woods realizing that she cannot take Lysander's love for granted. The lesson in *Two Gentlemen* is one of loyalty, as Valentine and Proteus learn the meaning of friendship, which it is to be hoped they will apply to their marriages, and Julia demonstrates her patience, perseverance, and faith in love.

The trials of *The Merchant of Venice* and *As You Like It* are of a different nature. Portia's father has left the caskets, which act the part of *senex iratus*, testing her suitors' character. The test spares Portia the vain and fortune hungry and gives her Bassanio, who has apparently undergone a transformation, learning to love Portia for herself and willing to "give and hazard all he hath" (II.vii.16). Another ordeal, the ring trick at the end of the play, confounds Bassanio and Gratiano, combining their friendship and admiration for the young lawyer and his clerk with their love for their wives. Once again, through trial, Shakespeare affirms the value of friendship and its place in any enduring love. *As You Like It* echoes this lesson. Having undergone a trial by ordeal in the forest, imposed initially by two *alazons*, her uncle and his brother, Rosalind and Orlando have grown in the knowledge of themselves and one another. As they are wed, Hymen tells them their love will endure: "You and you no cross shall part" (V.iv.137).

The lovers' personal development is to a great degree facilitated by the *alazons*, the intervening chaos contributing to the final comic balance and affirmation. The growth of the lovers, and in many instances that of their fathers, constitutes the comic gnosis or change in consciousness that leads to a new social order at the end of the play.

If the comedies are modeled after rites of passage, the final incorporation at the end of the play is both personal and social. On the social level, comedy combines conflicting characters into a final synthesis, presenting multiple marriages and sudden conversions as well as obtaining the father's blessing for the young couple. In *As You Like It* although Rosalind arranges nearly everything else in the play, in Act V she presents herself to her father to be given in marriage to Orlando, confirming the importance of the ritual transfer.[33] In *Two Gentlemen* the father's blessing is also ensured. No longer a *senex iratus*, the duke is reconciled to Valentine in the woods and gives him his blessing to marry Silvia. The energies in the play shift as he releases his retentive hold on his daughter so she can participate in love and the creation of new life. The creative forces of nature have a magical effect on more than one recalcitrant *senex iratus*. It is also in the woods that Egeus, along with Theseus and Hippolyta, comes across the two young couples sleeping peacefully. At the insistence of Theseus, Egeus allows Hermia to marry Lysander. In *Cymbeline*, Imogen's father accepts Posthumus in the general reconciliation at the end of the play. Venetian law requires that Shylock bequeath to Jessica and Lorenzo the remainder of his estate. If this reconciliation in *The Merchant* is forced and unsatisfactory, it represents at least a financial acceptance of his daughter and son-in-law. The feast at the end of *The Taming of the Shrew* symbolizes another paternal acceptance. C.L. Barber noted the extent to which Shakespeare's comedies end with weddings or feasts, rituals of incorporation, securing the father's blessing, resolving personal jealousies and hostilities, and affirming the bonds of love and commitment necessary to create a new society, the ultimate renewal in the comic mythos.[34]

Lear: A Father in Turmoil

King Lear is Shakespeare's most conflict-ridden and possessive father. Of the four categories of paternal imbalance, Lear has them all: He is *reactionary* in his desire to retain his daughters as obedient children to forestall his own aging and death. He is *mercenary* in his view of love, measuring it in quantitative terms. He is so *jealous* of his youngest daughter that he cannot release her in marriage without a ritual that requires her to promise the impossible. Finally, he is *egocentric* in his identification with his daughters, especially Cordelia, and his identity problems are severe.

Lear's announcement of his proposed retirement on the eve of his youngest daughter's marriage signals his awareness of the final stage of life. He knows he is an old man, "fourscore and upward" (IV.vii.61), and as he releases his last daughter, he contemplates a period of retirement:

> Know that we have divided
> In three our kingdom: and 'tis our fast intent
> To shake all cares and business from our age;
> Conferring them on younger strengths, while we
> Unburthen'd crawl toward death.   [I.i.38-42]

To Shakespeare's contemporaries, this announcement would have been shocking, grievously contrary to primogeniture and cosmic order. One did not divide up kingdoms. A similar suggestion from the rebels in *1 Henry IV* was presented as a horrifying mutilation of the body politic, revealing the otherwise engaging Hotspur and Glendower as serious threats to order. Similarly, one did not retire from his or her divinely appointed place in the hierarchy. The Tudors lived and died as monarchs of England.

From a historical perspective alone, we are immediately suspicious of Lear's motives, recognizing his proposed action as a dangerous threat to order in the realm. The lines themselves offer more subtle contradictions, indicating a schism in his psyche comparable to that which he later inflicts upon his kingdom. His determination to "shake all cares and business from our age; / Conferring them on younger strengths" is troublesome. His awareness of his own "age" in comparison to "younger strengths" is clear. But beneath this awareness lurks a desire to shed the responsibilities of age and return to an infantile state bereft of any "cares and business" in which he might thus "unburthened crawl toward death." In the Renaissance, the individual's spiritual growth *required* burdens; one could not simply shed them and return to infantile self-absorption. We sense, even here, Lear's ambivalent attitude toward his final developmental crisis. As he acknowledges the necessity of confronting death, he retreats from it, to "crawl" back into a comfortable infancy. Lear wants to hide in the emotional shelter of Cordelia's love, to rest in her "kind nursery" (I.i.125). He acknowledges but does not accept the challenge of integrity.

Years ago Freud analyzed Lear's confrontation with his three daughters in Act I, scene i, recognizing a mythic pattern similar to that of the three caskets in *The Merchant*. Lear's daughters represent man's three inevitable relations with women: "the woman who bears him, the woman who is his mate, and the woman who destroys him." These three are represented in world religions as the goddesses of motherhood, love, and death. Lear at the beginning of the play is an old man, a dying man, who must come to terms with death.[35] But even as he recognizes his grim summons, he resists it, clinging to the past. Unwilling to renounce this world and look within, he demands a continued assessment of his own worth in his daughters' vows of love. Retreating to infancy, he wants to immerse himself in their affection.[36] With Cordelia he seeks a mother's unconditional love; to Goneril and Regan he gives a parent's power and authority. As he releases his youngest daughter, he is supposed to move from middle life to the integrity of late adulthood. Instead, he clings to her desperately. His final challenge brings to the surface all his unresolved conflicts, and within the psyche of this old man a small child huddles in fear. Unwilling to hear the truth from her lips and face his own decline, he rejects this message, confusing the silent goddess of death with the mother goddess and the goddess of love. In his emotions he crawls desperately backward down the tunnel of time.

Freud's thesis pinpoints Lear's conflict and explains the iconography of the final scene. "Cordelia is Death. If we reverse the situation it becomes intelligible and familiar to us." She is "the Death-goddess," like the Valkyrie in German mythology who carry off the dead warrior.[37] Lear's progress appears in the complementary relation between the first and last scenes. Initially, Goneril and Regan compete for their father's favors; Cordelia's silence infuriates Lear, and he banishes her, refusing to listen to the truth from her lips. In the final scene, Goneril and Regan die competing for the love of Edmund, Lear's rejection of Cordelia turns to acceptance, and he dies pointing to her lips: "Look there, look there!" (V.iii.311). For centuries, critics have argued about what he sees. Is this final scene a nihilistic negation or a transcendent vision? I would argue that Lear sees and hears nothing, that same nothing which had infuriated him so long ago. This time he accepts his summons from "the silent goddess of death" and meets his fate in final affirmation.[38]

In the first scene, we see Lear confronting the crisis of old age and beginning a dialectic struggle between integrity and despair.[39] Terrified, he clings to Cordelia for comfort. Unfortunately, this is the time that Cordelia must become another man's wife. Lear's despair and gnawing insecurity drive him to arrange this public spectacle and provide for retirement with his favorite child.[40] But in proposing the love test, he sets himself up for ultimate failure.

Not only does Lear crave affection at the very time Cordelia looks toward new adult commitments. He also demands from his daughters an accounting of their love, an assurance of his own continued self worth—something which, first of all, cannot be measured, and a determination he must make for himself. The love test reflects Lear's immaturity and insecurity. As Jung has explained, "the infantile concept of loving is getting presents from others."[41] Lear wants his daughters to gratify him with elaborate speeches, verbal gifts, for which he will reward them with gifts of land. Threatened by old age and declining powers, he wants to know how much he is beloved, how important he remains. He craves exaggerated declarations of love, proof that he remains the dearest person in their lives. Since his married daughters will have at best "a divided duty" to father and husband (as Desdemona has expressed it in *Othello* I.iii.181), he is defying all reason and blatantly asking them to lie. But reason has very little to do with Lear's actions. Driven by his emotions, he wants to be the center of his daughters' universe, feed his despair with their adulation, and hide from death.

There are flaws not only in Lear's motives, but in the test itself. Since love cannot be quantified, the test is meaningless, an empty shell of pretense and flattery designed to justify giving the largest share of land to Cordelia and to gratify Lear's desire for love and self-worth. But the test cannot accomplish Lear's objectives because Cordelia is unable to lie or to flatter. It merely elicits rhetorical effusions from Goneril and Regan. Lear's love test makes him a pathetic auctioneer who will sell the largest share of his kingdom to the highest bidder. From Cordelia he expects a declaration even more extreme than those made by her sisters. He has reserved the largest share of his kingdom and the coronet for her. His first question sounds like a bribe: "What can you say to draw / A third more opulent than your sisters? Speak" (I.i.87-88). When she hesitates and answers inadequately, he coaches her: "How, how, Cordelia! mend your speech a little, / Lest you may mar your fortunes" (I.i.96-97). For Lear the task seems simple enough. She is to fit the proper words to her feelings and receive her fortune. Goneril and Regan have accommodated him by fitting their words to the fortunes they desire, an inevitable result in a contest which measures rhetoric, not affections.

But Cordelia disappoints him, answering:

Cordelia. Nothing, my lord.
Lear. Nothing!
Cordelia. Nothing.
Lear. Nothing will come of nothing: speak again.
[I.i.89-91]

She cannot lie; she cannot flatter. What, indeed, *can* she say? There is no way to describe accurately how much we love our fathers—or anyone else for that matter. They have a special place in our lives; we love them "no more nor less" (I.i.95). When Lear asks for more, Cordelia responds:

Good my lord,
You have begot me, bred me, lov'd me: I
Return those duties back as are right fit,
Obey you, love you, and most honour you.
[I.i.97-100]

Cordelia loves him but she will not flatter like her sisters, recognizing in their excessive protestations a love which, if true, would be incestuous:

Why have my sisters husbands, if they say
They love you all? Haply, when I shall wed,
That lord whose hand must take my plight shall carry
Half my love with him, half my care and duty:
Sure, I shall never marry like my sisters,
To love my father all.   [I.i.101-06]

Her sisters' words have made a mockery of their marriage vows, and Cordelia, soon to be married, will not prostitute the ritual.[42]

A rational father would recognize the truth in Cordelia's words. If Lear were emotionally balanced, however, he would not set up this spectacle in the first place, nor would he crave hyperbolic demonstrations of affection. Lear does not want truth. He wants to avoid truth: the truth of his own decline and approaching death. He wants love, tenderness, affection, and comfort. He is a frightened child inside an old man's body, desiring the security of maternal love. When this is not forthcoming, he feels only bitter rejection:

Lear. But goes thy heart with this?
Cordelia.   Ay, my good lord.
Lear. So young, and so untender?
Cordelia. So young, my lord, and true.
[106-9]

[67]

With the pain of a rejected child and the fury of injured pride, Lear turns on his favorite daughter:

> Come not between the dragon and his wrath.
> I lov'd her most, and thought to set my rest
> On her kind nursery. Hence, and avoid my sight!
> So be my grave my peace, as here I give
> Her father's heart from her! [123-27]

"So be my grave my peace"—as his dream of loving comfort in Cordelia's "kind nursery" vanishes, the grave once again gapes ominously before him. His anger and hurt mixed with terror, he disowns Cordelia, who he feels does not love him. She will not speak the words to save him from his cruel confrontation with mortality. Goneril and Regan apparently love him more, and between them he divides his kingdom.

By measuring love as a commodity, Lear casts himself adrift to learn a bitter lesson. The end of this scene presents another definition of love, which transcends earthly measure. In words that echo the beatitudes, France chooses the dowerless Cordelia: "Fairest Cordelia, that art most rich, being poor; / Most choice, forsaken; and most lov'd, despis'd" (253-54). The paradoxes in his language and the final oxymoron express the paradox of love that passes all human understanding: "Not all the dukes of wat'rish Burgundy /Can buy this unpriz'd precious maid of me" (261-62).

This is not a concept Lear learns easily. In II.iv he still sees love as an exchange of commodities, expecting gratitude in equal measure from Goneril and Regan because "I gave you all" (253).[43] His allotment of knights diminished by Goneril from one hundred to fifty, he turns to Regan, who will allow but five and twenty. His stock rapidly falling, he seeks to stabilize his losses. Turning again to Goneril, he determines:

> I'll go with thee:
> Thy fifty yet doth double five-and-twenty,
> And thou art twice her love.
> [II.iv.261-63]

In a bitter parody of the first scene, this cruel auction continues until they deny him any. Lear falls into a mad rage on the heath, confronting the elements and his own elemental nature, awakening from a false perception of himself and his world. Lear's error had been in attempting to measure spiritual values—to comprehend love and self-esteem—in material terms.

[68]

Stripped of his clothes, his worldly rank, and his possessions, he learns in his madness to discard those superfluities and his own superficial measure of human worth.

Lear's anger at Cordelia has long been seen as the response of a rejected lover. According to F.L. Lucas, his "contention with Cordelia seems as fantastic as a lover's quarrel." John Donnelly explains that "Lear expects his daughter to love him not only as a daughter but also as a lover. . . . It is the rational note in Cordelia's 'half my love' that produces Lear's reaction."[44] Lear's intense love for Cordelia reflects all the symptoms of pseudo incest.[45] In the absence of wife and mother, he centers all his cravings for feminine comfort upon his youngest daughter and responds with unbounded fury when she denies him. But this love surpasses sexuality, penetrating to the very core of his being. It is his deepest human bond, expressing the need to love and be loved. Cordelia is the one person in the world he does love, and he loves her possessively, tyrannically, and exclusively. He has made her his emotional security. Given this background and Lear's angst at his decline, it is apparent how Cordelia's impending marriage threatens him. Her suitors, France and Burgundy, "long in our court have made their amorous sojourn" (I.i.48) and must now be answered. Lear's words ring with desperate urgency. His repeated references to time and duration demonstrate that the immediate loss of Cordelia precipitates both the love test and his abdication:

> We have *this hour* a constant will to publish
> Our daughters' several dowers, that *future strife*
> May be prevented *now*. The princes, France and Burgundy,
> Great rivals in our youngest daughter's love,
> *Long* in our court have made their amorous sojourn,
> And *here* are to be answer'd.   [I.i.44-49, italics mine]

It is clear from Renaissance political philosophy that dividing up his kingdom would hardly prevent "future strife." But political security is not his meaning here. Lear is trying to avoid "future strife" in a personal sense, by providing a comfortable and secure home for himself with Cordelia.

As he turns to his cherished daughter, he reveals his continued sense of urgency with the repetition of the word "now" and demonstrates his hidden motives for the love test:

> *Now*, our joy,
> Although our last and least; *to whose young love*

[69]

The vines of France and milk of Burgundy
Strive to be interess'd;   [84-87, italics mine]

For the past few days and weeks, Lear has observed with obvious dismay France and Burgundy's courtship of Cordelia, their competition for her affections. Fearful of losing her, he is also frankly jealous. He has seen these two men courting her when he wants to remain the principal man in her life. Lear, moreover, is used to being the center of everyone's attention. He arranges this competition to satisfy himself, for now his daughters must court *him*, demonstrating their love in return for their dowries. It is again significant that Lear was unthreatened by the marriages of either Goneril or Regan. Only the loss of Cordelia drives him to this extreme.

On the eve of her betrothal, Lear simply cannot and will not let her go. He defies the accepted Elizabethan principle of primogeniture and the right order of succession, dividing his kingdom to ensure that he will not lose his beloved child. His scheme involves a built-in justification for violating tradition as well as considerable arrangement behind the scenes. His real reason for giving the largest third of his kingdom and the coronet to Cordelia is a desperate attempt to retain her love. The public justification is merit over inheritance. Instead of leaving the kingdom to his eldest, Goneril, he will divide it and give the largest share to Cordelia, rewarding the daughter who loves him most: "That we our largest bounty may extend / Where nature doth with merit challenge" (I.i.53-54). Furthermore, he arranges to give Cordelia the largest share to ensure her marriage with the mercenary Burgundy. Even without considerations of national unity, Lear's actions would be criticized by Shakespeare's contemporaries. William Gouge censured parents for the sin of partiality to one child, condemning even more severely those cases in which "a gripulous feeling of advantage to themselves maketh parents to disinherit the right heire."[46] But Lear pursues his plan in violation of all order.

In I.i.192-200, Burgundy indicates that he is ready to accept Cordelia's dowry as Lear has previously offered it. In fact, having just entered the room, Burgundy has no idea that anything is amiss: "I crave no more than hath your highness offer'd, / Nor will you tender less" (197-98). As his metaphors indicate, he has accepted Cordelia and assessed her worth in terms of her dowry. Cold, formal, and mercenary, Burgundy is a far more acceptable son-in-law than France. He is a lesser noble; thus, Cordelia could remain in England as regent with the coronet and Lear could live with her. Also, knowing Burgundy's character, Lear feels sure that if Cordelia were to marry Burgundy, she would certainly love her father more. A powerful man with his own kingdom, France is a threat. Politically, he is Lear's equal; with his charm and personal warmth, he might win Cordelia's love. He would take her away, moreover, to become the queen of France. Thus, Lear has arranged the more convenient alliance with Burgundy.

Apparently, Lear has arranged everything for his own future security. The flaw in his plan is the love test, which asks Cordelia to do the very thing she cannot. This sabotages all his careful planning and leaves him in the position he most feared: abandoned by his daughters and left alone to face the challenge of integrity. The question may be asked why Lear would devise this well-crafted scheme and simultaneously undermine it by requiring Cordelia to perform what for her would be impossible. The answer is that Lear created the plan in the image of his own ambivalence. While emotionally he realizes he has already lost her, he makes a desperate effort to retain her love, to deny time and necessity. His jealousy of the two men competing for her hand and his feelings of rejection as she prepares to marry another have left him with a deep sense of loss. The plan was consciously designed to ensure Lear's security but unconsciously intended to confirm the pain of rejection.

Whatever he consciously believes about the love test, Lear knows in his heart that Cordelia cannot flatter him. In accepting the courtship of other men, she has seemingly "rejected" him already. So she is bound by her very nature to reject him now. There are many possible reasons for Cordelia to have failed the test. As we have seen, she is too truthful to flatter. She may also have a speech impediment, unable to speak when deeply moved. She says: "Unhappy that I am, I cannot heave / My heart into my mouth" (I.i.93-94). In later passages, when emotionally moved, she has a trick of repeating words—"And so I am, I am," "No cause, no cause" (IV.vii.70,76). Does she stutter under pressure? If so, then all the more reason to believe that Lear intended his plan to fail. Desiring to mourn, to wallow in self-pity, he sets himself up for failure, creating a situation that matches externally the ineffable sense of pain and loss he feels. This explains the zest with which he disowns Cordelia in lines 110-25. He meets her rejection with ensuing rejection, taunting her by giving to his "beloved sons" what should have been hers.

The knowledge that another man will possess her torments him immeasurably; Cordelia has been her father's one great love. As he can no longer preserve their former relationship and cannot become her lover, he plans to retire, to become her surrogate child, to "rest" in her "kind nursery." But even that is not enough. What he really wants is the occasion to wallow in self-pity, to cry like an abandoned child, and to lament the intolerable loss he feels.

Lear's own consciousness splits as does the coronet in I.i, when he realizes Cordelia cannot give him the unconditional love he desperately craves. He undergoes a crisis of faith, a need no human love can satisfy, no matter how deep. Whatever she does, Cordelia cannot content him. At the final crisis of his life, Lear looks to his much-loved child for a complete union in love and finds only rejection. What he asks from her, he must ultimately find for himself. His emotional need has long been recognized in Christian marriage ceremonies. As C.L. Barber has explained, "*Lear* begins with a failure of the passage that might [have been] handled by the marriage service," had the context of the play been overtly Christian and his own consciousness sufficiently receptive. What a father surrendered in the marriage service, he would ideally be compensated for in the communion service that followed, as all present acknowledged their unity in the greater love of God.[47]

Lear's blindness to the loyalty of Cordelia and Kent in Act I, scene i, is caused by his egocentricity. The victim of ego inflation, he had perceived his daughters and subjects as extensions of himself, their function only to please or accommodate him. His bitter rejection of Cordelia in I.i.236-37 demonstrates this: "Better thou / Hadst not been born than not t' have pleas'd me better." His egocentricity extends far beyond that of the other fathers discussed in this chapter. Whereas Leonato and Shylock are neurotically attached to their daughters, Lear's egocentricity encompasses his entire world. As the fool tells him, he has grown old before learning essential developmental lessons (I.v.49).

In the final phase of life, confronted with the frightening prospect of death, Lear must cope with all earlier unresolved conflicts. He has not resolved his identity in the crisis of adolescence. He cannot dissociate himself from his authoritative roles of king and father. Nor has he learned intimacy and commitment in young adulthood. His inadequate perception of love confirms that. His parenthood, as well, has been superficial and incomplete. He has sired daughters but has never really known them.[48] He has failed in his commitment to the care and nurture of society, retreating into narcissistic self-absorption. In this weakened condition, he confronts the challenge of integrity. Unprepared, he recoils in terror, regressing to second childhood.

Psychologist-critics have noted Lear's infantilism, which leads him to make impossible demands of his daughters. They have pointed out that at "fourscore and upward" he "remains a great baby . . . a ranting, towering, very dangerous baby." But they have not fully examined Lear's crisis in its developmental context. Maturation involves a continued growth in altruism, reaching beyond the self-centeredness of childhood, from dependence through independence to interdependence.[49]

In this final stage, Lear must face all unresolved developmental crises. This means learning not only intimacy and identity, but basic trust, the earliest lesson of all. Threatened by the specter of death and his own inadequacy, Lear at the beginning of the play is a study in contrasts: his implicit assumption of absolute power clearly at variance with his abdication of political power to his daughters and his desperate need of their love.[50] A prideful, powerful man, he is spiritually impoverished. There are many references to the gods in this play, but most of them are curses. Lear's references before Act III reveal no trust in the benevolence of God or the universe.[51] Without basic trust, he can hardly have developed identity or intimacy.[52] Lear's very immaturity drives him back to the earliest stage of his development. This is at once his weakness and his salvation, for by finally learning the lesson of trust, he can grow into a more complete human being.

On one level, Lear commits the ultimate folly by making his daughters his mothers. He projects upon Cordelia his need for maternal love, asking her for more than she can give: he "destroys Cordelia by creating her presence in the image of his own need and imprisoning her in that image."[53] He also foolishly surrenders his political power to Goneril and Regan, vainly hoping to "retain / The name, and all th'addition to a king" (I.i.138-39). Renaissance philosopher William Gouge denounced parents who "in their folly . . . put themselves in their children's power, and let goe all their authority over them."[54] In his immaturity, Lear precipitates his tragedy. He brings his suffering upon himself by his initial refusal to face his own individuation, by seeking to hide his underlying conflicts beneath a facade of flattery and pretense. Yet the very retreat to childishness that precipitates his tragedy also facilitates his psychological development.

His desperate desire for a mother's love stems from his deep lack of trust. Faced by the prospect of death, he must return to that darksome void some affirmation of the meaning of life, and this is impossible without basic trust. His madness reduces and redeems him. On the heath, he strips off his clothing—in the Renaissance, a sign of rank and identity—and returns to the essential man, recognizing the "poor, bare, forked animal" (III.iv.115).[55] Reduced to his own basic elements as he nakedly confronts the storm, he is

[73]

transformed in a process of spiritual alchemy to his own vital essence. Reborn, returned in the image of a naked, wailing babe, Lear begins again the process of personal development, repeating the lessons he had missed.

For the first time, he reaches out in expressions of caring. He leads his poor fool into the hovel—"I have one part in my heart / That's sorry yet for thee" (III.ii.72-73). And then he kneels down to pray, in an affirmation of basic trust as well as compassion for the:

> Poor naked wretches, wheresoe'er you are,
> That bide the pelting of this pitiless storm,
> How shall your houseless heads and unfed sides,
> Your loop'd and window'd raggedness, defend you
> From seasons such as these?

In newfound empathy he realizes: "O, I have ta'en / Too little care of this!" (III.iv.28-33).

As his mind splits into kaleidoscopic patterns, he finds new aspects of himself in expressions of identity, intimacy, and generativity. He learns identity as he recognizes his human infirmity, the truth behind years of flattery: "they flattered me like a dog . . . they told me I was every thing; 'tis a lie, I am not ague-proof" (IV.vi.97,106-7). He learns generativity in caring for his poor subjects who must suffer as he is suffering. With these truths comes a new capacity for intimacy. He awakens from his ordeal, addressing Cordelia with honest humility:

> I am a very foolish fond old man,
> Fourscore and upward, not an hour more or less;
> And to deal plainly,
> I fear I am not in my perfect mind. [IV.vii.60-63]

No longer childish and egocentric, Lear can now ask forgiveness and can love Cordelia with a trust beyond his ability to measure. Yet he embraces her only to lose her again in death.

Even her death furthers his development, for Lear must learn that Cordelia herself is not the answer. He cannot cling to her, arrested in the state of intimacy, if he is to gain the wisdom of integrity. Act V, scene i, demonstrates Lear's excessive attachment. As he is led away to prison, he feels that he has everything he has ever wanted: Cordelia's love exclusively. The rest of the world may pass away, for he finally has her all to himself. His speeches sound more like those of a lover than a father. One recalls the concentrated personal world of Donne's *Songs and Sonets*:

Come, let's away to prison:
We two alone will sing like birds i' th' cage:
When thou dost ask me blessing, I'll kneel down,
And ask of thee forgiveness.   [V.i.8-11]

Have I caught thee?
He that parts us shall bring a brand from heaven,
And fire us hence like foxes.   [V.i.21-23]

Enclosed within the comfort of his daughter's love, Lear makes the same mistake he had made long ago: equating Cordelia's love with divinity itself. No matter how much she loves him, she cannot bestow ultimate meaning, for she is mortal. In her loving acceptance, she has taught him to love, but he cannot look to her for affirmation. That must come from Lear himself.

With Cordelia he demonstrates commitment. He is able to fight for her, killing the slave that was hanging her, and ultimately, to die with her in final recognition of the silent message on her lips. In his last moments, he finds his affirmation. Holding the body of his beloved child in his arms, he also reaches for the loyal Kent, drawing him close by asking him to "undo this button" (V.iii.309).[56] Affirming a love that cannot be measured or possessed, Lear leaves this life in a final gesture of caring.

CHAPTER FOUR

Dominated Daughters

S hakespeare offers three examples of young women dominated by patriarchal expectations. Ophelia, Hero, and Desdemona are victimized by
the traditional power structure that identifies women exclusively as
childbearers, insisting on a rigid model of chastity to ensure the continuity of
pure patrilineal succession. This requirement leaves women highly vulnerable. What matters is not that they are modest, chaste, and obedient, but that
men perceive them as such.[1] Imprisoned in their passive situation, women
cannot actively affirm or defend their honor. The more they seek to be good
women, conforming to traditional expectations, the more they are victimized.
Politically and psychologically, these dominated daughters remain children
in their innocence, obedience, and submission to authority. Because the passive feminine ideal denies them their autonomy, they fail to resolve the crisis
of intimacy, fail to become fully adult. By depicting their suffering, Shakespeare repudiates the traditional stereotype as confining and destructive, ar-
resting young women in their growth into healthy adulthood, and in some
instances even depriving them of their lives.

Ophelia: Fearful Domination

Traditionally, critics have seen Ophelia as a "pathetically weak character."[2]
She has been alternately pitied and condemned for her helplessness and
domination by her father. A.C. Bradley saw her as childlike, "so near childhood that old affections still have the strongest hold."[3] Critics have emphasized her innocence and dependence. "She has never been woman enough to
have a mind apart from [her father]."[4] She is "young and sweet and also very

[76]

passive," "pretty but ineffectual," "a timid conventional girl, too fragile a reed for a man to lean upon."⁵ "Like other simple-minded daughters who lack the strength of mind to rely on themselves," she has been characterized as "a puppet in her father's hands" and "a doll without intellect."⁶

Yet while their observations are valid from one point of view, the great majority of Ophelia's critics have been "Hamlet-critics," perceiving her as he perceives her, through their regret that she does not fulfill the needs and expectations of the tormented prince of Denmark. A feminist analysis of Ophelia's behavior demonstrates that she is not the simpleminded creature she seems. Traditional readings of her character have been as superficial as nineteenth-century productions, which portrayed her as a simple, pretty girl of flowers whose mad scenes were artfully sung and danced. As Helena Faucit realized and dared to play her to a stunned audience in 1844-45, Ophelia actually does go mad.⁷ There is pain and struggle beneath that sweet surface. Her misfortune merits not only our pity but our censure of traditional mores that make women repress themselves and behave like automatons.

Contrary to prevailing opinion, Ophelia is more than a simple girl, living in "a world of dumb ideas and feelings."⁸ The pity of it is that Ophelia *does* think and feel. A careful examination of the text in I.iii reveals that she loves Hamlet and thinks for herself, but is forced to repress all this at her father's command, conforming to the stifling patriarchal concept of female behavior that subordinates women to their "honor," their procreative function in male society.

Torn between what she feels and what she is told to be, Ophelia is tormented by the crisis of identity. As one critic pointed out long ago, "she is not aware of the nature of her own feelings; they are prematurely developed in their full force before she has strength to bear them."⁹ Caught in adolescent uncertainty between childhood and adulthood, she cannot enter the stage of intimacy and adult commitment because she does not yet know who she is. Carol Gilligan has pointed to the difficulties young women have in individuation. Raised with an emphasis on empathy rather than autonomy, girls tend to subordinate their own needs to those of others. Ophelia experiences severe role confusion in which her personal feelings are suppressed in favor of external expectations.¹⁰

At the beginning of the play, Ophelia is a healthy young woman with romantic feelings and a normal level of sexual awareness. This is apparent in her dismay at Laertes's warning about Hamlet; her comprehension of Hamlet's sexual innuendoes; and, finally, the sexual references that rise to the surface in her madness. As her initial liveliness in I.iii indicates, she is affectionate, expressive, ingenuous, as natural as the flowers she later embraces. In this scene, however, she comes face to face with that static and oppressive female virtue: chastity.

Both her brother and her father warn her repeatedly to defend her honor, her virginity, the fragile basis for woman's respectability and personal value in patriarchal society. They have defined her in the traditional role of nurturer and caretaker, while simultaneously devaluing that role, subordinating care to masculine power.[11] Their obsession with female chastity and the accompanying double standard reflect the patriarchal concern for legitimate issue, the demand that young women be presented as chaste vessels by their fathers to future husbands, sacrificing personal identity to their function as childbearers. Women in this sense are "womb men," reduced to walking repositories for the male seed. In order to perform their sacred function, they must remain clean, chaste, and hermetically sealed until the marriage act, which ensures the continuity of patrilineal succession for another generation. Then their husbands must see that they remain pure. It is not only Hamlet, Laertes, and Polonius who are acutely concerned with woman's chastity. The issue looms large in *Othello*, and the preponderance of cuckold jokes among the men, even in Shakespeare's comedies, reveals their concern with legitimate issue, their underlying fears and suspicions of female sexuality.

The patriarchy upholds the traditional ideal of the sweet, innocent, and fundamentally passive young woman who obeys her father and elder brother. Their duty is to defend her honor that she may procreate only within patriarchal bounds. To a great extent, woman's reproductive function has led to her domination. The ideal of feminine virtue is static—the preservation of her chastity—while masculine virtue is dynamic, active, developmental. Men may add honor to their names by noble deeds and accomplishments, while women may only defend the small shred of honor they have, which once gone is irrevocably lost.

In his protective, masculine role, Laertes confronts his sister and warns her about the danger in her love for Hamlet:

> Then weigh what loss your honour may sustain,
> If with too credent ear you list his songs,
> Or lose your heart, or your chaste treasure open
> To his unmast'red importunity.
> Fear it, Ophelia, fear it, my dear sister.
>
> [I.iii.29-33]

His fearful warning later echoes in Ophelia's ears when she confronts an impassioned Hamlet in her closet. Her father warns her more abruptly: "You do not understand yourself so clearly / As it behoves my daughter and your honour" (I.iii.97-98). She is his child, his property, a vessel of procreation, no more but so. As the play progresses, Shakespeare shows us Ophelia's acceptance of this role and the tragic consequences.

At the beginning of I.iii, she is still the young and spirited girl Hamlet has loved. When Laertes maligns Hamlet's motives, calling his courtship but "a fashion and a toy in blood," Ophelia is stunned and hurt, responding, "No more but so?" (10), for she had believed in Hamlet's love. She listens to her brother's advice but knows him well enough to ask that he practice the restraint he preaches, denouncing the operative double standard and showing herself a perceptive, spirited young woman. To the young fashion plate Polonius later suspects of "drabbing" in Paris, Ophelia adds:

> But, good my brother,
> Do not, as some ungracious pastors do,
> Show me the steep and thorny way to heaven;
> Whiles, like a puff'd and reckless libertine,
> Himself the primrose path of dalliance treads,
> And recks not his own rede.   [46-51]

Ophelia realizes that not all male authority figures practice what they preach. Seeing beneath appearances, she recognizes the ugly reality of hypocrisy. Although young and inexperienced, Ophelia most assuredly is not simple. She does not lack intellect, nor does she automatically take everything at face value.

But when Polonius adds his lengthy warning in the same scene, Ophelia begins to doubt herself. Her brother, then her father, has frightened and insulted her about her love for Hamlet. The two authority figures in her young life, they undermine her trust in love, making her doubt Hamlet's intentions and her own awakening sexual feelings. What had once seemed so wonderful becomes progressively more frightening. Her protestations that Hamlet has "importun'd [her] with love / In honourable fashion" and sworn to her "with almost all the holy vows of heaven" (110, 113) are met by the sordid cynicism of Polonius. As Iago poisons the mind of Othello, so do Laertes and Polonius poison Ophelia's mind, presenting a view of human sexuality that is gross, animalistic, degrading, and terrifying.[12] Hamlet's vows, they tell her, are merely a means to satisfy his lust, "springes to catch woodcocks" (116), and she has stupidly believed him, made herself his helpless prey and risked losing her honor, her very identity in patriarchal society. The image of courtship Polonius paints for her is nothing less than calculated rape.

Her dream of love lies shattered at her feet; she tells Polonius, "I do not know, my lord, what I should think" (104). According to Gilligan, moral development in women "proceeds from an initial concern with survival to a focus on goodness and finally to a reflective understanding of care."[13] Ophelia is concerned with survival in what seems a brutal, hostile world. Frightened and disillusioned, she seeks safety in the passive role assigned to women for generations. Her father tells her to stay away from the danger that Hamlet represents, and she submits: "I shall obey, my lord" (136). Her submission is not only a surrender to convention, but an act of self-preservation by a young woman for whom sexuality has become a frightening animalistic threat. Ophelia succumbs to severe security anxiety.[14] Her ensuing actions reflect a compulsive defense of her chastity in a world that appears blatantly brutal and aggressive. Ophelia's fearful withdrawal and subsequent deterioration represent an implicit accusation of a society that defines men as active sexual aggressors, condoning their promiscuity while valuing women only for their chastity which must be defended at all costs. Retreating behind the false self the patriarchy has created for her, Ophelia represses her feelings and obliterates her own reality, collapsing into a schizoid divided self and moral confusion. As R.D. Laing wrote of her: "there is no one there. She is not a person. There is no integral selfhood expressed through her actions or utterances. Incomprehensible statements are said by nothing. She has already died."[15]

Ophelia has been condemned for letting her father dominate her, for failing to "observe the fundamental responsibilities that hold together an existence."[16] But let us consider the situation from her point of view. As a young woman, she is, first of all, more inclined to defer to the wishes of others than to follow her own feelings.[17] Ophelia errs in trusting her father, but she is not the only person in the play who has taken a parent at face value. Hamlet failed to recognize his mother's moral weakness until her marriage to Claudius. Furthermore, reverence for one's parents was expected of Renaissance youth. As Harley Granville-Barker emphasized, "we may call her docility a fault, when, as she is bid, she shuts herself away from Hamlet; but how not to trust to her brother's care for her and her father's wisdom?"[18] Like Othello, Ophelia errs in trusting the wrong moral guide: in his case a friend who had shared dangers on the battlefield, in hers a father to whom convention bound her duty and obedience. Polonius's warning, seconded by her brother's, gains greater credibility. But most significant, her moral guides have not only told her how to behave; they have redefined her entire universe, inculcating in Ophelia a view of human sexuality as nasty and brutish as that which infects Othello. Ophelia sees herself in a world in which sexuality transforms human beings into beasts, with men the predators and women their prey.

If the play had offered any moral alternative, she might have been able to think more clearly and trust her love. Romantic heroines in Shakespeare's comedies defy corrupt patriarchal authority, think for themselves, and affirm their love because their moral guides or close friends uphold a nobler view of human nature. Rosalind has Celia's friendship; Portia, Nerissa's. Hermia has Helena's friendship and the example of Duke Theseus in love. Even Jessica, flawed as she is, finds a moral alternative to her father's values in Christianity and later in Portia herself. Juliet has the moral influence of the friar, who sees her marriage to Romeo as a means to greater harmony. Even the isolated and tormented Hamlet finds a friend in Horatio. But Ophelia has no one: no friar, no friend, not even a positive role model in Gertrude, the only other woman in the play. Everything around Ophelia only confirms her father's words. Her next experience with Hamlet is a case in point. When she sees him in II.i, she runs in to her father crying, "O, lord, my lord, I have been so affrighted" (75). After she concludes her description of the disheveled Hamlet, Polonius asks, "Mad for thy love?" and her answer, "My lord, I do not know; / But truly, I do fear it" (85-86), reflects her fear and confusion. No longer a romantic dream, love has become a violent and fearful thing. We know that Hamlet has confronted his father's ghost in the previous scene and that either this or his antic disposition explains his behavior. But Ophelia does not know this. The very personification of love melancholy, Hamlet rushes into her chamber in frantic disarray, grabs her by the wrist, holds her close, and stares into her eyes. He finally releases her with a sigh and backs out of the room, his eyes still riveted upon her. During all this time, not a word is exchanged. In this unfortunate encounter, Ophelia fails to give Hamlet the reassurance he seeks and confirms his suspicions about women. But for Ophelia, Hamlet's actions cannot fail to confirm what her father and brother have told her: that men's sexual passions are fearful things, transforming them into beasts. Terrified—Is he here to rape her?—she is unable to speak a word to him and runs to her father for protection.

In III.i not only Polonius but also the king and queen reinforce for Ophelia the importance of obeying her father to rescue Hamlet from the madness her love has driven him to. She succumbs to convention, becoming a puppet in their hands. But she plays her role awkwardly, revealing her inner conflict. She is understandably nervous when confronted with the violent effects of love melancholy, and her actions contradict her father's plan. Polonius has arranged this as a chance meeting with Hamlet, handing her a prayer book as a prop to ponder as she waits. But Ophelia has brought with her all Hamlet's "remembrances," and since Polonius fails to mention these, we are to assume that this is her idea. She returns the gifts with what has been called the "completely inappropriate little maxim":[19] "Take these again; for to the noble mind / Rich gifts wax poor when givers prove unkind" (100-101). To Hamlet, the gifts reveal that the encounter is not chance but contrivance, and the maxim makes no sense, for *she* has rejected him. From Ophelia's point of view, however, the maxim is quite appropriate: he had given her these gifts and promises of honorable love when he had really intended to seduce her. The prince has been unkind indeed; Ophelia feels betrayed and disillusioned. Then, in confirmation of her fears, Hamlet torments her verbally, declaring, then denying, his love. Her answer to his "I did love you once" reveals her disillusionment: "Indeed, my lord, you made me believe so" (116-17). In these lines she denies the reality of her previous perceptions; Hamlet never loved her. He had only sought to use her. This, too, he seems to confirm as he responds, "You should not have believed me; for virtue cannot so inoculate our old stock but we shall relish of it: I loved you not." She answers, "I was the more deceived" (118-21). Heartbroken, Ophelia hears the man she loves denounce her, insult her, and fall into wild ravings, the sexual nausea in his words reinforcing and confirming her own.

Her speech at the end of this encounter expresses her guilt, dejection, and despair. As Hamlet exits, raving at her, she laments:

> O, what a noble mind is here o'er-thrown!
> . . . .
> And I, of ladies most deject and wretched,
> That suck'd the honey of his music vows,
> Now see that noble and most sovereign reason,
> Like sweet bells jangled, out of time and harsh;
> That unmatch'd form and feature of his blown youth
> Blasted with ecstacy: O, woe is me,
> T'have seen what I have seen, see what I see!
> [III.i.158, 163-69]

In her misery, she loves him still. This passage resonates with recognition. Rejected by her love, taken in by his "music vows," and guilty by complicity in the love that drove him to madness, she regrets what she has been and done. The devastated and emotionally exhausted Ophelia now perceives love as a poisonous dream, which attracts like honey but transforms men to beasts. Hurt, disillusioned, and troubled by her own sexual feelings, she is ashamed that her beauty has awakened such appetites in Hamlet. Claudius may not believe love has caused Hamlet's madness, but Ophelia most certainly does.

Hamlet's gross language during the play scene reinforces her impression of his lust. Insulted and humiliated by his sexual innuendoes, she keeps up a brave front, responding to him with terse formality:

> No, my lord . . .
> Ay, my lord . . .
> I think nothing, my lord . . .
> What is, my lord? . . .
> You are merry, my lord . . .
> Ay, my lord. [III.ii.120-31][20]

Stunned into a fear of her lover and a childlike dependency on her father, Ophelia suddenly has them both removed, and even her brother is out of the country. She collapses into madness because she knows not where to turn for guidance. As one critic explained, "she was like a tender vine, growing first to the trellis of filial piety and then to that of romantic love. When these two are removed and she is left unsupported, she cannot stand alone, and falls."[21] But there is more to it. Interspersed between her songs of unfaithful lovers and dirges for dead fathers, we find this telling admission: "They say the owl was a baker's daughter. Lord, we know / What we are, but know not what we may be" (IV.v.41-43). This fragile flower has not only been deprived of her props, she also feels guilt and complicity in her father's death. What emerges here is the devastating awareness of her own repressed sexuality, the shock of "what may be" in herself combined with the horrible transformations wrought by romantic love. Hamlet has desired her and she has desired him as well, loved the man who later killed her father, and, most horribly, it was her love that drove him mad. Distributing her flowers, she gives both Gertrude and herself rue, emblematic of repentance and regret.[22] In her madness, her repressed sexuality finally breaks through the conventional false self of enforced modesty, chastity, and decorum.[23] In addition to the imagery in her risqué songs, Elizabethans would have recognized the flowers she clutched to herself when she drowned as definite phallic symbols, indicative of her repressed longings.[24]

[83]

The symbolism in her drowning is itself an emblem of the inner conflict which drove her to madness. She drowns in her "fantastic garlands," woven of buttercups, daisies, nettles, and long purples, flowers that represent her innocence, pain, and sexuality, woven together here in madness as she had been unable to do in her life. Unable to combine her conflicting fears and desires into an integrated sense of self, she drowns. Encircled by this tangle of discordant meanings, surrounded by water—symbol of the unconscious[25]—gradually pulled down by her clothes, that external self which finally became too heavy to bear her up any longer, she slips beneath the surface, into madness, into death.

Hero: Slandered Innocence

Like Ophelia, Hero in *Much Ado* has been both praised and criticized for her innocence. Her passive vulnerability has inspired pity in some and boredom in others. According to William Hazlitt, Hero "leaves an indelible impression on the mind by her beauty, her tenderness, and the hard trial of her love." Others have called her "as pure and tender as a flower" or "rather a boring girl."[26] In two modern studies she has been characterized as "shadowy and silent," an ineffective heroine who lacks credibility.[27] All have found her mild and quiet, and "vulnerably passive."[28]

Hero is numinous, archetypal in her innocence, the silent woman of legend and the chaste and obedient Renaissance ideal. So silent is she that the majority of critics accord her only a passing reference, giving their attention instead to the more dynamic Beatrice, Benedick, and Claudio. In critical studies, as in the play itself, Hero's role is silent and symbolic. "Throughout the courtship, misunderstandings and all, Hero herself has hardly anything to say: she is essentially a figure in the pattern whose chief dramatic function is to stand there and look beautiful."[29] In her silence and modesty, she exemplifies the perfect Renaissance woman. As an individual, she is conspicuous by her absence. This can be better understood by noting exactly how her character functions in the text. In I.i she is present during the opening scenes but has only 1 line to Beatrice's 45. For more than 150 lines Hero simply stands there in silence. Even when her father introduces her to Don Pedro at line 103, she speaks not a word but probably curtsies dutifully. In II.i, during which she is told by her father of Don Pedro's presumed intentions, is courted by him, and agrees to help trick Beatrice into realizing that she loves Benedick, she has only 8 lines to Beatrice's 97.

Claudio falls in love with her image. In I.i he refers to her as "a modest young lady," "the sweetest lady that ever I looked on" (164,189), and determines to marry her. She is his silent goddess, his anima symbol, and the image of his dreams.[30] Unlike Beatrice, she has revealed no individuality to obscure the pure abstraction he desires in her.

The model young woman, Hero listens in silent and modest obedience to her father's instructions about her marriage in a manner Juan Luis Vives would have applauded.[31] Her silent figure stands looking on while her father and uncle discuss her future and Beatrice dazzles with her witty exposition on marriage. All the while, Hero speaks not a single word:

> *Antonio.* [*To Hero*] Well, niece, I trust you will be ruled by your father.
> *Beatrice.* Yes, faith; it is my cousin's duty to make curtsy and say "Father, as it please you." But yet for all that, cousin, let him be a handsome fellow, or else make another curtsy and say "Father, as it please me."
> *Leonato.* Well, niece, I hope to see you one day fitted with a husband.
> *Beatrice.* Not till God make men of some other metal than earth. Would it not grieve a woman to be overmastered with a piece of valiant dust? To make an account of her life to a clod of wayward marl? No, uncle, I'll none; Adam's sons are my brethren; and truly, I hold it a sin to match in my kindred.
> *Leonato.* Daughter, remember what I told you: if the prince do solicit you in that kind, you know your answer.
> *Beatrice.* The fault will be in the music, cousin, if you be not wooed in good time.
>
> [II.i.55-73]

If Beatrice is the dynamic rebel who rejects the traditional woman's role, Hero is the archetypal good woman who follows it to the letter. She is "the embodiment of the courtly concept of ideal daughter and bride. Emblem of the sheltered life—crowned by beauty, modesty, and chastity—she is bred from birth for a noble alliance which will add luster to her lineage."[32] Psychologically, her character follows Erikson's description of traditional female development. She "holds her identity in abeyance as she prepares to attract the man by whose name she will be known, by whose status she will be defined, the man who will rescue her from emptiness and loneliness by filling 'the inner space.'"[33] But her obedience and archetypal purity avail her little. No matter how good or innocent she is, she cannot influence her fate. Her identity depends upon men's perceptions of her, and the illusion of doubt can quickly sully even the most virtuous reputation, leaving her no defense.

In III.i, a scene without male authority figures, Hero has a suprising 76 lines. Plotting with the other women to trick Beatrice into realizing that she loves Benedick, Hero is spirited, gregarious, and much more verbal. Apparently, she is not naturally shy or phlegmatic; her silence at other times merely reflects her breeding as a lady. Before men she is silent and deferential, while with her cousin and other women she may relax and be more herself. In III.iv, we see her again interacting with women. Dressing for the wedding, she exchanges witty banter in some 14 lines, although troubled by nervousness and forboding.

In IV.i, when exposed to public scandal in the church, she courageously affirms her innocence:

> *Hero.* O, God defend me! How am I beset!
>   What kind of catechising call you this?
> *Claudio.* To make you answer truly to your name.
> *Hero.* Is it not Hero? Who can blot that name
>   With any just reproach?
> *Claudio.*   Marry, that can Hero;
>   Hero itself can blot out Hero's virtue.
>   What man was he talk'd with you yesternight
>   Out at your window betwixt twelve and one?
>   Now, if you are a maid, answer to this.
> *Hero.* I talk'd with no man at that hour, my lord.
> *Don Pedro.* Why, then you are no maiden.
>
>   [IV.i.78-88]

Not only has she been betrayed; she is powerless to exonerate herself. Regardless of what she says or does, she cannot actively prove her innocence. The staged deception of the night before has soiled the image of her chastity. Because of the dualism implicit in men's perception of women, when the shadow of doubt clouds her radiant image, she ceases to be a virgin in their eyes and automatically becomes a whore. Hero's protestations of innocence, like Desdemona's, are seen only as further proof of her guilt. Don Pedro then describes the shameful encounter at her window—as we know, an illusion. But one illusion can destroy her, so fragile is a woman's honor, so tenuous her position in man's world. Unless she is beyond suspicion, she becomes a tainted outcast.

Claudio's repudiation of her in the church may seem unduly rash, but he barely knows her. Far more shocking is her father's rejection. How quickly Leonato believes the slander about his child. Apparently, all those years in which Hero was the model daughter—chaste, silent, obedient, and submissive—have not enabled him to trust in her character.[34] Leonato sinks into anger and despair, and only Beatrice rallies to Hero's defense.

In her study *The Slandered Woman in Shakespeare*, Joyce Sexton pointed out how Hero's predicament illustrates the insidious nature of slander, an attack for which woman has no defense.[35] She cannot actively regain her honor and good name with noble deeds like a courtier who has fallen out of favor. Because of their procreative function as chaste mothers in patriarchal society, women cannot earn or acquire more honor; all they can do is behave according to patriarchal expectations. Hero is trapped by the traditional concept of virtuous womanhood, which is untenable and unhealthy. As Gilligan observed, "the notion that virtue for women lies in self-sacrifice has complicated the course of woman's development by pitting the moral issue of goodness against the adult questions of responsibility.[36] This play demonstrates how easily woman's passive virtue comes to naught and how helpless she is to defend it.

Hero's restoration, like her repudiation, is not contingent upon her actions. As a traditional woman, her identity depends upon men's perceptions of her. Fortunately, a man, Borachio, confesses, redeeming her tarnished reputation. In V.i, when Claudio discovers that Hero has been unjustly slandered, his words reveal just what she means to him: "Sweet Hero! now thy image doth appear / In the rare semblance that I lov'd it first" (259-60). It is only her image that he loves. In V.iv the repentant Claudio receives at her father's hand another Hero. Now ceremoniously transferred from father to husband, Hero lifts her veil and reveals herself, revived, restored to life and honor. But so fragile is her identity in patriarchal society that when she fails to match men's dreams of perfection, she becomes a victim of their deepest fears and doubts. Implicit here is Shakespeare's criticism of the traditional feminine stereotype as a static and passive ideal, which represses women and makes them far too vulnerable to the oft-observed antinomy between appearance and reality.

Desdemona: Love's Sweet Victim

Alternately canonized and criticized for loving Othello, Desdemona has been praised for her devotion and censured for her sexuality, described as deceptive, proud, and manipulative or as helplessly passive. She is herself a tragic paradox. A spirited, courageous young woman, Desdemona is moved by the depth of her love to conform to a static and fatal ideal of feminine behavior. Among those critics for whom she shines as a saintly ideal, Irving Ribner said that "in the perfection of her love Desdemona reflects the love of Christ for man," and G. Wilson Knight found her a "divinity comparable with Dante's Beatrice."[37] Yet W.H. Auden observed "One cannot but share Iago's doubts as to the durability of the marriage," predicting that "given a few more years of Othello and of Emilia's influence and she might well, one feels, have taken a lover." Jan Kott, too, found her strong sexuality disturbing: "Of all Shakespeare's female characters she is the most sensuous. . . . Desdemona is faithful but must have something of a slut in her."[38]

Beyond a doubt, Desdemona is affectionate and sensual, but this does not make her a slut any more than the absence of sexuality would sanctify her. Too often her critics themselves have fallen victim to the virgin-whore complex, the false dilemma that dominates the perception of women in traditional society. A few critics have recognized the simple fact that Desdemona is both a virtuous and a passionate woman.[39]

The elopement has been cited as proof of her courage or evidence of her deceptive nature: "a measure of her determination to have a life that seems to offer the promise of excitement denied her as a sheltered Venetian senator's daughter"; "her deception of her own father makes an unpleasant impression." We may laugh at Thomas Rymer's oversimplified reading of the play as "a caution to all Maidens of Quality how, without their Parents consent, they run away with Blackamoors" and "a warning to all good Wives, that they look well to their Linnen."[40] Desdemona's critics range from the sublime to the ridiculous. Predominantly male, they have seen her as either willful and manipulative or helplessly passive: "a determined young woman . . . eager to get her own way;" her advocacy for Cassio demonstrating her desire to dominate Othello, revealing a strong case of penis envy."[41] Arthur Kirsch saw her advocacy as concern for her husband, realizing that his continued alienation from Cassio was "unnatural and injurious to them both," while Auden called this merely another demonstration of her pride: "In continuing to badger Othello, she betrays a desire to prove to herself and to Cassio that she can make her husband do as she pleases." Bradley, by contrast, found her "helplessly passive," an innocent, loving martyr:

> Desdemona is helplessly passive. She can do nothing whatever. She cannot retaliate even in speech; no, not even in silent feeling. And the chief reason of her helplessness only makes the sight of her suffering more

exquisitely painful. She is helpless because her nature is infinitely sweet and her love absolute. . . . Desdemona's suffering is like that of the most loving of dumb creatures tortured without cause by the being he adores.

In a similar vein, Bernard McElroy wrote, "The inner beauty and selflessness of her character are exactly what render her most vulnerable to the fate that overtakes her." As Carol Thomas Neely observed, for traditional critics, "the source of her sainthood seems a passivity verging on catatonia."[42]

The history of Desdemona on the stage parallels these changing critical estimations. Until Fanny Kemble, Helena Faucit, and Ellen Terry endowed her with a new dynamism, Desdemona was portrayed as a pathetic girl, not a tragic heroine. In the nineteenth century her part was diminished by extensive cuts, and William Charles Macready tried to dissuade Fanny Kemble from playing it, arguing that this was no part for a great actress. Kemble persevered, creating a Desdemona who was softly feminine but also forthright and courageous. Her Desdemona, like Helena Faucit's, fought for her life in the final scene. According to Ellen Terry, most people believed that Desdemona was "a ninny, a pathetic figure," that "an actress of the dolly type, a pretty young thing with a vapid, innocent expression, is well suited to the part," but she felt that Desdemona was "a woman of strong character," requiring the talents of a great tragic actress.[43]

As these actresses recognized, Desdemona is a young woman who transcends any stereotype. In her courage and compassion, she is androgynous; in her boundless love and goodness she sees beyond the artificial divisions of the patriarchal hierarchy. Like Hamlet, she values people, not for their social rank, but for themselves. She has been praised for "a man's courage . . . an extreme example of that union of feminine and masculine qualities that Shakespeare plainly held essential for either the perfect man or the perfect woman."[44] Her "downright violence and storm of fortunes" demonstrate her courage and defiance of convention as well as the strength of her love (I.iii.250). She loved Othello "for the dangers [he] had pass'd," recognizing in his bold spirit a counterpart to her own, longing for adventure denied by her confining role as a Venetian senator's daughter. Othello "lov'd her that she did pity them," her feminine compassion equal to her masculine courage (I.iii.167-68).

She is by nature unconventional, a sensuous and virtuous woman in a culture that prized a cold, chaste ideal. Dynamic and courageous when the traditional feminine norm was passivity, she transcends patriarchal order and degree, reaching out in loving kindness to all. Desdemona behaved with daughterly decorum in her father's house but revealed her assertiveness and magnanimity in her love for Othello. Her enthusiastic and affectionate nature are evident in Othello's description of their courtship, especially in the Folio version. This apparently docile maiden would rush from her household chores to "devour" his stories "with a greedy ear," (I.iii.150,149). She was fascinated by this man of men and the adventurous life he led. So far was she from Brabantio's conventional "maiden never bold" (94) that she gave Othello for his pains "a world of kisses," (159) in the Folio reading far more assertive than the Quarto's "sighs."[45]

It is this magnanimous woman who stands resolutely before her father and the duke in council, declaring her love for which she had defied all convention. But this young woman now places her love into the traditional perspective, speaking of her "divided duty" between father and husband in which filial obedience is transferred from one authority figure to the next. As one critic has observed, "Desdemona's description of the transfer of her feelings from her father to her husband, with its invocation of her own mother as her example, touches in almost archetypal terms upon the psychological process by which a girl becomes a woman and a wife."[46] Othello inherits the father's title, "my lord":

> My noble father,
> . . . you are the lord of duty;
> I am hitherto your daughter: but here's my husband,
> And so much duty as my mother show'd
> To you, preferring you before her father,
> So much I challenge that I may profess
> Due to the Moor my lord.   [I.iii.180-89]

In her elopement, Desdemona "successfully defies the Father," Brabantio himself and "the symbol of Authority and Force" he represents. Harold Goddard contrasts her to the submissive Ophelia and Hamlet, who fail to break free from paternal authority.[47] True, her love liberates her long enough to elope with Othello, but in her concept of marriage she again succumbs to the yoke of convention, adopting the traditional role inherited from her mother, a relationship in which the wife becomes her husband's submissive, obedient subject.[48] She fails to make the psychological transition to adulthood, conforming to Vives's injunction that "the woman is as daughter unto her husband."[49] As Gilligan would explain it, Desdemona's moral development is arrested at the level of altruistic self-denial. Her every action reflects a desire to demonstrate goodness over selfishness.[50] Denying her own authority, she submits to the traditional pattern, ironically out of her deep love for Othello and her desire to be the perfect wife. As she declares, "My heart's subdu'd / Even to the very quality of my lord" (I.iii.251-52).

Critics have found an echo of the traditional father-daughter relationship, pointing to Othello's age, which makes him a father surrogate, and noting that he was her father's friend before the elopement.[51] Some psychological critics have seen her choice of him as motivated by an Oedipus complex, in which she sought either to marry someone like her father or to punish her father for being faithless to her in childhood. They explain her subsequent passive behavior as "moral masochism," motivated by guilt for her incestuous urgings.[52] But one need not resort to incest and Oedipus complexes to explain Desdemona's behavior. We have seen in her love for Othello a highly idealistic strain as well as a passionate attachment, an almost religious fervor and dedication. All her young life she had longed for a heroic mission, a cause. Because she is a woman, unable to pursue her heroic ideals, she finds her cause in loving Othello, subordinating herself in her role as his wife, even as he subordinates his ego to the demands of war. It is not only Othello who "agnize[s] / A natural and prompt alacrity . . . in hardness" (I.iii.232-34). Desdemona, as well, longs for heroic commitment and sacrifice. Given the limits of her culture, she can find this only indirectly, some would say masochistically, by devoting herself to Othello.[53]

Thus we have the paradox that explains Desdemona's contradictory image. She is courageous, heroic, passive, and vulnerable. She is both extremes because of her love, which makes of her an oxymoronic "excellent wretch" (III.iii.90). On the altar of holy love she sacrifices her dynamic self to the image of her dreams, becoming not a "moth of peace" (I.ii.257) but an equally diminished shadow of herself. As she rejects the "wealthy curled darlings" (I.ii.68) of Venice, leaving her father and embracing the man of her dreams, it would seem that she has resolved for herself the crisis of identity. But in her marriage she does not commit herself with the dynamic energy that flourished in her courtship and elopement. She chooses a new identity, a controlled, ever modest and obedient self, not Desdemona but the model wife, because this is what she feels Othello deserves. She becomes a victim of the convention she embraces, a neurotic self-effacement amounting to slow suicide.[54] She, too, loves "not wisely, but too well" (V.ii.344), affirming a static ideal, a polished surface of behavior that will not withstand the tempests her marriage faces on Cyprus.

As discussed at length in chapter two, the relation of a traditional Renaissance wife to her husband was like that of an obedient child. Although some critics censure Desdemona for failing in her wifely role, I would argue that her tragic fate stems from slavish conformity, an excess of altruism to which she sacrifices her own being.[55] After marriage, Desdemona conforms to the traditional norm for feminine behavior, as expressed by William Gouge.[56] This norm involves: "1 Acknowledgement of an husband's superioritie" and "2 A due esteeme of her owne husband to be the best for her, and worthy of honour on her part." Desdemona announces that her "heart's subdu'd / Even to the very quality of my lord" (I.iii.251-52), and in III.iv she berates herself for chiding him, even in her thoughts. Other wifely attributes are "3 An inward wive-like feare," "4 An outward reverend cariage towards her husband which consisteth in a wive-like sobrietie, mildnesse, curtesie, and modestie in apparell," and "5 Reverend speech to, and of her husband." Desdemona is gracious, poised, and respectful in her actions and speech. She refuses to speak ill of Othello after his shameful behavior in III.iv and when he strikes her in IV.i. In the former scene, she attributes his behavior to state business; in IV.ii she confesses to Emilia and Iago that she knows not what she has done to displease him but loves him still and ever will. Even when Othello comes to murder her, she behaves toward him with traditional wifely reverence.

Gouge lists "Obedience" as requirement 6. "Whate'er you be, I am obedient," Desdemona says in III.iii.89, choosing to follow his command rather than think for herself. This is also evident in her obedient departures at his command in III.iii and IV.i, and her coming at his bidding in IV.ii. Even in his jealous rages, she addresses him with love and respect. Gouge's requirement 7 is "Forbearing to doe without or against her husbands consent, such things as he hath power to order, as, to dispose and order the common goods of the familie, and the allowance for it, as children, servants, cattell, guests, journies, &c." Although some would criticize her for asking to accompany Othello to Cyprus, this request does not reflect willfulness on her part so much as an eagerness to begin married life. Most important, in asking this she does not go against Othello's wishes. Gouge also recommends "8 A ready yeelding to what her husband would have done. This manifested by her willingnesse to dwell where he will, to come when he calls, and to doe what he requireth." So attentive is Desdemona to Othello's desires and welfare that she does not even notice when she drops her hankerchief in III.iii, for she is concerned about his headache. She comes dutifully when he calls, bears his torments before Lodovico in IV.i, and seeks in every way to please him, even dismissing Emilia and retiring when her forebodings are apparent in the willow song.

Requirement 9 is "A patient bearing of any reproofe, and a ready redressing of that for which she is justly reproved." Desdemona patiently bears Othello's reproofs, although she cannot understand them and admits herself "a child to chiding" (IV.ii.114). She criticizes herself as an "unhandsome warrior" (III.iv.151) and tells Emilia that her "love doth so approve him, / That even his stubbornness, his checks, his frowns . . . have grace and favour in them" (IV.iii.19-21). Gouge also recommends "10 Contentment with her husbands present estate." Desdemona loves Othello for the dangers he has passed and accompanies him to the wars. Moreover, she even accepts his present *mental* state:

> And ever will—though he do shake me off
> To beggarly divorcement—love him dearly,
> Comfort forswear me! Unkindness may do much;
> And his unkindness may defeat my life,
> But never taint my love.　　　　[IV.ii.157-61]

Gouge's final requirements are "11 Such a subjection as may stand with her subjection to Christ" and "12 Such a subjection as the Church yeeldeth to Christ, which is sincere, pure, cheerefull, constant, for conscience sake."[57] Desdemona's undying love for her husband is apparent even in her death, when she speaks not to accuse but to protect him. Her last words are: "Commend me to my kind lord: O, farewell" (V.ii.125). In her devotion, she becomes once again "the sweet and submissive being of her girlhood," adopting the pattern of neurotic compliance traditionally praised in women.[58]

Othello is the bleakest of tragedies, for although these two people love each other dearly, their love is not enough. They fail because they do not know who they are. Othello knows only what it means to be a soldier, a heroic leader who makes decisions on the battlefield, in an instant discerning friend from foe and taking violent action. Like Coriolanus, he is one of Shakespeare's warrior heroes who calls the heroic ideal into question. The same behavior that makes him a hero on the battlefield only destroys him in peacetime. Desdemona knows how to be a dutiful daughter, the traditional role she rejects in courageously following Othello and her heroic dreams. Her short-lived self-affirmation in love, however, turns to bondage in marriage. In I.iii she acknowledges the ritual transfer that makes her not her father's but her husband's chattel, surrendering her dynamic self for the passive feminine ideal. Both Othello and Desdemona err in conforming to traditional male and female stereotypes, adopting persona behavior which prevents real intimacy and trust. Desdemona's chastity becomes more important to both of them than Desdemona herself. Othello kills her and she sacrifices herself to affirm the traditional ideal. As we have seen in considering Hero, nothing the traditional woman can do will alter men's misperceptions of her. In the world of traditional male-female roles, males act and females react. Desdemona cannot change Othello's perceptions. Her loving unselfishness becomes compulsive compliance which actually prevents her from defending herself.[59]

Iago's assessment of Desdemona is correct. She attempts to please everyone, fulfilling the role of the good woman. She: "is of so free, so kind, so apt, so blessed a disposition, she holds it a vice in her goodness not to do more than she is requested" (II.iii.325-28). Desdemona's error is that of the traditional woman who lives for others, choosing goodness over selfishness.[60] In attempting to nurture everyone around her, she fails herself. She pleads eloquently to the duke about her love for Othello. In her boundless empathy, she pleads for Cassio, but, characteristically woman, she cannot plead for herself. Unable to speak in her own behalf, Desdemona "becomes practically monosyllabic."[61]

Even her lie about the handkerchief can be explained as altruism. She subordinates truth to the main priority in her life, pleasing her husband. Gilligan notes how often excessively altruistic women will compromise truth to avoid hurting others. Desdemona knows the handkerchief is missing but intends to find it again without troubling Othello.[62] Emilia does not mean to hurt anyone either. She takes the handkerchief to please her own husband and had meant to return it once the work was taken out. But these small dissimulations combine in a fatal pattern.

Enslaved by the traditional ideal that not only dominates her behavior but distorts her perceptions, Desdemona sinks into passivity until in IV.ii.98 she tells Emilia she is "half asleep" in shock. Attempting to conform to "what should be," she fails to see "what is," refusing to recognize Othello's jealousy and the danger it represents. The traditional norms have given her no means of defending herself. She is told only to bear chiding with all patience and obedience, and so she does. The idealism and all-consuming nature of her love lead her into a closed-image syndrome not uncommon among battered wives: she refuses to believe all this is happening. Othello cannot really be jealous; she never gave him cause. Every shock to her system is met with a new denial, a new affirmation of her innocence and obedience in the role of perfect wife.[63] Her inability to accept Othello's jealousy is compounded by her previously sheltered life, which did not prepare her for anything like this. In loving Othello, she has risked everything, given up home, father, and country. Her identity as Othello's wife has become her *only* identity; her belief system at this point will not tolerate his rejection, which would make her a nonentity and turn her world to chaos.

A significant line early in the play is Othello's response to the street brawl: "Are we turn'd Turks, and to ourselves do that / Which heaven hath forbid the Ottomites?" (II.iii.170-71). Are we, he asks, our own worst enemies? His accusation holds true for all the principal characters in the play. Iago betrays his humanity in his murderous revenge. Cassio betrays himself by drinking to excess. Othello loses his faith in Desdemona's love, betrayed by his own insecurities. In his *anagnorisis* he acknowledges this, executing justice upon himself as he had done to the "turban'd Turk," arch enemy of the Venetian state (V.ii.353). Desdemona, too, has been an enemy to herself in slavishly following the traditional ideal of female behavior, which undermines her self-esteem.[64] Her unselfish devotion to Othello makes her a martyr to love. Desdemona's last words have been read many ways: a final act of loving kindness, a benevolent lie to protect Othello. As Emilia asks her who has done this deed and Desdemona answers, "Nobody; I myself" (V.ii.124-25), there is surely some truth in her admission. She dies upholding the impossible standard of the good woman, impossible because even though she was innocent and chaste, the man she loved failed to perceive her so.

Like Ophelia and Hero, Desdemona is in her own way a dominated daughter, a dominated woman in a patriarchal society that will not allow women to grow up, to assert themselves in their adult lives, or even to act in their own defense.[65] In her attempt to be a good wife, she loses her vitality and self-confidence, drawing her identity from her husband's perceptions. Despite her forebodings, she lies in bed waiting for him in V.ii. And as he murders her, she becomes the ultimate embodiment of the feminine ideal: silent, cold, and chaste, as beautiful as a marble statue: "Cold, cold, my girl! / Even like thy chastity" (V.ii.275-76). The element of necrophilia in Othello's adoration of her sleeping form is no accident ("Be thus when thou art dead, and I will kill thee / And love thee after" [18-19]). Carried to its logical extreme, the traditional ideal represents a woman's denial of her thoughts and desires, her very essence, an ultimate obliteration of the self. In her death, Desdemona finally becomes the "perfect" Renaissance woman.

CHAPTER FIVE

Defiant Daughters

Seventeen of Shakespeare's plays address the crisis of intimacy, when daughters leave their fathers for the commitment of marriage. This creates identity crises for them as well as for their parents. In what Erikson has seen as "the stage of life crucial for the emergence of an integrated female identity," young women leave behind the secure bonds of childhood and go forth into the unknown, risking lifelong commitment to a stranger in the adventure of awakening love.[1] Most of Shakespeare's daughters defy their fathers to make this commitment, actively affirming new values and priorities. With the sole exception of Ophelia, once their hearts are touched by romantic love, these young women embrace it as their destiny, rejecting patriarchal bonds and childhood commitments. In this chapter I shall examine the defiance of Hermia, Silvia, Julia, Desdemona, Imogen, Ann Page, Jessica, Goneril, Regan, Cordelia, and Katharina. All leave behind traditional filial obedience, affirming something new in its place. Some move from what Gilligan called "a focus on goodness . . . to a reflective understanding of care as the most adequate guide to resolution of conflicts in human relationships." Unlike Hero and Desdemona, these young women are able to care for themselves as well as others, moving from the dependence of childhood to interdependence and an affirmation of human community.[2] Their defiance constitutes part of a comic pattern of thesis, antithesis, synthesis, which leads to new social harmony. Other daughters polarize the needs of self and others, precipitating a destructive conflict in which nothing is affirmed but their own egos, creating discord and chaos, both personally and politically.

Romantic love takes young women from childhood to adulthood. It is "a crucial moment, when development must move one way or another, marshalling resources of growth, recovery, and further differentiation."[3] This developmental crisis and its effects—the daughter's revolt, the father's reaction, and the values affirmed—form the structural core of at least nine tragedies and comedies. Daughters in these plays choose love over paternal obedience, affirming personal choice over enforced duty. Yet while Shakespeare dramatized the limits of traditional order, he recognized the need for other bonds to prevent its opposite, rampant greed and social chaos. In his plays he consistently condemns both slavish obedience and unbridled appetite, upholding a personal bond of love and trust as the only moral basis for enduring human commitment.

Romantic Love and Comic Defiance

In Shakespeare's romantic comedies, the daughters' defiance leads to personal and social renewal. The frustrated, grasping fathers function as *senes irati*, subjecting young lovers to a trial by ordeal to test and prove their love. The lovers grow in self-awareness and develop their relationships as the older generation plays its "vital role as sanctioners and critics."[4] In the archetypal conflict that develops youthful dreams into adult commitments, parents must play the rigid role of Authority, upholding an order against which young people can exercise their emerging sense of self. Paternal authority provides the initial thesis in this developmental dialectic of personal growth and social renewal.

Like John Milton a few decades later, Shakespeare recognized that human development arises through conflict, that in challenge we strengthen and define ourselves: "That which purifies us is trial, and trial is by what is contrary."[5] Shakespeare's concern is developmental, his concept of adulthood surprisingly modern. His daughters are not static ideals but dynamic characters who actively search for adult commitment. Love for them is a process of growth in which they discover a new sense of self and affirm a value system based on mutual respect and trust.[6]

Shakespeare dramatized this clash of traditional and progressive perspectives in I.i of *A Midsummer Night's Dream*. In answer to her father's insistence that she marry Demetrius, Hermia declares, "I would my father look'd but with my eyes." Literally, she argues for her point of view; the man she loves is Lysander. Figuratively, she stands for the progressive view of marriage: not a dispassionate family arrangement, but a personal commitment between two individuals. Speaking for traditional authority, Theseus counsels, "Rather your eyes must with his judgement look" (I.i.56-57). In keeping with the fifth commandment, a daughter was to let her father's judgment determine her actions. Traditionalists prized obedience over reason and initiative, while humanists and Puritans defined virtue more actively. Empowered by her love, Hermia speaks to the duke as Desdemona does in *Othello*. Rejecting the silent passive model of female virtue, she dares to make her own decisions. Like Renaissance scientists, she refuses to accept established authority, considering all available data before reaching her own conclusion. Hermia realizes that her behavior is unconventional. She apologizes for her seeming breach of modesty while inquiring about the penalty for disobedience:

> I do entreat your grace to pardon me.
> I know not by what power I am made bold,
> Nor how it may concern my modesty,
> In such a presence here to plead my thoughts;
> But I beseech your grace that I may know
> The worst that may befall me in this case,
> If I refuse to wed Demetrius.   [I.i.58-64]

Learning that her alternatives are death and perpetual celibacy, she affirms her integrity, refusing to be a mere property passed from father to husband. She will not let an unloved man possess her body:

> So will I grow, so live, so die, my lord,
> Ere I will yield my virgin patent up
> Unto his lordship, whose unwished yoke
> My soul consents not to give sovereignty.
>   [I.i.79-82]

Hermia rejects forced marriage to "his lordship," the "unwished yoke" and "sovereignty" of traditional arranged marriage in which women too often became their husbands' sexual slaves. She affirms her right to consent, echoing Renaissance Puritans, who enabled young women to veto their father's choice, choosing to obey God over their fathers. As Gilligan explained, "the concept of rights changes a woman's conceptions of self, allowing them to see themselves as stronger and to consider directly their own needs," changing personal relationships "from a bond of continuing dependence to a dynamic of interdependence."[7]

Hermia later escapes with Lysander from the tyranny of Athenian Law. Their elopement leads them, along with Helena and Demetrius, through a surrealistic ordeal in the woods, which teaches them that love can be threatened, not only externally but internally. They must temper their passions and overcome adolescent egotism to make an adult commitment. In IV.i they awaken to a new vision. Hermia sees "with parted eye, / When every thing seems double" (IV.i.193-94). Through their ordeal they overcome the egocentric illusions of adolescence, the young men's need to prove themselves in competition for the most desirable young woman,[8] and the young women's insecurities about their attractiveness. Seeing beyond tradition, illusion, and appearance, they develop their faith in a love they cannot rationally explain.

Silvia in the early *Two Gentlemen of Verona* is another progressive young woman. Like Desdemona, she initiates the courtship, asking Valentine to write a love letter to an unnamed friend, then presenting it to Valentine himself. Although her jealous father locks her up in a tower at night, she plans to elope with Valentine, using a rope ladder. After Proteus reveals their plan, Silvia remains loyal, rejecting the advances of her father's wealthy favorite and the inconstant Proteus, whom she lectures on his infidelity to Julia. She then runs away to join Valentine in Mantua, demonstrating courage and commitment. In some rather unbelievable turns of plot, this comedy concludes with affirmations of friendship and forgiveness, matching each young man with his original lady and obtaining the blessing of Silvia's father.

In what resembles a comic plot, Desdemona defies her father to affirm her love for Othello. Her elopement trumpets to the world the depth of her love, demonstrating individual choice, courage, and commitment. But in this tragic world there is no father's blessing to bring the lovers back into society. There is only Brabantio's warning, a bitter parody. In marrying Othello, Desdemona has divorced her family and country. Her father disowns her and dies in despair, as she goes with Othello to an alien land. In her new role as wife, she clings to the ideal of traditional womanhood, pathetically accepting Othello's verbal and physical abuse with sweetness, patience, and passivity. Her attempts at wifely obedience and feminine perfection ironically ally with Iago's efforts to undermine the trust essential for intimacy. A victim of cross purposes and impossible ideals, Desdemona is caught squarely in the transition between traditional and progressive concepts of marriage and womanhood.

Juliet is another tragic heroine whose love begins with the familiar pattern of comic defiance. The young lovers are at odds with their elders, who function as *alazons*, their feud creating impediments to young love. Critics emphasize the fact that love matures Juliet, turning her almost overnight from a child to a woman. For Irene Dash, Juliet's youth gives her additional independence, for she has not yet accepted the docile, subordinate role of the traditional woman that girls accept when they grow older.⁹ I would not attribute Juliet's independence to her youth, however. As we saw in chapter two, women were indoctrinated from childhood with submission and obedience. Children, male and female, were considered their parents' property. The only difference was that one day boys grew up, while girls remained docile and obedient children, the virtues of the good child and the good woman being almost synonymous.

Juliet develops from her first appearance in I.iii, when we see her as a child who comes at her mother's command and considers marriage "an honour that I dream not of" (65). What develops her independence and maturity is her love for Romeo. She is willing to listen to Paris's offer, but once she exchanges her true love's vows with Romeo, she is committed irrevocably to the love that rules her life. No longer a child, she accepts the world of adult commitment and sexuality, taking the initiative and proposing to Romeo in II.ii. Once married, she anticipates her love's consummation in III.ii, her young blood stirring in a manner that would distress other less sanguine maidens. Like Hermia, she reserves the right to commit herself and her body to the man of her choice. She later affirms her love beyond any ties of family loyalty or childhood security. With a burst of indignation, she rejects her nurse's offer of bigamy and maintains her fidelity to Romeo. At fourteen, abandoned by all she has ever known, this is courage indeed. Ultimately, she chooses union with Romeo in death over the friar's offer of life in a convent. Rejecting all compromise, she upholds love as the basis of her existence. In her courageous defiance of convention for love, Juliet resembles the young women of romantic comedy, but her love blossoms in a tragic universe, a world poisoned by hate, in which there can be no redemption, only *anagnorisis* and remorse.

Imogen in *Cymbeline* is another defiant daughter who chooses love over filial obedience. As the play opens, she has incurred her father's displeasure but has won the admiration of the court by rejecting the foolish Cloten for the more worthy Posthumus. Cymbeline banishes Posthumus and imprisons Imogen, calling her a "disloyal thing" (I.i.131) and encouraging Cloten to court her. Throughout these indignities and the greater trials that follow, Imogen affirms her love. She tells her father, "I am senseless of your wrath; a touch more rare / Subdues all pangs, all fears" (I.i.135-36). Like the other young women discussed in this section, she regards marriage not as an arrangement to please her father, but as a personal commitment. She claims Posthumus as her soul mate, in the progressive spirit advocated by Puritans, explaining to Cymbeline, "You bred him as my playfellow, and he is / A man worth any woman" (I.i.145-46). She repels the advances of Cloten and the temptations of Iachimo, running off to meet Posthumus in Milford Haven, where even the plot against her life cannot quench her love. Donning a page's garments, she follows her heart through fantastic adventures in the forest and finally returns to claim her husband and receive her father's blessing. Faithful in love despite the thousand shocks she encounters, Imogen merits the name of her alter ego: Fidele.

Romantic love in the comedies is an irresistible force, inexplicable as grace itself, which draws young people into marriage, providing them with a partner for life. These plays reflect the Puritan definition of love as a gift of God, a force of inspiration and renewal. In *The Merry Wives of Windsor*, Ann Page elopes with Fenton, rejecting the suitors her parents have chosen. Fenton's speech in V.v articulates the progressive view of marriage:

> You would have married her most shamefully,
> Where there was no proportion held in love.
> The truth is, she and I, long since contracted,
> Are now so sure that nothing can dissolve us.
> Th'offence is holy that she hath committed;
> And this deceit loses the name of craft,
> Of disobedience, or unduteous title,
> Since therein she doth evitate and shun
> A thousand irreligious cursed hours,
> Which forced marriage would have brought upon her.
>   [V.v. 235-43]

"Th'offence is holy that she hath committed"—consistently Shakespeare moves beyond the plot machinations of new comedy and portrays romantic love as a matter of conscience over parental obedience. As William Gouge, Robert Pricke, and Thomas Gataker had argued, children were not to obey their parents in anything contrary to true religion.[11] In choosing to follow her heart, Ann Page "shun[ned] / A thousand irreligious cursed hours" in the hell of a forced marriage. Repeatedly, Shakespeare's daughters reject the old order and affirm a new, more personal morality.

Selfish Defiance: Revenge and Domination

In upholding individual choice, Shakespeare does not condone unbridled selfishness. As Milton later observed, there is a great difference between liberty and license.[12] Some of Shakespeare's daughters affirm nothing more than resentment and personal greed. For this tendency Shakespeare provides both comic and tragic examples. Jessica's elopement in *The Merchant* is riddled with selfish spite; Goneril and Regan's defiance of their father in *Lear* demonstrates the bestial extremes to which human relationships can descend when they are uninformed by love and personal commitment.

Jessica's elopement has received mixed reviews from critics. Some see her as a romantic heroine imprisoned by a wicked father, her flight motivated by love or religion. According to Martin Holmes, "Jessica is nowadays more hardly judged than the playwright seems to have intended. To a less sophisticated audience she was the Fair Heathen, the daughter of the Sinister Oriental, whose function was to run away with a Christian lover in the best fairytale style, taking a certain amount of her father's treasure with her."[13]

One wonders whether Shakespeare's contemporaries regarded Jessica with such a romantic suspension of their mores. Although progressive marriage tracts justified a daughter's defiance of her father for love, I have found no such justification for a daughter who steals his money, even when it is ostensibly her dowry. William Gouge emphasized conscience in matters of religion. Yet he heartily condemned children who "privily take away and purloine what goods, money, wares, or any thing else they can come by of their parents. This the holy Ghost accounteth plaine theft." He also condemned those children who "riotously spend their portion, like the prodigall childe, and runne into debt, and so make their parents either to pay it, or to leave them to the law."[14] Sir Arthur Quiller-Couch found Jessica "bad and disloyal, unfilial, a thief; frivolous, greedy, without any more conscience than a cat," and H. B. Charlton maintained that "she flippantly desecrates all that Shylock holds sacred," demonstrating "a cruel indifference to her destruction of his family happiness."[15]

Agnes MacKenzie's assessment of Jessica's character points to her real motivation. Jessica "is an efficient little sketch of shallow, pretty charm, eager for pleasure and horribly bored by her prim seclusion as the only daughter of a wealthy Jew."[16] Bored, restless, and superficial, eager for the acceptance of her peers and resentful of her father, Jessica is a typical adolescent. She embodies the worst qualities of youth without its fervent idealism. Psychologists have noted the frequency with which adolescents rebel against their parents in order to assert themselves, getting into trouble in flagrant defiance of their parents' values.[17] Jessica's adolescent rebellion is also a bid for social acceptance. She becomes a Christian because in Venice all the "right people" were Christians. She resents her father for her strict upbringing, for his thrift, even for being a Jew. In rebellious self-assertion, she throws her father's casket of jewels down to Lorenzo and stuffs her pockets with his gold in an act of psychic vandalism. She is ashamed only that her elopement has compelled her to dress in boy's clothes, an affront to her vanity. In her travels she continues to torment her father, by squandering his money and pawning his turquoise ring.

Some have excused Jessica, arguing that frivolity is not a sin on festive occasions and that Shylock had not really prized the ring since he was not wearing it.[18] But her actions are prompted by adolescent vengeance, not festive celebration, and Shylock is obviously devastated. She has not only rejected him personally, but profaned his values, all that he lives for. Bitterly, he mourns the loss, which he feels as symbolic castration and his daughter's denial of her parentage. Such spiteful defiance was not the intention of even progressive tracts on matrimony, which told children to leave their parents and cleave to their spouses. In her theft and callous prodigality, Jessica has "symbolically disavow[ed] the sanctity of the conjugal bond."[19] This is not liberty but unbridled license.

Austin Dobbins and Roy Battenhouse maintain that Jessica merely follows the advice of contemporary commentators who counseled children to obey their parents "in the Lord," only so long as parental dictates accorded with Protestant theology. Since Shylock is Jewish, they argue, Jessica is justified in leaving him to seek true religion.[20] Children in the Renaissance were reminded of their primary duty to God, but Jessica's motivation for becoming a Christian is superficial at best. Nowhere do we see her studying the Bible or asking theological questions. In II.iii.21 she says in soliloquy that Lorenzo will make her "a Christian and thy loving wife." For the wrong reasons, one may be "a heretic in the truth."[21] Her conversion, more secular than spiritual, does not justify her flagrant violation of order. As we have seen, other daughters defy their fathers for love, but their love extends beyond selfishness and revenge. Celia in *As You Like It* rejects her father to comfort her banished cousin. Repudiating her father's usurpation of the dukedom, she swears to restore to Rosalind her rightful inheritance after his death. Jessica could practice Christian charity by relieving the suffering of others with her father's wealth, but she affirms no such alternative. Her love for Lorenzo "is lawless, financed by theft and engineered through a gross breach of trust."[22] Violating the traditional filial bond, Jessica affirms only ego and infatuation. This comedy ends with Portia affirming the love and trust which raise individuals beyond appetite, integrating human society. Love as Jessica expresses it, how-

ever, is not an acceptable alternative to tradition. Her rebellion and the egoism it represents are antisocial and destructive, at least as destructive to the
human soul as narrow and oppressive tradition. Shakespeare was progressive,
but no anarchist. He realized that without some bonds of trust between individuals, society as we know it would not endure.

Nowhere is this message more apparent than in *King Lear*. His daughters
undermine both his sanity and the social order. In this grim account of filial
ingratitude, defiance and sadism, Shakespeare portrays the savagery to which
human life would descend without essential bonds of love and respect. Goneril and Regan's treatment of Lear demonstrates the devastating effect of
relationships based only on hierarchical power. In I.i, when he has political
power as well as control of their inheritance, they flatter him with hyperbolic
declarations of love. Their loyalty is to themselves alone; they kowtow to Lear
only so long as his power exceeds theirs. As Shakespeare reveals again in the
case of Edmund and Gloucester, hierarchical order without love and respect
is at best only a temporary breakwater to keep conflicts at bay, a Hobbesian
Leviathan that may too easily be seized and subverted by unscrupulous Ma-
chiavels.

Goneril and Regan are motivated only by appetite. Once Lear's power
advantage is gone, there are no human bonds. At the end of I.i the two sisters
huddle together, coldly assessing their father's faults and plotting their future
strategy now that they have him in their power. "'Tis the infirmity of his age,"
Regan concludes (I.i.296). Lear's aged immaturity has made him a child
again, and he is now politically their inferior. Their speeches reveal a hierarchical power void of all empathy. Without love or respect, Goneril eyes her
father coldly as an "idle old man / That still would manage those authorities /
That he hath given away" (I.iii.15-17). He is for her merely a superfluous old
fool without worth because he has no official status in the hierarchy.[23] So it is
in any society that measures individual value by social status. Retirement
precipitates an identity crisis because older citizens are no longer socially
useful. Goneril resents her father's continued presence in her home, ration-
alizing her harshness in hierarchical terms. Having given away his adult identity, Lear has become a helpless, irksome child: "Old fools are babes again;
and must be us'd / With checks as flatteries" (I.iii.19-20). Rejected by Goneril, Lear goes to Regan and receives the same response:

> O, sir, you are old;
> Nature in you stands on the very verge
> Of her confine: you should be rul'd and led
> By some discretion, that discerns your state

Better than you yourself.

[II.iv.148-52]

I pray you, father, being weak, seem so.

[II.iv.204]

A parable of what can become of human relationships when motivated only by greed, power, and appetite, the Lear story is filled with historical and psychological significance. The story itself parallels a lawsuit in 1603 involving Sir Brian Annesley and his three daughters. The older two were married; the youngest, unmarried, was named Cordell. His eldest daughter and her husband, in an effort to seize his property, attempted to have him declared incompetent. But Cordell resisted, engaging Sir Robert Cecil in her father's defense.[24] Shakespeare was undoubtedly familiar with this contemporary case of filial ingratitude.

Stephen Reid proposed a psychological case study, attributing Goneril and Regan's savage behavior to frustrated Oedipal desires and sibling rivalry. Goneril, the eldest child, has grown up jealous of her father's affection for her mother and her younger sister Regan. Because Lear's temper would explode whenever she attempted to express her feelings, she became cold and dispassionate. Regan's case paralleled her sister's. Repressing her feelings, she joined with Goneril in resentment of the youngest child, Cordelia. Reid argues that their mother must have died in childbirth or shortly thereafter, so only Cordelia received her father's love without Oedipal jealousy. The elder sisters' resentment has been buried for years until Lear's rejection of Cordelia brings it to the surface.[25] As the two assess their father's actions, Goneril's remark recalls years of bitterness and envy: "he always loved our sister most" (I.i.293).

Goneril and Regan have become sociopaths, individuals without conscience or empathy, motivated only by power and appetite.[26] Their father's recent abdication has given them unlimited power to avenge themselves and they lash out sadistically. Regan throws him out into the storm with the words:

O, sir, to wilful men,

The injuries that they themselves procure

Must be their schoolmasters. Shut up your doors.

[II.iv.305-07]

For the orgy of inhuman cruelty that follows, critics have called them "monsters" and "witches."[27] Reversing the hierarchical structure, they strike out at their father and all men who have been in power, "determined to master [them] . . . and reduce them to inferiors." In a "masculine protest," Shakespeare's evil women—Goneril and Regan, Lady Macbeth, and Volumnia— attempt to "outman" their fathers, sons, and husbands.[28] In all three cases, however, the logic of the plays condemns them, not because they rebel against traditional feminine passivity, but because in so doing they become cruel and inhuman tyrants.

Relishing the exercise of raw power in the fury of filial revenge, Regan takes the initiative, insisting that Kent stay in the stocks "Till noon! till night, my lord; and all night too" (II.ii.142). She reduces her father's retinue of knights with the vindictive "what need one?" (II.iv.266) and cruelly turns her father out into the cold with the rationalization that "this house is little: the old man and's people / Cannot be well bestow'd" (291-92). As they capture Gloucester, Goneril sadistically suggests, "Pluck out his eyes" (III.vii.5). But it is Regan who remains behind to accomplish this heartless deed.

The vindictive sisters descend to the level of animals. They are "she-foxes" (III.vi.24); "tigers, not daughters" (IV.ii.40); "dog-hearted" (IV.iii.47), pelicans, vultures, and kites, and their "sharp-tooth'd unkindness" (II.iv.137) horrifies all who hope for more from humanity. Shakespeare's contemporaries would have recalled the biblical reference to Mark 13, in which children rise up against their parents, and the Homily of 1574, *Against Disobedient and Wilful Rebellion*, shuddering in fear as the dissension between parents and children warned of decay in the body politic and the threat of universal chaos.[29]

As Cordelia returns to England, her sisters turn their attention from revenge to competition. In their lust for Edmund, they reenact an earlier sibling rivalry for their father.[30] Finally, in frenzy and desperation, Goneril poisons Regan, then stabs herself and "all three / Now marry in an instant" (V.iii.228-29) in a union wrought of blood and violence. "Yet Edmund was belov'd," sighs their paramour (239) in a tragic ending that parodies the group weddings in the comedies, emphasizing the absence of comic unifying love and demonstrating the destructive effects of hatred and egoism.

Edward Dowden, long ago, saw in Goneril and Regan "the destructive force, the ravening egoism in humanity which is at war with all goodness," and more recently Phyllis Rackin recognized a concept of human interaction all too familiar today, in which "there is no duty higher than self-aggrandizement and no standard of value but quantitative measurement—or price."[31] The lesson is obvious. Without mutual respect and personal commitment, society is structured by conflict, not cooperation. Our "ravening egoism" must be tempered by love, our animal appetites balanced and guided by angelic reason, or human existence, as exposed so brutally in *Lear*, becomes a Hobbesian nightmare in which life is "solitary, poor, nasty, brutish, and short."[32] Shakespeare recognized that hierarchical domination too often brings with it either repression of the individual or its opposite, ruthless defiance and revenge. Beyond the alternating cycles of power that pit individuals in competitive struggle, he recognized the need for a new social order, based not on fear and oppression but on personal bonds of love and respect. This vision transcends hierarchy, affirms our higher selves, and promises new harmony to our world.

In Cordelia we see another kind of defiance and its resolution into precisely these bonds of love. Many reasons have been proposed for Cordelia's inability to flatter her father in I.i, and critics have called her everything from a saint to a spoiled child.[33] Among Cordelia's critics are those who point to her "stubbornness and lack of sympathy," "boastful self-righteousness," and "hot-headed pride."[34] In her defiance of her father's love test, Cordelia initially ignores the old man's need for love. More concerned with herself, with proving that she is no hypocrite like her sisters, Cordelia lacks charity. In her adolescent absolutism, she will not compromise. Like Isabella in *Measure for Measure*, she recoils from anything less than her ideal of truth. To Lear's stunned, "So young and so untender?" she answers resolutely, "So young, my lord, and true" (I.i.108-9). She stands firm in her own defense, proudly telling France that no immorality has deprived her of her father's favor,

> But even for want of that for which I am richer,
> A still-soliciting eye, and such a tongue
> As I am glad I have not, though not to have it
> Hath lost me in your liking.   [I.i.233-36]

She rejects the absurd love game and her hypocritical sisters. Her lack of empathy, however, brings tragic consequences upon herself and the insecure old man, her father. She fails to respond to his crisis of old age and desperate need of reassurance. She has always been her father's favorite and sees no need to prove that now. She resents her sisters for their lies and resents Lear for imposing this test. So intent is she on proving her virtue that she breaks her poor father's heart. She is stubborn, proud, unyielding, very much her father's daughter. As Paul Jorgensen has pointed out, "stubbornness and inflexibility run in the entire Lear family."[35]

Like her sisters, Cordelia suffers from sibling rivalry. She must define herself in contrast to her hated sisters. Lear's and Cordelia's developmental needs clash violently, devastating them both. Lear begins his descent into madness, and Cordelia is unable to make the transition from identity to intimacy. She is later driven by excessive altruism, the need to prove herself the good child, deserting her husband and returning to her father for his blessing in IV.vii.[36] Although hailed by some as a Christ figure, a saint and martyr, Cordelia would have been criticized by Shakespeare's contemporaries. William Gouge severely rebuked "children who so respect their parents, as they neglect their husband or their wife," citing biblical references and arguing that if one's spouse and parents were both on their deathbeds, a child's first loyalty lay with the marriage partner.[37]

In her eagerness to do the right thing, Cordelia once again confuses her priorities. Like her father's, hers is a case of arrested development. Although married and Queen of France, her identity remains juvenile. She is neither wife nor queen, but her father's child.[38] All other responsibilities she abdicates, pursuing her father's love in the later scenes as single-mindedly as he had once demanded hers, determined to rescue him and prove, by abandoning husband and country, that she loves her father all. She dies affirming what she had earlier defied, repairing the broken bond between father and daughter. Departing in I.i with his curses echoing in her ears, she cannot move on to intimacy and commitment in marriage. She returns to redeem not only her father but herself, to make amends for the callous rejection that had stunted her own psychic growth. Now she affirms not cold truth but "love, dear love, and our ag'd father's right" (IV.iv.28).

Her death has shocked legions of critics. For years the play was performed with a happy ending, reuniting her with Lear and marrying her to Edgar. But Cordelia is more tragic than transcendent or pathetic. In I.i she defies her father, refusing to meet his needs and in this *proairesis* precipitates a tragic sequence that catches her inexorably in its wake. She, like Lear, must regress in time to amend the mistake. He dies, clutching her lifeless form and looking intently at her lips for the message of love that both of them have finally learned to affirm.

Defiance of Convention: The Taming of the Shrew

Until quite recently, feminists have been uncomfortable with *The Taming of the Shrew*, a play that subtly satirizes traditional relationships. Whether Katharina is tamed at the end of the play and what this taming means has been argued in interpretations that range from sheer farce to dramatic irony.[39] Despite conflicting critical opinion, at least two points are obvious: Katharina the shrew and her sister Bianca change places at the end of the play, and the induction tells us to look beyond appearances, for human relationships are seldom what they seem.

As the play opens, Bianca is apparently the model daughter, Katharina's "painfully insipid younger sister."[40] The men in the play perceive her as an anima figure, their ideal of beauty, sweetness, and modesty.[41] Her father's favorite, she is pursued by admirers, and when Lucentio sees her, he too is taken in by her appearance:

> Tranio, I saw her coral lips to move
> And with her breath she did perfume the air:
> Sacred and sweet was all I saw in her.
> [I.i.179-81]

Stupified by her beauty, the archetypal ideal he perceives, Lucentio neglects his studies at the university. He changes roles with Tranio to become her servant Cambio and a slave to love, willingly dominated by her charms. Bianca, we find, is much more than sweet and insipid. She is a shrew in sheep's clothing, a spoiled and indulged youngest child, used to getting what she wants. In her own way, she is just as tyrannical as her father. She manipulates men with her beauty and another feminine weapon, her tears. In II.i, tormented by her sister, Bianca gets her father's sympathy and affection: "Poor girl! she weeps" (24). He virtually ignores Katharina when she weeps in frustration a few lines later.

Bianca makes weakness her strength, demonstrating how feminine opportunists use the traditional stereotype to advantage. This fact, as much as the patriarchal domination of Hero, Ophelia, and Desdemona, represents a serious accusation of traditional patterns that either oppress women or encourage hypocrisy. Individual women can only conform to a stereotype by denying themselves or dissembling. In dissembling, they use appearances to manipulate men, the battle of the sexes continuing covertly, with hierarchical power replaced by more subtle deception and intrigue.[42]

Bianca dominates the men around her. In her courtship she quickly takes charge, announcing that she will "learn my lessons as I please myself" (III.i.20). She listens to her disguised suitors' respective offers and dismisses Hortensio while encouraging Lucentio. Lucentio is, of course, the wealthiest suitor, a fact that does not escape this daughter of the mercenary Baptista. He also employs a Latin translation as a cover, and she answers him in kind, maintaining the upper hand. Hortensio, however, is much cleverer—too clever, in fact, for Bianca. In his more imaginative suit he has prepared a new gamut for her, rearranged it to begin on G instead of C, the first note of the natural scale, and interlaced it with a plea for his love.[43] Bianca is annoyed by his presumption and apparent condescension. She is tired of playing scales and sees his lesson as an attempt to dominate her. She wants no imaginative rearrangement of this scale or anything else, telling Hortensio, "Old fashions please me best; I am not so nice / To change true rules for old inventions" (80-89). Katharina and Petruchio will rearrange old patterns of power and dominance into a new cooperative mode, but Bianca prefers the "old fashions" and the advantage they give her.

Bianca and Lucentio steal off to marry in secret, while Tranio makes all the official arrangements with her father. Such an act is typically Bianca, who uses appearances to obtain what she wants. On the social level, Lucentio is playing her game, while on the interpersonal level, he is playing *into* her game. He knows her only superficially. There is no intimacy between these lovers. She has deceived him with appearances as she has deceived everyone else— everyone, that is, except her sister, who sees through her feminine wiles with seething resentment.

Katharina, the apparent shrew of this tale, has been called everything from "the archetypal gifted woman in an unsympathetic society" to "a naughty girl in her teens."[44] She rebels against her father's favoritism and traditional expectations for women, unable to play Bianca's game, although she sees through it. Like Cordelia, she is disgusted by her sister's hypocrisy and too honest to descend to her level. She becomes a shrew in a desperate plea for attention and self respect.

In frustration she torments her sister and tells her father, "Her silence flouts me, and I'll be reveng'd" (II.i.29). Rejected by her father, who dotes on Bianca, Katharina is, frankly, jealous and hurt. Hers is an extreme case of sibling rivalry. Baptista showers his affections on Bianca, the baby of the family. In a plea for attention, Katharina does as frustrated older children are wont to do: throwing tantrums, she accepts even negative attention to confirm her identity. She wants a relationship, not the sham of superficial obedience, dominance, and subtle manipulation she observes all around her. Resenting Bianca's hypocrisy, she torments her in an effort to break through the façade and learn what she really feels. Tying Bianca's hands behind her, Katharina orders her sister to give her, this once, a straight answer: "Of all thy suitors, here I charge thee, tell / Whom thou lov'st best; *see thou dissemble not* (II.i.8-9, italics mine). Bianca merely taunts her with conventional sweetness, and finally Katharina strikes her in frustration.

As we find her in the beginning of the play, Katharina is friendless, unloved, lashing out in anger at everyone around her. She is jealous of the great ado made of her sister's courtship, for she too would like to find a husband, someone to take her away from this miserable family and perhaps even recognize her for who she is. Bitterly, she tells Baptista:

> She is your treasure, she must have a husband;
> I must dance bare-foot on her wedding day
> And for your love to her lead apes in hell.
> Talk not to me: I will go and weep
> Till I can find occasion of revenge. [II.i.32-36]

Alienated from those around her, she fears becoming a social outcast, an old maid at least as much as she fears being married against her will.[45] Katharina is in a predicament. While her objections are valid, her violent protest has locked her into a self-perpetuating negative cycle. She has established her identity as a shrew, and that very identity has prevented any real intimacy. Her rebellion has gained her attention, made her a minor celebrity in her town, but it has made her feared, not loved. Her behavior is destructive, not only to others but to herself. It has gained her, however, one significant concession from her father: he will not marry her against her will.[46] As he tells Petruchio in II.i.128, he must obtain "her love; for that is all in all." The fury she would raise against an unwanted match obviously terrifies Baptista. Katharina has gained recognition and respect, but she needs to redirect her energies into less violent forms of protest to build a healthy relationship.

Enter Petruchio at this point to rescue the fair maiden from the dragon of wrath. But when we meet our hero, he himself is no model of deportment. As Coppélia Kahn aptly pointed out, "if Petruchio were female, he would be known as a shrew and shunned accordingly."[47] This is precisely the point: Petruchio *is* a shrew. Like Katharina, he is restless and too prone to spend his adolescent energies in violence. When we first meet him, he is beating his servant Grumio for nothing more than a simple misunderstanding. Stubborn, willful, cast loose by the death of his father, he is a bored adolescent male without direction who comes to Padua to seek his fortune. He pursues what he thinks he wants, a rich wife, and finds what he really needs: a challenging relationship that channels his otherwise destructive energies. Like Bassanio in *The Merchant*, he is educated away from earlier motivations. He approaches Katharina for her promised wealth, but learns to respect her for herself, finding a worthy partner in wit, energy, and imagination, someone who also takes a devilish delight in flouting convention.[48]

Katharina initially perceives Petruchio as a rude madcap, but at least not the kind of man to be taken in by Bianca's tricks. He speaks to Katharina in her own idiom, in an exchange of wit and sexual innuendoes that apparently fascinates them both. Katharina realizes she cannot intimidate Petruchio, and he is attracted by her beauty and fire. He also treats her with respect. She slaps him, but while he threatens, he does not return the blow. He flatters her, moreover, with unfamiliar compliments and words of love.

In II.i.294 his assessment is accurate: "If she be curst, it is for policy." Katharina is not naturally choleric. Spirited, witty, intelligent, and sensitive, she has become a shrew out of frustration. He teaches her another way and discovers for himself how to replace violence with wit and humor. Petruchio recognizes the importance of positive reinforcement. Mercenary fortune hunter that he is when we first see him, he is the first, indeed the only person in the play, to say anything positive about Katharina. And she is starved for it. She knows too well the sound of criticism, demonstrating her hypersensitivity by bashing Hortensio over the head for correcting her during a music lesson. Petruchio marks this well, deciding to:

> woo her with some spirit when she comes.
> Say that she rail; why then I'll tell her plain
> She sings as sweetly as a nightingale:
> Say that she frown; I'll say she looks as clear
> As morning roses newly wash'd with dew.
> [II.i.170-74]

Petruchio holds constant in this practice, never criticizing, but complimenting her, swearing that he does everything in care of her. Somewhere in the process, his compliments turn from fiction to fact, his attention to love and respect. In later scenes he asks her for a kiss, desiring her willing acceptance, not patriarchal domination.

He recognizes the rebel in her because he is a rebel too. Bored by convention, he delights in satirizing it. This he does in mocking hyperbole or open defiance. The former explains his description of his wife as:

my goods, my chattels; she is my house,
My household stuff, my field, my barn,
My horse, my ox, my ass, my any thing.
[III.ii.232-34)[49]

Their unorthodox courtship—which follows the wedding ceremony—redirects his rebellion as well as hers into an affirmation of caring and commitment.

Although Petruchio's courtship has been criticized as ruthless domination, it is not nearly so brutal as it seems.[50] He manipulates the external situations to advantage but continues to treat Katharina with respect. Never does he strike or dominate her physically. In contrast with the other shrew literature of the time, his taming is remarkably mild. What he does do is redirect her antisocial defiance into more creative channels by teaching her lessons of empathy, love, and play. The first lesson he teaches by example. Perhaps he has learned by her example how pointless and hurtful his own temperamental outbursts have been. He throws himself into an exaggerated portrayal of a shrew, beating his servants because the house is not prepared, the meat is burnt, and so forth. Seeing what such behavior does to others, Katharina empathizes, speaking up in their behalf. This lesson alone takes her out of her previous self-absorption.

The lesson of love is more complex. We have discussed their initial fascination in II.i. Act III, scene ii, depicts Katharina as troubled when he does not appear on time for the wedding. At least a part of her wants to marry him or she would be rejoicing, not weeping. He finally does appear in old clothes, flouting conventional expectations and personifying the contrast between appearance and reality that is at the heart of the play. "To me she's married, not unto my clothes" (III.ii.119), he declares, affirming not the letter but the spirit of matrimonial law: the partnership between two individual souls. The contrast between appearance and reality prevails as Petruchio's words say one thing, his actions, another. He calls her his goods, his chattel, and other exaggerated descriptions of the wife in a traditional marriage. Yet if he really saw her as only a physical body to dominate, he would not refrain from raping her on their wedding night.[51] Instead of physical domination, Petruchio mirrors her extreme choleric behavior to demonstrate its destructiveness. Throughout the farcical taming scenes, he affirms respect for her in his restraint. He provides the structure but waits for her to redirect her spirit into more acceptable channels of wit and imagination.

[113]

In the sun-moon exchange, Katharina suddenly recognizes that she may answer Petruchio in kind while affirming her own integrity simply by employing comic irony. No longer defiant, neither is she dominated, nor is she manipulative like her sister. She offers Petruchio a witty answer that includes them both:

> Then, God be bless'd, it is the blessed sun.
> But sun it is not, when you say it is not;
> And the moon changes even as your mind.
> . . . .
> Pardon, old father, my mistaking eyes,
> That have been so bedazzled with the sun.
> [IV.v.18-20, 45-46]

She learns in play the spirit of cooperation.[52] By adopting the ironic mode, Katharina retains her independence and intellectual freedom, winning Petruchio's respect. They find between them a creative synthesis in humor, which offers an alternative to competition for power. These two rebels join forces to mock convention and appearances, but their mutual respect will prevent sarcastic bickering.

Thus, Katharina has discovered a new identity by affirming her intellectual energies—her wit and imagination—and Petruchio has tamed his own misdirected energies, discovering a partner who can play his game with finesse. Her final speech, when seen in this context, can be nothing less than ironic hyperbole.[53] Engaging in the witty play Petruchio has taught her, she performs what to the two of them is irony, while to her sister and the widow the speech is an explicit condemnation of their own selfish attitudes.

The play ends with Petruchio's "kiss me, Kate" and the promised consummation of their marriage (V.ii.180). They leave behind the other couples, whose main concern is social conformity, having affirmed something paradoxically less and more. Katharina's wit demonstrates that she is most assuredly not tamed in the traditional sense, nor would Petruchio wish her to be. While defying all social mores, they have yet discovered the spirit of love in partnership.[54] Rejecting patriarchal domination, they have created a dynamic relationship that allows for surprises, ironies, and jests, but above all the spirit of cooperation. Friends and intellectual equals as well as husband and wife, they provide an alternative to both domination and defiance, affirming in a sense truer than tradition the purpose of love in marriage.

CHAPTER SIX

Androgynous Daughters

Shakespeare's comic heroes stand in dramatic opposition to their tragic counterparts. The tragic personality is dominated by what A. C. Bradley called "a marked one-sidedness," a fatal predisposition to one mode of behavior while comic heroes are versatile, dynamic, and resourceful.[1] They demonstrate a vast repertoire of behavioral modes, varying from formal to informal, rational to emotional, masculine to feminine. Tragic personalities are beset by mental illness and aberration; comic heroes consistently demonstrate the resourcefulness that characterizes the mature and healthy personality.[2] While the majority of Shakespeare's tragic heroes are men, his comic heroes are women, whose intelligence, wit, and versatility transcend conventional gender stereotypes and provide new models of adulthood. Attaining a dynamic equilibrium by successfully confronting external challenges, these women become forces of harmony and transformation.

Shakespeare's plays uphold intelligence and assertiveness as admirable qualities in women, winning praise from modern feminists. He has been called "as much a feminist as an Elizabethan can be," his plays anticipating the women's movement by four hundred years.[3] His women heroes are revolutionaries who transcend accepted patterns of female behavior, raising questions about conventional norms and the masculine power structure. These women grow and mature in the context of their experience and discover new potentials for human depth and maturity. They educate and redeem their men from the folly of limited vision and self-absorption, teaching their audience as well to reach beyond convention, to risk the adventure of love, intimacy, and adult commitment. Solving problems in law, medicine, and human relations, these young women bring new order to their world.

Critics have noted a family resemblance among Portia, Viola, and Rosalind, suggesting that the same boy actor originally played all the roles.[4] Shakespeare certainly exploited the convention of the boy actor, emphasizing the high spirits of his women heroes by dressing them in doublet and hose.[5] But boys also played Ophelia, Hero, and Desdemona—all Shakespeare's women. His heroes triumph in their androgyny, combining an active, witty assertiveness with their capacity for empathy. Androgyny liberates them from the traditional expectations that so oppress Ophelia and Hero. They are free to travel, discovering new possibilities and confronting men on their own terms.[6] Their androgynous balance enables them to resolve social discord, performing with finesse the roles traditionally assigned to men.

The concept of androgyny was prevalent in the Renaissance, appearing throughout alchemical lore, poetry, and the visual arts. The female knight Britomart in Spenser's *Faerie Queene*, the slim boyish figures of Botticelli's goddesses, and the ideal Renaissance man in Castiglione's *Courtier*—poet and lover, soldier, scholar, and statesman—are only a few examples. Androgyny liberates individuals from conventional stereotypes, offering them a wide spectrum of behavior and expression. It "suggests a spirit of reconciliation between the sexes" as men and women find a means of affirming the anima or animus of their unconscious, men discovering greater sensitivity and feeling, and women greater strength and intellectual assertiveness.[7]

Shakespeare "was the most androgynous of men" according to Carolyn Heilbrun.[8] Throughout his plays, he objected to "the extreme polarization of sex roles and the contradictions underlying it."[9] As an artist, he recognized the creative power of androgyny. Realizing that healthy men and women naturally display "a variety of impulses," some "masculine," some "feminine," he equated androgyny with emotional balance.[10] In contrast to women impoverished by conformity to sex roles, Rosalind, Portia, and Viola are all successful, healthy, and vital. Each fulfills the essential requirements for becoming an independent personality. "Instead of being only the feminine counterpart of a man, she . . .[brings] up to consciousness her own masculine qualities," going out into the world and submitting to disciplines that activate her animus.[11]

Interestingly enough, Shakespeare's fatherless daughters are the most androgynous. Free from the dilemma of domination or defiance, they are able to express their energies in other, more creative directions. As Dusinberre observes, "Portia, Viola, and Beatrice are women set free from their fathers, and their voice is that of the adult world, where Hero is still a child."[12] The missing fathers and single-parent families in Shakespeare reflect actual conditions in his time. Among the English aristocracy in the sixteenth and seventeenth centuries, one child in three had lost a parent by the age of fourteen. Among the lower classes, the ratio was even higher.[13] But Shakespeare's plays do more than reflect current conditions, they demonstrate the effect of the missing parent upon the children. Unlike Hamlet and Coriolanus, Shakespeare's daughters are not traumatized by the loss of their fathers. Rosalind, Viola, and Portia incorporate their fathers' talents, strength, and character into their own personalities. Spared the struggle of active filial rebellion by paternal death or absence, these daughters move on to affirm their own inner authority. Developing the father within themselves, actualizing the animus, or masculine potential, they perform many of the father's functions in society.

Many of these androgynous women adopt masculine attire. Boy's clothing protects Julia, Rosalind, and Viola from "the loose encounters of lascivious men" (*Two Gentlemen* II.vii.41) when they travel.[14] It also allows them greater expression and development. Once liberated from her long skirts, boned stays, and farthingales, the comic hero can move about freely in the Forest of Arden or the law courts of Venice, manifesting greater physical and psychological freedom. Assertive female behavior becomes more acceptable in doublet and hose. Audiences enjoy Rosalind's and Viola's saucy wit but often perceive the assertiveness of Beatrice and Katharina as hostile and aggressive. Paradoxically, for women to express themselves fully, they must do so in disguise, an implicit accusation of gender stereotypes.[15]

Julia, in *Two Gentlemen*, is the first of Shakespeare's women to disguise herself as a boy.[16] Harold Goddard notes Shakespeare's apparent delight in this complex intermingling of masculine and feminine: "One feels the author reveling in this contrivance like a child who has just learned to play hide and seek. In one scene, for instance, we have a boy actor playing the part of a girl, who, disguised as a boy, tells how he disguised himself as a woman in a play. . . . The young Shakespeare evidently delighted in this artifice of disguise within disguise."[17] Like Rosalind, Julia shows her independence and resourcefulness by traveling in masculine garb and has a female confidante, her waiting woman, Lucetta. She also wins Silvia's sympathy. While the men in this play betray their friends, the women are constant and true. Like Viola in *Twelfth Night*, Julia is sent by the man she loves to court another woman. Since she is Proteus's "true-confirmed love," having exchanged rings and vows, Julia is more devastated than Viola:

> I am my master's true-confirmed love;
> But cannot be true servant to my master,
> Unless I prove false traitor to myself.
> Yet will I woo for him, but yet so coldly
> As, heaven it knows, I would not have him speed.
>   [IV.iv.108-112][18]

In the final scene, which anticipates the ring exchange in *The Merchant*, Julia faints when she hears Valentine offer his beloved Silvia to Proteus, who has just tried to rape her. Silvia, understandably, is speechless. Regaining consciousness, Julia offers Proteus the ring he gave her originally. This revelation brings him to his senses; he recognizes Julia in his long-suffering page and repents. The play ends with their projected marriage and the giving of their rings once more in a solemn exchange of true love's vows. An early play, *Two Gentlemen* contains several essential elements that reappear in Shakespeare's festive comedies: the heroine in boy's clothing, the lover whom his lady must educate or redeem, and the forces of love and friendship, all of which are developed more fully in later comedies.

Through same-sex friendships, adolescents learn loyalty while reinforcing their identity and self-worth. Their peers help them discover who they are and what they believe in. In their struggle to find "something or someone to be true to," they learn the lesson of fidelity, which they will later apply to their adult commitments.[19] Shakespeare's early comedies offer many examples of same-sex friendship challenged by the advent of romantic love. In *Two Gentlemen*, Proteus betrays his friendship with Valentine to court Silvia. In *Love's Labour's Lost*, the King of Navarre and his noblemen swear to avoid all women for three years, but the visiting Princess of France and her ladies cause the subsequent defection of these celibate scholars. Masculine loyalty gives way to sexual fascination. A similar male camaraderie is altered in *Much Ado*.

A Midsummer Night's Dream portrays feminine friendship through the eyes of the frustrated Helena. Incensed that Hermia would "join with men in scorning your poor friend" (III.ii.216), she reproaches her, recalling their long-standing "school-days' friendship, childhood innocence" when they would sit on one cushion, stitching a single flower:

> Both warbling of one song, both in one key,
> As if our hands, our sides, voices and minds,
> Had been incorporate. So we grew together,

Like to a double cherry, seeming parted,
But yet an union in partition. [III.ii.206-10]

With their "two seeming bodies, but one heart" (212), they had embodied that Renaissance ideal of friendship: one soul in bodies twain. So they were united in affection until these strangers, these men, raised new passions in their hearts. Helena may complain bitterly, but she too has betrayed her friend in I.i, telling Demetrius of Hermia's elopement in a desperate plea for his attention.

Shakespeare affirms the value of friendship in the sonnets and throughout his plays. In his androgynous comic heroes, he gives us young women who function as companions and confidantes to their lovers. The forces of love and friendship, opposed in the early comedies, are combined in the synthesis of friendship and romance which constitutes enduring love.

As You Like It

Having lost her father to banishment, Rosalind is spared any active rebellion. Yet he has been the most significant man in her life. She thinks of him in the same breath with her newfound love, Orlando, shifting her affections and loyalties from father to future husband. In I.iii, Celia asks about her apparent depression:

Celia. But is all this for your father?
Rosalind. No, some of it is for my child's father.
[I.iii.10-11]

Coleridge saw Rosalind's answer as a textual error, "a mistake for 'my father's child,' meaning herself," agreeing with Theobald that "a most indelicate anticipation is put into the mouth of Rosalind without reason;—and besides, what a strange thought, and how out of place, and unintelligible!"[20] Yet in the psychology of fathers and daughters, Rosalind's remark is both intelligible and significant. In some inexplicable insight or prescience, Shakespeare's daughters often mention their fathers and future husbands in the same breath. Unconsciously, they seem to recognize an intrinsic correlation between the two most significant men in their lives and anticipate the necessary transition. The words *father* and *husband* are vital links in an archetypal pattern that transforms them from girls to women.[21] In this sense, Desdemona announces her "divided duty" to the Venetian senate, explaining that:

> I am hitherto your daughter: but here's my husband,
> And so much duty as my mother show'd
> To you, preferring you before her father,
> So much I challenge that I may profess
> Due to the Moor my lord.   [*Othello* I.iii.185-89]

And Cordelia asked:

> Why have my sisters husbands, if they say
> They love you all?
>
> . . . .
>
> Sure, I shall never marry like my sisters,
> To love my father all.   [*King Lear* I.i.101-6]

This shift of primary loyalties represents for Shakespeare's daughters their developmental destiny as they make the transition from childhood to adulthood. Some daughters embrace their marriage partners in an adult commitment; others make them merely surrogate fathers, but the momentous transition is there. Rare is the daughter who does not perceive some subliminal connection between father and husband.

The archetypal connection continues in *As You Like It*, as Rosalind explains her sudden love for Orlando to Celia—and to herself—with the words "The duke my father loved his father dearly," to which Celia responds logically: "Doth it therefore ensue that you should love his son dearly? By this kind of chase, I should hate him, for my father hated his father dearly; yet I hate not Orlando" (I.iii.30-33). But love is beyond logic. It is much easier to explain Frederick's hatred for his niece. By reminding his subjects of the absent duke, she constitutes a threat to his power. He banishes her with the words, "Thou art thy father's daughter; there's enough" (60).

In the Forest of Arden, the disguised Rosalind encounters her father. Their reunion is reduced to a witty exchange, for in her heart she has already left him behind: "I met the duke yesterday and had much question with him: he asked me of what parentage I was; I told him, of as good as he; so he laughed and let me go. But what talk we of fathers, when there is such a man as Orlando?" (III.iv.36-42).

Affirming friendship over filial obedience, Celia defies her father to defend her cousin. She has been banished too, the loyal Celia tells Rosalind, for they are united in soul: "thou and I am one . . . / And do not seek to take your change upon you, / To bear your griefs yourself and leave me out" (99-105). Celia's friendship teaches Rosalind loyalty and commitment, contributing to her celebrated spirit. Her sense of adventure emerges when Celia proposes a journey to the Forest of Arden. Cheered by her support, Rosalind proposes to dress as a male, laughing at the contradictions between her "swashing and . . . martial outside" (122) and the underlying reality.

When they reach the forest, Rosalind could shed her disguise, but she has obviously begun to enjoy it. She remains in her doublet and hose, developing inner strength while educating Orlando. Their mock courtship serves as a "trial by ordeal" for them both.[22] Rosalind learns to trust Orlando and her own feelings; Orlando tempers his ardor with witty realism. The role of Ganymede also helps Rosalind develop greater strength of character. When she enters the forest, hungry and exhausted, she comforts Celia, her doublet and hose summoning courage and resolution: "I could find it in my heart to disgrace my man's apparel and to cry like a woman; but I must comfort the weaker vessel, as doublet and hose ought to show itself courageous to petticoat" (II.iv.3-8). As psychological studies have shown, playing a role actually develops similar tendencies within the individual.[23]

Rosalind's disguise enables her to examine Orlando's motives, allowing her to say and do things that traditional feminine modesty would not permit.[24] She scorns the static role of goddess on a pedestal, refusing to be victimized by idealization and traditional expectations. Unlike Hero and Desdemona, Rosalind has no desire to sacrifice herself to become the perfect Renaissance woman. She warns Orlando of his Rosalind's potential for shrewishness or fickleness to inform him that she will not always meet his expectations.[25] Reserving the right to remain herself, she rejects the traditional feminine stereotype, the inevitable artifice and limitations it inflicts upon couples, affirming a new kind of partnership.

In their witty exchanges, Rosalind is alternately herself, Ganymede, and Ganymede playing Rosalind, manifesting a variety of voices and responses. In IV.i, she is genuinely hurt by Orlando's lack of punctuality and fears he does not love her. Can she trust this stranger to whom she has given her heart? Her disguise allows her to reproach him: "Nay, an you be so tardy, come no more in my sight: I had as lief be wooed of a snail" (51-53). As Ganymede playing Rosalind, she teases him about cuckoldry to get even and to test his feelings about fidelity. With his constant vows of love, he reassures her. Smiling through her disguise, she tells him, "And I am your Rosalind" (63), stepping back into character at Celia's insistence. "Then love me, Rosalind," cries the smitten Orlando. "Yes, faith, will I," answers Rosalind, covering her vulnerability with Ganymede's rejoinders—"Fridays and Saturdays and all," "Ay, and twenty such" (114-15, 119).[26]

Rosalind is both realistic and romantic. She controls her romantic excess beneath the mask of Ganymede, giving rein to her emotions with Celia, confessing "how many fathom deep" (IV.i.214) she is in love, and admitting, "I cannot be out of the sight of Orlando: "I'll go find a shadow and sigh till he come" (IV.i.222-23). Rosalind strikes a marvelous balance among the extremes she encounters, which mitigate against any real trust and partnership. Her friendship with Celia saves her from the isolation and excessive subjectivity of Jaques; her romantic idealism is in contrast to both Touchstone's earthiness and Silvius's Petrarchan excess. In her response to Phoebe, she recognizes the cruelty of feminine pride and egocentric disdain.[27]

By the end of IV.i, Rosalind is ready to rehearse commitment in marriage. At her request, Celia officiates as "priest" but actually serves as witness as the couple exchange spousals *de futuro* and *de presenti*:

Rosalind. You must begin, Will you, Orlando—'
Celia. Go to. Will you, Orlando, have to wife this Rosalind?
Orlando. I will.
Rosalind. Ay, but when?
Orlando. Why now; as fast as she can marry us.
Rosalind. Then you must say, 'I take thee, Rosalind, for wife.'
Orlando. I take thee, Rosalind, for wife.
Rosalind. I might ask you for your commission; but I do take thee, Orlando, for my husband: there's a girl goes before the priest; and certainly a woman's thought runs before her answers.

[IV.i.130-41]

Although she is married in the more traditional group ceremony at the end of the play, this exchange not only assures Rosalind of Orlando's love, but also approximates a legal marriage.[28] Like Shakespeare's other spirited daughters, Rosalind takes the initiative in courtship. Like Juliet, Helena, and Olivia, she arranges her own wedding. Transcending traditional stereotypes, Shakespeare's assertive daughters give themselves in marriage with courage and commitment.

Orlando initially lacks education, but makes up for this in his progress through the play. Betrayed by his jealous elder brother and kept rustically at home, he has learned neither court manners nor fidelity. His unmannerly demand for food from the Duke Senior demonstrates his lack of etiquette. More important, until Adam accompanies him to the forest, Orlando has not known the trust and generosity of a friend. With this old man he learns fidelity, and his demand for food in II.vii only reveals his concern for Adam's life.

Rosalind and Orlando apply the lesson of friendship to their love. When they are ready for greater commitment, Rosalind's disguise gradually wears away. In IV.iii, she faints at the sight of Orlando's blood, and Oliver sees through her masquerade. She cannot counterfeit her love and concern for Orlando. After overcoming the serpent of envy and the lion of wrath separating him from his brother, Orlando, too, is able to see more clearly. In the next scene he recognizes Rosalind through her disguise, telling her: "I can live no longer by thinking" (V.ii.55). He now proposes in earnest; at this point the game is over. Rosalind replies, "Believe then, if you please, that I can do strange things" (V.ii.62), promising to unite all the lovers in marriage.

Her androgyny enables "Rosalind of many parts" (III.ii.156) to unite the forces of romance and friendship. On a personal level, she is a creative balance of masculine and feminine that anticipates Jung's concept of individuation. This inner balance enables Rosalind to harmonize the conflicting forces around her.[29] At the beginning of the play, the two *alazons*, Oliver and Frederick, relate to others with hatred and violence, representing men's relationships in a purely masculine hierarchy. Brothers are divided by envy and enmity; relationships are based on competition, power, and domination. At the end of the play, the brothers are miraculously renewed by the healing power of love. Orlando rescues his brother from the lion—and his own wrath—with the love he has learned in the forest. Frederick experiences a religious conversion by merely entering the magical Forest of Arden, where cooperation and camaraderie prevail. The power of androgyny radiating from Rosalind combines opposing forces into greater harmony. Discovering her animus or inner authority, she performs what has traditionally been the father's function, arranging her marriage and those of the other couples. In V.iv, she approaches her father for his ritualistic blessing, but, as we know, she has long since plighted her troth to Orlando. Thus, in *As You Like It*, love conquers hate, and competition turns to cooperation as Rosalind and Orlando affirm a partnership that transcends the need for domination, force, and violence.

Twelfth Night

Critics have praised Viola's devotion, seeing her as "a representative of ideal love . . . as patiently devoted as Griselda" and "a remarkable mind in which intelligence is enriched by love and a sense of duty and honor."[30] According to Harold Goddard, "Though she wears masculine attire, Viola is no boy-girl as Rosalind was. She is purely feminine."[31] More than conventionally feminine, Viola is also plucky, resourceful, androgynous. An orphan shipwrecked in a strange land, Viola takes action, unlike Olivia who retreats from the world in grief. As Dorothy Tutin played her, Viola huddles in a blanket, dripping wet, yet meets adversity with courage and initiative. She is a realist, accepting the possibility of her brother's death and the necessity of making her way in this foreign land.[32] She hopes for the best, awaiting news while determining how to live in Illyria. Asking who governs here, she plans to serve the duke, disguised in boy's clothing. The mention of Orsino's name brings us again that mystical connection of father and future husband. Viola has never seen Orsino, yet the convergence of these two men in her mind is more than coincidental:

> Orsino! I have heard my father name him:
> He was a bachelor then.   [I.ii.28-29]

Androgynous in her independence and self-reliance, Viola becomes even more so in her disguise, which allows her to express the assertive and witty aspects of her personality. She develops her animus, or masculine potential, by imitating Sebastian's manner and attitude as well as his garments. In effect, she becomes her twin as a means of coping with his loss.[33] Developing her animus apparently frees Viola as well as Rosalind and Portia from the difficulties with relationships that trouble other fatherless daughters. Viola is empathetic, responsive to the feelings of both Orsino and Olivia. Witty, independent, assertive, and brave, she combines these traits into a dynamic balance that makes her a healthy and attractive person. She detaches herself from her troubles long enough to care for others. Through all the confusion, Viola maintains her basic optimism, faith, and sense of humor.

While Orsino and Olivia are arrested in melancholy isolation, Viola is vibrant and versatile. Her spirit attracts both of them, excelling in what they lack. She is a catalyst, enabling them to find a balance in themselves. When Orsino asks her to help him court Olivia, Viola responds:

I'll do my best
To woo your lady: [*Aside*] yet, a barful strife!
Whoe'er I woo, myself would be his wife.
[I.iv.40-42]

She affirms with Orsino the loyalty of friendship. Yet his request puts her into a paradoxical position, which leads to comic conflict and complexity.

The Countess Olivia, who has also lost her father and brother, is a foil to Viola. With no masculine relative to dominate her, Olivia is an independent woman. Although mistress of her household, she is in a state of emotional confusion. Hiding behind her veil, refusing any man's suit for seven years, Olivia demonstrates the difficulties with relationships that are common among fatherless daughters.[34] Yet in I.v she is already bored and restless, wearing her veil only to receive Orsino's emissary. Her mourning is a public stance, a retreat from emotional commitment by a woman afraid to love—she has recently lost both father and brother. She repels the advances of Orsino as coldly as Phoebe does those of Silvius. She is the hard-hearted lady, he the lover languishing in despair. Both young people are arrested in extremes: she in defensive defiance, he in masochistic emotionalism. In a reversal of sex roles, she has become cold and rational, he has succumbed to passive emotionalism. Viola, however, unsettles them both, tempering Orsino's emotional excess with witty companionship and invoking from the cold Olivia a heated rush of passion.

Like Phoebe, the vain Olivia falls for a scornful boy, someone who refuses to worship her and actively points to her faults. In poetic justice, Olivia "is punished for being in love with herself by falling in love with her mirror image—another woman."[35] But there is more than poetic justice in her attraction to Cesario. As we have seen, Olivia has withdrawn from life; she has been emotionally dead. Fascinated by the insistent boy at her gates, she agrees to see him, hoping for some escape from her monotonous existence. She responds to the vivacious charms of Viola/Cesario, who is dynamic, witty, *engagé*, sensing in the young page a quality she herself lacks. Olivia is ready for emotional commitment. Unfortunately, Viola is the wrong person. She must await her masculine counterpart in Sebastian.

Although Orsino is Duke of Illyria, we never see him actively ruling his country. Rejected by Olivia, he has retreated into emotional passivity; the only orders he gives are for sad love songs to feed his melancholy. A recognized illness in the Renaissance, melancholy was dangerous to his health and that of the state. Only Cesario's friendship and empathy draw him out of egocentric isolation. As he says in I.iv.12-14, "Cesario / Thou know'st no less but all; I have unclasp'd / To thee the book even of my secret soul." Enervated by melancholy, he does not even actively court Olivia, but languishes at home, sending emissaries. In Cesario he recognizes a personable attractive quality that he feels will move his lady, as indeed it does.

Viola's friendship revives Orsino. He engages in active conversation only with Cesario, his other speeches limited to melancholy posturing. Their friendship also supports a growing attraction between them. In an early scene Orsino has noted "Cesario's" feminine beauty:

> Diana's lip
> Is not more smooth and rubious; thy small pipe
> Is as the maiden's organ, shrill and sound,
> And all is semblative a woman's part.
> [I.iv.31-34]

He regards her closely, nearly seeing through her disguise. Were he not so self-absorbed, he would recognize her for what she is.

Viola plays a difficult double role. While remaining Orsino's friend and continuing to court Olivia, she gradually reveals her own thinly disguised love. In II.iv she gives him several clues, saying that she loves someone of his years and complexion, insisting to the sexist Orsino, who has only his experience with Olivia to inform him, that a woman's love may be as deep as any man's:

> *Viola*. Aye, but I know—
> *Duke*. What dost thou know?
> *Viola*. Too well what love women to men may owe:
>   In faith, they are as true of heart as we.
>   My father had a daughter lov'd a man,
>   As it might be, perhaps, were I a woman,
>   I should your lordship.
> [II.iv.106-112]

Juliet Dusinberre said that "Orlando and Orsino develop love for a playfellow and confidant rather than for a sexual opposite—Erasmus's idea of love born from the harmony of like minds."[36] While Shakespeare portrayed companionship as an essential element in marriage, this does not preclude sexuality. He recognized the need for a vital balance. Sonnet 129 depicts the violence of sexuality reduced to lust: the "expense of spirit in a waste of shame" demonstrating how sex without respect and partnership can lead to degradation and domination. Orsino's Petrarchanism and sexual fantasies have been unhealthy, separating him from both a realistic relationship and his own good judgment. His ardor must be balanced by friendship and good sense. In the conclusion of this play, his passion is tempered but not quenched. He insists upon seeing Viola in her "woman's weeds" and promises that "when in other habits you are seen," she will become "Orsino's mistress and his fancy's queen" (V.i.280, 396-97). He wants to relate to her as a beautiful woman, his romantic attraction balanced this time by the solid bond of friendship. Orsino's new lady is no alien goddess to torment him, but a kind and loving partner.

Much Ado About Nothing

Beatrice and Benedick delight audiences with their witty, independent spirits. In this pair, "sex-linked differences of intellect and originality appear nonexistent."[37] Both are highly articulate, dynamic individuals who pride themselves on their nonconformity. Beatrice offers a lively contrast to the conventional hero. When Leonato plans Hero's wedding, Beatrice answers wittily, "Yes, faith; it is my cousin's duty to make curtsy and say 'Father, as it please you.' But yet for all that, cousin, let him be a handsome fellow, or else make another curtsy and say 'Father, as it please me'" (II.i.57-59). Beatrice clearly has a mind of her own. Refusing to be dominated, she flaunts her independence, preferring to keep merry company with the bachelors in heaven. Yet her first concern, cloaked by witty sarcasm, is that Benedick has returned safe from the wars. The mutual attraction is obvious. No two people would spend so much time talking about each other without more than a passing interest. Yet both hide their interest beneath a "merry war" of aggressive bantering.

While some critics have called Beatrice a shrew and others have accused her of intellectual pride,[38] I see both lovers caught up in a frustrating approach-avoidance conflict, attracted but defensive, afraid of being hurt. In two early lines, Beatrice reveals her doubts about Benedick's constancy. As we learn in I.i.109, he has a reputation as a ladies' man. Fearing that he cannot be true in his relationships, Beatrice asks suspiciously, "Who is his companion now? He hath every month a new sworn brother," adding "He wears his faith but as the fashion of his hat; it ever changes with the next block" (I.i.73-75). One critic sees in II.i.283-91 a reference to an earlier courtship in which Beatrice was rejected.[39]

Both Beatrice and Benedick are afraid to trust a member of the opposite sex. Angela Pitt says they are trying to cope with the vulnerability of being in love. "One way of attempting to exert control over the situation is to deny that it exists, acting as though what is in reality most loved, is most despised." Persons with "a strong intellect and forceful personality" are most prone to such defensive self-deception, she explains, "for they rationalize away their tender feelings."[40] Another important factor is Beatrice's status as a fatherless daughter, which psychologists claim leaves young women shy, defensive, excessively assertive, and unable to relate to men.[41] Beatrice uses her rapier wit as a defense to keep men from getting too close. Benedick tells Claudio that she "exceeds [Hero] as much in beauty as the first of May doth the last of December" (I.i.193-94) but he is obviously hurt in II.i.254: "She speaks poniards, and every word stabs."

With an illusion, their friends uncover the love beneath their defensive façades. Beatrice and Benedick repent of their pride and resolve to requite one another's love, but it takes a real crisis to bond them. Both have been arrested in the developmental search for identity. Performing an elaborate masquerade to hide their vulnerability, they have portrayed themselves as scorners of marriage, the opposite sex, and one another. Their witty performances have become part of their self-proclaimed identities. When their friends hold up a critical mirror, which condemns them as selfish and proud, the lovers discard their defenses, leaving themselves open to their mutual attraction. Their concern for Hero leads them to greater intimacy and commitment.

Much Ado portrays same-sex friendships between Hero and Beatrice as well as among the men. Real friendship involves loyalty and trust, however, which the women affirm, while the men are caught in a constant interplay of competition, envy, and suspicion. Not only does the evil Don John betray his brother and Claudio, but even men with good motives suffer from lack of trust. Claudio is suspicious of Don Pedro's offer to court Hero for him and later accuses Leonato of offering him a "rotten orange" in his daughter (IV.i.34). This distrust casts a dark shadow upon possibilities for love and commitment. Only Beatrice affirms her faith in Hero, declaring, "O, on my soul, my cousin is belied!" (IV.i.148). Later Benedick comforts Beatrice, sharing her faith in Hero's innocence: "Surely I do believe your fair cousin is wronged" (261). As a proof of his loyalty, Beatrice demands the extreme: "Kill Claudio" (291). His masculine loyalty recoils: "Ha! not for the wide world" (Iv.i.292). But he finally agrees, taking the women's part in an alliance with Beatrice.

Since it would turn this comedy to tragedy, Beatrice's request remains, happily, unfulfilled. But in asking this, she is testing Benedick's loyalty, "eliciting from him a guarantee of his moral integrity and concern."⁴² Ralph Berry sees her request as symbolic. "'Kill Claudio' is to kill the Claudio in oneself—to kill the forces of distrust."⁴³ Through their ordeal, Beatrice and Benedick develop trust and commitment, which so strengthen their love that while external conditions change, their love remains. This dynamic relationship is set against the pale conventionality of Hero and Claudio in the double marriage that closes the play. Benedick takes Beatrice for pity and she yields, "partly to save [his] life" (V.iv.95). Their teasing and laughter have changed from competition to cooperation, their wit only underscoring greater intimacy.

The Merchant of Venice

The most androgynous of Shakespeare's women, Portia not only personifies harmony, she takes upon herself the role of judge, establishing order in the masculine world of politics. She has long been praised for her balanced and varied character. Edward Dowden wrote that she "charms us not by the power of one predominant attitude, but by the harmony of many qualities rarely found in union," praising her strong intellect, ardent heart, and self-mastery.⁴⁴ Vera Jiji pointed to her androgyny and consummate control: "Not only does she control events throughout the play, she controls her sex at will. She moves from female to male and back to female not under the pressure of events from outside (as Julia, Viola, Rosalind, and Imogen do), but by her own choice of time and circumstance."⁴⁵

In I.ii., Portia has yet to learn this balance. Restless and frustrated, she chafes against the confining strictures of her father's will; "O me . . . I may neither choose who I would nor refuse who I dislike; so is the will of a living daughter curbed by the will of a dead father" (25-26). Her father's shadow falls across his daughter's choice in marriage. At first, the casket test seems to be another father's possessive attempt to withhold his daughter, requiring from her suitors a demanding trial by ordeal.⁴⁶ So "the will of a dead father" seeks to dominate the "will" of his daughter. The pun on "will," or antanaclasis, underscores the conflict. The father's will is, at least, primarily, his last will and testament, the daughter's will her own desire or volition. As Shakespeare used it in sonnet 135, however, *will* had yet another meaning in the Renaissance: that of sexual appetite.⁴⁷ Thus is the sexual desire of the daughter curbed by her father's decree, or even by his jealous paternal desire. Although her father is dead, his will functions as *senex iratus*.

Portia confronts the same moral dilemma of love and duty faced by many young women in Shakespeare's time. During the course of the play, she resolves this dilemma, learning to trust beyond her own will. In I.ii she cynically catalogues her suitors' excessive behavior or ridiculous apparel, referring primarily to externals. The casket test, which reveals the underlying motives and temperament—I take *complexion*, II.vii.79, in this sense—of Arragon and Morocco, educates Portia, refining her own "will" from an attraction based on appearances to an appreciation of character. Portia recognizes in the test her father's desire to protect her from fortune hunters and ensure that she marry someone who loves and respects her.

As he appears in I.i, Bassanio is apparently the last person to pass the casket test. A thriftless prodigal, continually squandering his means and borrowing from friends, Bassanio's initial attraction to Portia is mercenary. She is the "lady richly left," the "golden fleece," a way to recoup his losses (161, 170). He has regarded only her wealth and beauty—externals; he has yet to recognize her wisdom and personal worth. A venal person at the beginning of the play, all that Bassanio has to recommend him is his friendship with Antonio, and even that is suspect, gilded by many loans.

Nerissa describes Bassanio in I.ii.126 as "a scholar and a soldier," however, the image, at least, of the perfect Renaissance man: active and contemplative. A scholar he may prove. One hopes that he, too, "is not so old / But [he] may learn" (III.ii.162-63) to value more than golden appearances. Although Sir Arthur Quiller-Couch insisted "that a predatory young gentleman such as Bassanio would *not* have chosen the leaden casket," Larry Champion has seen a moral development in Bassanio brought about by Portia's love, which "kindles the best sparks in his character. Certainly by the time he is forced to choose between the caskets, his scale of values has undergone a significant change."[48]

Bassanio's motives in the casket scene are crucial. As Ralph Berry has observed, "if it can be established that Bassanio was given the secret of the caskets, our whole assessment of Belmont collapses." Portia's motives are no less important. If she breaks her word to her father and reveals the secret, our belief in her integrity is shattered. Her later determination of justice in the courtroom would strike us as supremely ironic.[49] The casket scene tests both lovers. Portia is honorable; she will not be forsworn, but she loves Bassanio. Their conversation reveals the trust and intimacy that has grown during his three months in Belmont. "I would not lose you; and you know yourself / Hate counsels not in such a quality," she tells him (III.ii.5-6); "I could teach you / How to choose right, but am then forsworn; / So will I never be" (11-12). After admitting their love, the two can live no longer in uncertainty. In an act of faith, Portia places her trust in a force higher than herself. "Away, then!" she urges, "I am lock'd in one of them: / If you do love me, you will find me out" (40-41). Some argue that she reveals the secret in the song that follows, for three final words rhyme with "lead."[50] The scene could easily be played this way, undercutting any deeper meaning. But the song also tells how sensuous love, engendered merely in the eyes, cannot last. As John Donne put it, "dull sublunary lovers love / (whose soule is sense)" is superficial and mutable.[51] True love transcends both sense and surface.

Does Bassanio act upon any clues from Portia? A close consideration of this scene demonstrates that it is far otherwise. If he hears the words at all, it is only unconsciously, for while the song is playing, he is meditating on his choice in a long philosophical soliloquy, concluding that "So may the outward shows be least themselves: / The world is still deceiv'd with ornament" (III.ii.73-74). Unlike Arragon and Morocco, Bassanio looks beyond both Portia's beauty and her wealth, spurning what other men desire, their choice revolving around mere appetite. Schooled by love, he chooses instead with his heart and soul. No longer a fortune hunter, his love transcends all sense. While Morocco and Arragon regard Portia only as "a valuable acquisition," Bassanio reflects Castiglione's philosophy of love in which "only one who looks with the eyes of the mind can judge rightly upon these matters; only a true lover can win the hand of Portia."[52] His descant upon Portia's picture further confirms his higher motives:

> yet look how far
> The substance of my praise doth wrong this shadow
> In underprizing it, so far this shadow
> Doth limp behind the substance.   [III.ii.127-30]

The chiasmus, repeating the words *substance* and *shadow*, underscores his awareness of the essential difference between appearance and reality. He recognizes the platonic truth, or substance, beneath the shadow surface. Inspired by Portia, whom he calls the substance, Bassanio has learned the truth of platonic love, which places all surface, all materiality, at nought. "Who chooseth me must give and hazard all he hath" (II.vii.9) is an apt definition of love in the mystical sense in which an individual risks all he or she has known or believed to seek a higher truth. Love is always a gamble. In marriage, lovers make a leap of faith, a commitment that makes no logical sense. They must give themselves, risk all they have for the rest of their lives—and for what? For something that cannot be weighed, measured, or explained, for a love that passes all understanding.

Like Bassanio, we must look beneath the surface to apprehend the meaning of this scene. In what seems the epitome of traditional wifely obedience, Portia pledges herself and all her worldly goods to Bassanio:

> Myself and what is mine to you and yours
> Is now converted: but now I was the lord
> Of this fair mansion, master of my servants,
> Queen o'er myself; and even now, but now,
> This house, these servants and this same myself
> Are yours, my lord's: I give them with this ring.
>   [III.ii.168-73]

Thus does Portia give and hazard all she has. Yet she does not give herself in traditional subservience. Her concept of marriage is partnership, and she gives herself, not to be dominated by Bassanio, but to share with him.[53] As a close examination of this scene reveals, Portia is assertive and androgynous during the entire courtship and marriage. Actualizing her father's image or animus, she has consistently played the male role: in managing her household, arranging her marriage, and later, in administering justice.[54] Like other spirited young women in Shakespeare, she takes the initiative in her courtship, not only proposing to Bassanio but pledging herself with the words:

> One half of me is yours, the other half yours,
> Mine own, I would say; but if mine, then yours,
> And so all yours.   [III.ii.16-18]

These words, spoken in the present tense before witnesses, constitute at the very least a proposal, at most, part of a formal spousal.[55] Thus she gives herself to Bassanio *before* her father's test, trusting that love will inspire him to choose correctly. Their conversation also indicates that she has taken the lead in their relationship, giving him lessons in moral philosophy that teach him a new set of values. She says that were she not forsworn in so doing, she could "*teach* you / How to choose right" and he answers later, "O happy torment, when my torturer / Doth *teach* me answers for deliverance" (10-13, 37-38, italics mine). Portia has been his moral teacher, a role traditionally assigned to the father. With her blessing, she leads him to her father's test. When he succeeds, with no father to give her in marriage, she gives herself, again taking the masculine role. In fact, a careful examination of her seemingly traditional statement of wifely love indicates its exact opposite: far from being a submissive bride, Portia is playing the groom's role. Gently and graciously but nonetheless assertively, she seals their marriage contract with a ring, the "visible pledge" of fidelity rendered by the groom in Renaissance marriage ceremonies dating back to the prayer book of Edward VI. She then further enacts the groom's part, in lines 166-71, by endowing Bassanio with all her worldly goods.[56] She continues to define her marital role in the more active masculine sense: "to love and to cherish" rather than the submissive "to love and obey." When she hears that Antonio is in danger, she moves quickly to cherish this friend of Bassanio's, his "semblance" or other self (III.iv.20). Rather than surrendering herself in a traditional marriage, Portia retains her independence and ingenuity.

Her effort to save Antonio is a more obvious exercise in androgyny. Combining empathy with decisiveness, she postpones the consummation of her marriage and sends her husband off to help his friend: "For never shall you lie by Portia's side / With an unquiet soul" (308-9). She combines her feminine empathy with an active pursuit of the good. As she tells Lorenzo: "I never did repent for doing good / Nor shall not now" (III.iv.10-11). Affirming a higher virtue than obedience, Portia enters the masculine world of action and accomplishment.

Like Rosalind, she enjoys the opportunity to play a man. It affords her greater scope of action, a joyous liberation of spirit. Their husbands, she tells Nerissa, will see them:

> in such a habit
> That they shall think we are accomplished
> With what we lack. I'll hold thee any wager,
> When we are both accoutred like young men,
> I'll prove the prettier fellow of the two.
> (III.iv.60-64)

While other women in Shakespeare adopt men's attire to protect themselves or follow their lovers, Portia seeks more than personal happiness. She leaves the domestic realm assigned to women to enter the law courts of Venice, the world of men. In this move, Shakespeare was "suggesting something very daring" according to Angela Pitt.[57] Portia's brilliant success represents a direct accusation of the traditional social order, in which it was assumed that men were naturally more competent and suited to public life, while women's "tender natures" predisposed them to child care and domesticity. Strong, precise, and intellectually creative, Portia can see more justice in the law than any man in Venice, even the duke himself. With a flash of brilliant irony, Shakespeare denies the validity of gender stereotypes. Portia is none of the traditional feminine virtues: soft, docile, obedient, passive, maternal. She is strong, decisive, and infinitely wise. She clearly has the best mind in this assembly, better than all the men and better than the duke, her social superior.[58] With this scene, Shakespeare defies the patriarchal hierarchy, denying the validity of stratification by either sex or social class.

With the wisdom of androgyny, Portia enters the courtroom in dignity even as the men around her are reduced to passionate extremes of fear, grief, or sadistic vengeance. She recognizes that to maintain social order she cannot openly violate the bond, for this would set a dangerous precedent. She offers an eloquent plea for mercy and then by looking more closely at the bond draws from it a justice stricter than even Shylock had dreamed of:

> if thou dost shed
> One drop of Christian blood, thy lands and goods
> Are by the laws of Venice, confiscate. [IV.i.309-11]

She cites the death penalty for any alien who threatens the life of a Venetian, converting this justice into mercy in a reconciliation between Antonio and Shylock, Shylock and Jessica. Acting with the responsible care that constitutes Gilligan's highest level of moral development, Portia exposes "the limitations of the contractual conception of justice."[59] Wiser than the men who see life in terms of competing polarities: Antonio *or* Shylock, mercy *or* justice, Portia sees through this false dilemma, apprehending the possibility for both principled morality and human care, a creative synthesis of justice and mercy that points to new patterns for human relationships.

In the ring trick, Portia brings about another creative synthesis. The ring itself is highly symbolic, representing the circular action of the play. The circle inscribed by the plot is a symbol of completeness and perfection, the alchemical quintessence or perfect balance of all the elements that Jung later adopted as his model of individuation. In the art of many cultures, the circular mandala has represented the reconciliation of conflicting urges within us all: the paradigm of androgyny.[60]

[134]

After rescuing Antonio from the hands of Shylock, the disguised Portia asks Bassanio for his ring. He refuses twice until Antonio intervenes with:

> My lord Bassanio, let him have the ring:
> Let his deservings and my love withal
> Be valued 'gainst your wife's commandement.
> [IV.i.449-51]

At his friend's request, Bassanio hands the young attorney his ring of gold, the purest metal, representing in its circularity the eternity of conjugal love. Although this incident is played for comedy, Bassanio has erred in undervaluing the marriage bond, which he should place before all prior claims of family and friendship, "forsaking all other."[61] He has not yet made a complete commitment. Portia and Nerissa taunt their husbands for giving their rings away, threatening to cuckold them with the lawyer and his clerk. Cuckold jokes abound in Shakespeare's comedies, underscoring a basic distrust between the sexes, arguing the need for greater fidelity and trust in marriage. A "ring" in contemporary jest books was equated with the vagina.[62] By giving away his wife's "ring," Bassanio has undervalued their bond of sexual intimacy, subordinating conjugal love to male friendship.

Witnessing this marital discord, Antonio finally swears he will "be bound again" (V.i.251) to secure Bassanio's faith. Portia then reveals herself as the judge, giving Antonio the ring to give to Bassanio in an interaction that can be seen on at least two levels. In an allegorical sense, Portia continues her unconventional role reversal in marriage. An older friend, Antonio functions as Bassanio's father. He has financed Bassanio's courtship, providing, as it were, a dowry. He is now called upon to give Bassanio in marriage, guaranteeing his virtue and truth as the traditional father brings his daughter to the altar. The threat of infidelity is thus dispelled and the couple receives Antonio's blessing. More literally, Antonio is a friend whose participation corrects Bassanio's earlier mistake in choosing friendship over marriage. Bassanio weds Portia twice: first as her feminine self and then as friend and partner. After the first ceremony, Bassanio's friendship with Antonio superseded his loyalty to his wife; in the second, Antonio is included in the bond. Encompassing both love and friendship, romance and mutual respect, the circle is now complete. At the conclusion of this play, Portia has not only resolved her own relationship but has brought greater harmony to her world. With the creative power of androgyny, Portia, like Rosalind, constructs new social patterns out of the materials of the old, affirming the possibility for love, trust, and a more inclusive social order.

All's Well That Ends Well

Helena in *All's Well* is Shakespeare's most problematic woman hero. While she is admired for her virtue, her actions make many people uncomfortable. She is praised for her "devotion to her lover, insight into his snobbery and lustfulness, strength of will, unflinching self-confidence and unperturbed resourcefulness." A combination of active and passive, masculine and feminine, she is at times "modestly shy," docile, obedient, and respectful to her social superiors; at other times in her courage and independence she defies the hierarchical order entirely: "aggressively determined to chart her own path."[63]

She was Bernard Shaw's favorite among Shakespeare's women; justified by her ability to reform Bertram; praised for her "Griselda-like . . . obedience to her husband," and seen by some as fitting "perfectly the role of the romantic heroine."[64] Elizabethans, it has been said, would have accepted her tricks and Bertram's change of heart as a romance convention.[65] But E. K. Chambers was repelled by her persistence and powerful will, which he ascribed to desperate sexuality. Hardly a romantic heroine, what she does, according to Chambers, is "drive a man, who not merely does not love her but loves someone else, into a forced marriage by a trick, and then by another trick to substitute herself in her husband's bed for the mistress whom he wishes to seduce," all of which constitutes "not Helena's triumph but Helena's degradation." She follows "the imperious instinct of sex . . . through unworthy paths to a profitless goal, [turning from] man's tender helpmate . . . into the keen and unswerving huntress of man."[66] While Shakespeare's other androgynous women are unequivocally praised, Helena makes more than a few critics nervous, and many find this play deeply disturbing. Has Shakespeare's development of androgyny gone too far in Helena? An examination of her character raises some provocative questions about the fate of progressive women in sexist society.

Like many young women, Helena has made the developmental transition from father to husband. In I.i everyone believes that she weeps for her dead father, but she reveals:

> I think not on my father . . .
>   . . . What was he like?
> I have forgot him: my imagination
> Carries no favor in't but Bertram's.
>   [I.i.90-94]

Both Bertram and Helena are fatherless, but his mother is still living, and as a minor of noble birth, he becomes a ward of the king. Helena is without parents entirely. Having internalized the authority of her father, she becomes autonomous, responsible only to herself. Like Shakespeare's other fatherless daughters, she affirms androgyny in her independence. She is high-spirited like Beatrice. Like Rosalind and Portia, she arranges her own marriage. Like Portia, she moves from the domestic sphere to perform an active function in society, using her father's prescription to cure the king. With her wit, courage, and superior ability, she wins the admiration of those around her, including the king and countess. For all her admirable qualities, however, she only repels the man she loves. The reason lies less in her androgyny than in the manner of her courtship.

Viola courts the melancholy Orsino in disguise, winning first his friendship, then his heart. Helena courts Bertram much more directly. A fatherless daughter who behaves inappropriately in relationships with men, Helena offends his pride.[67] Openly playing the male role, she becomes a female Petrarchan lover in an idolatry as extreme as that of Silvius and Phoebe. She laments:

> That I should love a bright particular star
> And think to wed it, he is so above me:
> In his bright radiance and collateral light.
> [I.i.97-99]

Like other Petrarchan lovers, she degrades herself and concentrates on the beauty of her beloved, "his arched brows, his hawking eye, his curls" (105). She loves him for his beauty, not his accomplishments, valor, or character. Like many a misguided young man in Shakespeare—Orsino in *Twelfth Night*, for example—Helena loves not a real person but a projected archetype, a beautiful person who promises by platonic analogy a beautiful soul. As Cymbeline is deceived by his beautiful but wicked queen, so Helena falls for a pretty but ineffectual youth. Weakened by pride and self-indulgence, his character lacks the depth, courage, and integrity of her own. Yet as Mariana, in *Measure for Measure*, remains devoted to the cold and hypocritical Angelo, so Helena devotes herself to Bertram. Inspired by his handsome face and noble carriage, she sees not what he is but what he may be and loves him for her own animus projection.

He is distant and disdainful, like many a coy mistress, so Helena becomes the active one in their courtship. Their sex roles remain reversed. Helena has inherited from her father more than medical skill. She has absorbed the active optimism of a physician who believed that people could be cured and problems solved with the proper remedy. Her father has raised her like a son, educating her in his profession, and making her supremely self-reliant, unwilling to submit to any obstacle or surrender to traditional feminine patience and passivity. This conditioning makes her even more masculine in her behavior than Shakespeare's other androgynous women. Traditional psychologists would say that she has "missed a crucial stage in [her] feminine development."[68] Thinking more like a son than a daughter, she affirms a humanistic faith in individual responsibility, free will, and the power of reason:

> Our remedies oft in ourselves do lie,
> Which we ascribe to heaven: the fated sky
> Gives us free scope, only doth backward pull
> Our slow designs when we ourselves are dull.
> [I.i.231-34]

With her tremendous optimism, Helena sets out like a young knight on a quest to win her love with noble deeds:

> Impossible be strange attempts to those
> That weigh their pains in sense and do suppose
> What hath been cannot be: who ever strove
> To show her merit, that did miss her love?
> The king's disease—my project may deceive me
> But my intents are fix'd and will not leave me.
> [I.i.239-44]

If we admire the heroes of romance for their courage and determination, do we find Helena any less admirable because she is a woman?[69] We esteem Petrarch's devotion to Laura and Dante's to Beatrice, yet criticize Helena for finding inspiration in an unworthy man. We know very little of Laura and Beatrice. It is the poets' ideal we see in both. The projection of anima or animus has more to do with the perceiver than the perceived; it is Helena's own ideal that she sees in Bertram. If we admire the vision of poets and the heroism of the Redcrosse Knight while misprizing Helena's actions, we measure virtue according to gender stereotypes. By reversing the roles of men and women in romance, Shakespeare tests his audience, forcing us to examine our own models of virtuous behavior.

Like her male counterparts, Helena sets out to win her love and for this has been called selfish and aggressive. Her methods in the first two acts are direct and unabashedly masculine; she uses no feminine wiles. As Hazelton Spencer observed, "she is utterly without and above feminine artifice."[70] Helena's approach is admirably honest. Yet in so directly adopting the masculine role in her courtship, she proves unsuccessful. We may admire her for accomplishing noble deeds, but sexual attraction is based upon far "more than cool reason ever comprehends" (*Midsummer*. V.i.6).

Helena carries androgyny to its extreme, going "beyond the bounds of behaviour acceptable in a woman."[71] This play asks us how we respond to someone who so blatantly defies gender stereotypes and reveals the underlying assumptions of society. Androgyny violates convention. Independent women may affirm inner freedom and active initiative, but this does not free them from the anger and resentment of those with vested interests in sexist society. Hugh Richmond wrote that in *All's Well* Shakespeare was demonstrating "that a dominant woman is likely to be a destructive force, rather than a creative influence" in society.[72] If such a woman is destructive, it is not in herself that she is so, but in the fact that old values and beliefs die hard. By excelling in a man's world, by outperforming men, she threatens any male insecure enough to lean on tradition.

In her actions and accomplishments Helena succeeds. She cures the king by using her medical skill, at the risk of her life, and the king is apparently secure enough to accept his cure at her hands. In Bertram's reaction, however, tradition, sexism, and class prejudice combine as he recoils in disgust from the virtuous Helena. Insecure in the extreme, he runs from this successful, assertive woman, seeing his marriage as an insult to his manhood and his class, unable to appreciate her nobility of character because of his pride and insecurity. He is an immature, arrogant adolescent, too intent on proving himself to recognize anyone else's accomplishments. A shallow and superficial character, he cannot prize what he does not understand. Although forced by the king to wed Helena, he casts her away in violent resentment.

Helena succeeds only partially in her active quest for love. She performs a noble deed, but fails to win Bertram's love, becoming his wife in name only and winning a Pyrrhic victory, a marriage even the legality of which is in question.[73] In her idolatry, Helena has committed an error familiar among amorous men. She has worshipped Bertram, put him on a pedestal and objectified him. With total disregard for his feelings, she has pursued him and won the prize but has failed to build a relationship. In her energetic quest for her goal, she has completely overlooked the ritualistic significance of courtship. The lovers in Shakespeare's happy comedies are educated through a mutual trial by ordeal. Rosalind and Orlando develop by facing personal hardships, learning trust and commitment. When he is forcibly married to Helena, however, Bertram has neither developed personally, nor has he known her as anything more than a servant in his mother's household.

Throughout his comedies, Shakespeare emphasizes the significance of the courtship in developing any love relationship. In *The Tempest* Prospero in his wisdom devises a trial for Ferdinand and Miranda, taking upon himself the role of *senex iratus* because he realizes:

> this swift business
> I must uneasy make, lest too light winning
> Make the prize light.   [I.ii.449-51]

The courtship of Hero in *Much Ado* graphically illustrates this lesson. In an effort to help his friend, Don Pedro woos Hero by proxy, presenting her to Claudio, who cannot rightly prize what he has not earned. His relationship with Hero remains superficial. He is easily suspicious, inclined to doubt, because he does not know her. In *The Merchant*, Bassanio learns that love itself is a trial, in which one must "give and hazard all he hath" (II.vii.9).

Helena has risked her life to win Bertram's hand, but Bertram himself has risked nothing. In their psychological development, they are at cross purposes. Helena is ready for commitment in intimacy, while Bertram is still caught up in the identity crisis of adolescence.[74] He is eager to leave home for the court and foreign wars, to define himself in active endeavor. Helena represents to him the pull of home and mother. In a surge of adolescent egotism, Bertram demands his freedom. He must learn a great deal about himself and others before he is ready for any commitment. In I.i, he is the pampered only child of the Countess of Rousillon, a pretty boy, not a man. He is exceptionally handsome, as we know not only from Helena, in I.i.105ff., but also from Diana, in III.v.83. Spoiled and indulged for his attractiveness, Bertram is conceited and condescending. This, combined with the arrogance of adolescence, produces a shallow, underdeveloped young man. His immaturity is recognized by his mother, who says to him:

> Be thou blest, Bertram, and succeed thy father
> In manners, as in shape.   [I.i.68-69]

She sees him as yet "an unseasoned courtier" (80). The king, as well, notes his outward resemblance to his father, marking that he has not yet developed the corresponding strength of character:

> Youth, thou bear'st thy father's face;
> Frank nature, rather curious than in haste,
> Hath well compos'd thee. Thy father's moral parts
> Mayst thou inherit too.   [I.ii.19-22]

His moral development will take much seasoning and maturing, as Bertram is both arrogant and naive. He chooses as his friend the dissolute and faithless Parolles. Unlike the friendships in Shakespeare's other comedies, this one teaches Bertram no lesson of fidelity. An opportunist and libertine, Parolles brings out Bertram's egotism and lust. Only in the Italian wars does Bertram perceive nobility in other men and recognize the faithless Parolles for what he is.

Bertram has imitated Parolles's attitude toward women, regarding sexual attraction as appetite. In personal relations he has learned no limits, order, loyalty, or responsibility. He rebels against the authority of the king with a tantrum, insisting upon his own choice in marriage. To satisfy his lust for Diana Capilet, he compromises even his ancestral ring, his family honor. In faithless ardor, he complains of his forced marriage and vows to be eternally true (IV.ii.15-17). But his words are only a means to an end, his passion merely "lust in action." Unchecked by reason or allegiance to higher values, Bertram's lust drives him to its satisfaction; once satisfied, it turns to satiety and disgust. He discards Diana after one night of dalliance. When he sees her again in France, he calls her a common camp follower, covering himself with the excuse of youth and the double standard (V.iii.210-13).

Such is the shameless performance of a young man without fidelity or personal honor. Bertram is saved only by his participation in the wars, where he learns a measure of discipline from the Duke of Florence. He has learned courage and discipline, defining himself as a good soldier with a reputation for "worthy service" (III.v.51). His behavior in personal relations, however, is still despicable and his pride extreme. His exposure in V.iii is not unlike that of Angelo in *Measure for Measure*. Publicly humiliated, each is redeemed by the rejected wife who stood in for the virgin he supposedly seduced. Angelo acknowledges Mariana and Bertram swears to love Helena "dearly, ever, ever dearly" (317), but Shakespeare's audiences are less than cheered by these marriages. Certainly both Angelo and Bertram have developed to some degree; their pride is crushed and they are united to selfless, devoted women. Yet Angelo would prefer to die rather than live in dishonor, and Bertram clings to Helena more out of relief than real devotion. Shakespeare has brought these couples together, but he cannot make them happy.

Bertram is "doubly won" (315) by the persistent Helena, first by direct, then indirect means. When her efforts as the knight errant prove unsuccessful, she becomes a clever Griselda, who performs to the letter all her husband's commands. She uses anything to accomplish her purpose: her rumored death, disguise, dissimulation, humiliation, and taking another's place in her husband's bed. She changes her image from that of the active androgyne, who threatens his masculine pride, to the dutiful and pregnant wife who stands before him, her body swollen with their progeny. Bertram may prize her fertility and constancy when he could not appreciate her more active virtues, but the conclusion of the play is imperfect. He has developed to some degree from the conceited boy of I.i, but he remains a limited and conventional man. If he does prize Helena, he is not mature enough to admire her for courage and heroic androgyny, but for taking "the woman's part" as his long-suffering wife. This, then, is Helena's degradation, that she would demean herself in order to win this man's love. If there is verisimilitude in this play, it must be taken as Shakespeare's accusation of the patriarchal dualism that subjugates women and the women who, in loving, weaken and succumb to it.

CHAPTER SEVEN

Redemptive Love and Wisdom

While Shakespeare's mature comedies are focused on androgynous women heroes, his romances emphasize the corresponding need of the fathers for balance and integration. In three romances, a father loses his daughter through his own folly and goes through a period of penitential suffering. He is reunited with her at the end of the play, finding spiritual renewal, individuation, and integrity.[1]

Because the dramatic point of view shifts to the father's perspective in the romances, their daughters serve a symbolic, numinous function, more significant for what they represent than as characters in their own right. As one critic pointed out, they seem more like medieval heroines than Renaissance women.[2] In their youth and saintly innocence, they stand like icons, evoking a desire to cherish them as incarnations of the eternal feminine. These daughters are "the female as the male would dream her: young, pure beyond belief, loving, and with no trace of hypocrisy or guile in her nature."[3] Like Petrarch's Laura or Dante's Beatrice, they become spiritual guides, leading their fathers to wholeness and integration, enabling them to acknowledge the feminine side of their natures. They epitomize mercy, grace, and renewal, not the troublesome sexuality of Shakespeare's tragic women. The daughters of romance are shimmering emblems of purity, who overcome danger and chasten men's lust with a transcendent, spiritual power.[4]

Many critics have posited an autobiographical motive in these plays, a "proof that the . . . father-daughter relationship was assuming increased importance in Shakespeare's mind toward the end of his life." As he approached retirement and faced his own final developmental crisis, Shakespeare presumably "looked wistfully to his daughters for continuance of his line."[5] Frank Harris claimed that the romances were inspired by Shakespeare's rediscovery of his younger daughter, Judith, who would have been twenty-two in 1608, that her portrait appears in Marina, Perdita, and Miranda, who are all dutiful, modest, sweet, and innocent. Hans Sachs argued that the incestuous note in the final plays expressed Shakespeare's strong paternal feelings for his favorite daughter, Susanna, who inherited New Place and the greater share of his estate.[6]

For all the critical conjecture, Shakespeare's personal motivations remain a mystery. We have only what he left us in the romances: an affirmation of moral development and psychic integration in the fathers that complements his portrayal of Rosalind, Portia, and the other androgynous women. But while the young women of comedy delight in their doublets and hose, joyfully expressing their male potentiality, the male heroes of romance must suffer to acknowledge their feminine side, painfully learning the qualities of love and compassion, which alone will make them whole. The comedies depict lighthearted journeys to a liberating green world, while the romances record a painful pilgrimage of guilt and uncertainty before their protagonists finally discover the feminine principle within themselves.

In Jungian terms, as Shakespeare's women heroes acknowledge the animus, his heroes of romance must come to terms with the anima, the universal figure of woman, which looms in their unconscious: "formed by the human experience of Mother and of all other aspects of womanhood, whether mother, witch, mate, seductress, beloved, virgin, or harlot, that have impinged on man from the very beginning of time."[7] In nonandrogynous, nonintegrated men, the anima remains unconscious and is projected on the women around them. They see women as either the benevolent or malefic anima, which accounts for the familiar virgin-whore complex.[8] Psychologically, what we do not control controls us. The projection of the anima indicates unresolved forces in the unconscious that lead men to worship women as saints or condemn them as sluts and witches. A man out of touch with his own sexual feelings too readily projects these troublesome desires upon women. He is unable to befriend or feel emotionally close to any woman. "He does not wish to know any woman well because he is afraid to know himself well—especially the less masculine aspects of himself."[9] Blaming women for his lust, he perceives them as harlots, temptresses, witches, who draw him to his doom like the Lorelei. Women have become the emblem of irrationality, persecuted by men as scapegoats for feelings they cannot accept in themselves. Frequent episodes of witch burning, fear, and misogyny throughout history bear wit-

ness to the human tendency to project "the ev
others who are in some way different, the chief
Male protagonists in at least three roman(
animas, uncomfortable with emotions traditi
cious of their sexuality, which makes them vu
incest or cuckoldry, they fear and mistrust
preponderance of lust and jealousy in these
world.[11] In his tragedies, Shakespeare provided simila.
tegrated man. Othello's sudden loss of faith in Desdemona reveals n.
controlled perception. His uneasiness with his own sexuality is apparent, not
only when he believes her a whore, but even earlier, when the newly married
Othello announces that he desires Desdemona's companionship but "to be
free and bounteous to her mind" (I.iii.266). The misogyny of Hamlet and
Lear is rampant. As one critic noted, "the loathing of the flesh variously spat
out by a Lear, Hamlet, Timon, or Posthumus represents a coarsened sexual
sensibility that blames life's ills on a force outside oneself and beyond male
comprehension."[12]

Historians have noted the dominance of misogyny in Western civilization:
"wherever sex was regarded as a weakness on man's part and rigid codes of
sexual morality were adopted, women were feared and mistrusted for their
very attraction. A final element in misogyny lies in the nature of patriarchy
where males dominated, females were 'other,' secondary, inferior." Germaine
Greer explained that "as long as man is at odds with his own sexuality and as
long as he keeps woman as a solely sexual creature, he will hate her, at least
some of the time."[13]

If the romances are dramas of redemption, what the protagonists are redeemed *from* is their limited vision, their lack of *anima* integration, their
sexism. When seen in a developmental context, their sexism reveals a limited
perception of themselves. In mistrusting women and their own emotions,
these men have "cut themselves off from an understanding of the fullest range
of human experience." Their redemption occurs with their discovery of androgyny as their daughters lead them to acknowledge their animas and attain
emotional wholeness.[14]

C. L. Barber argued that Renaissance Protestantism had a profound effect
on English drama, for it removed the cult of the Virgin Mary, leaving men
with no ritual resource for coming to terms with the anima.[15] For Catholics,
Mary had been the image of the benevolent anima, balancing the malefic

life and legend. Protestants retained only the malefic anima, in of Eve, witches, and the Whore of Babylon. Shakespeare's contemporaries were forced to redefine the benevolent anima for themselves, which explains in part the apotheosis of Elizabeth I as Gloriana, the Virgin Queen. This need was also filled by Shakespeare's chaste and redeeming heroines of romance.

Androgyny was a dominant concept in the Renaissance, expressed variously in art and philosophy. Significant for our purposes was its role in alchemy, which Jung saw as an allegory of individuation. The "state of grace" in alchemy required a perfect balance in the individual: the marriage of sulphur and mercury, conscious and unconscious, masculine and feminine. Androgyny was a prerequisite for hermetic wisdom, the redemption of the soul from base and unregenerate matter.[16]

Shakespeare's romances are profoundly mystical, with hermetic magic producing "'theophanies' or new revelations of the divine."[17] They are parables of individuation, integration, and spiritual growth. Women "die" and are miraculously "reborn"; the psyches of paternal protagonists are redeemed through regeneration of the anima, or feminine principle. Pericles reclaims his anima in his daughter Marina and regains his lost wife, Thaisa. Leontes reclaims his feminine principle in his daughter, Perdita, and the statue of his dead wife, Hermione, miraculously comes to life before his eyes. In *Cymbeline* two men achieve greater wholeness. Cymbeline is reunited with his daughter, Imogen, and redeemed from the evil influence of his malefic queen. Posthumus discovers the feminine quality of mercy and is reunited with Imogen, who has symbolically died three times during the play. In Shakespeare's final romance, *The Tempest*, Prospero has acquired integration and psychic wholeness by living for twelve years on an island, caring for his daughter Miranda. His integration makes him a powerful magus, able to bring comic renewal out of potential tragedy.

Pericles

Shakespeare's romances are filled with incest and misogyny, reflecting the protagonists' lack of integration. According to Paula Berggren, incest "is the obverse of misogyny," revealing "the narcissism underlying the vilification of the female."[18] While incest lies beneath the surface in many father-daughter relationships, it confronts us directly in *Pericles*. In Act I, when young Prince Pericles courts the beautiful daughter of Antiochus, he is faced with the shocking specter of father-daughter incest. As the riddle reveals, this young woman to whom he has been so strongly attracted is a "glorious casket stor'd with ill" (I.i.77). The trials of Pericles and the ensuing action of the play flow from this "primal threat to family and social structure."[19] Pericles leaves Antioch abruptly, going on a long journey to avoid the wrath of Antiochus. Throughout his wanderings he carries with him an underlying suspicion of women and sexuality. In Antioch Pericles has constellated the malefic anima and found a father who possessed his own child, succumbing to those dark paternal passions hinted at in *Hamlet*, *Othello*, and *Lear*. In his journey through life, Pericles must choose for himself between images of the Good Father and the Bad Father and recognize the two sides of the anima. Repelled by the malefic and seductive anima he finds in Antioch, Pericles loses sight of the benevolent alternative until he is redeemed by his daughter Marina.

Pericles is washed ashore in Pentapolis after a great storm—tempests abound in Shakespeare's romances, symbolic of unresolved psychic energies. His father's armor, his patrimony, is retrieved by helpful fishermen. With his active male persona, his conscious self, Pericles has no difficulty.[20] As his successful battle in II.ii demonstrates, he is in touch with his masculinity, like his father performing noble deeds. It is his unconscious, his anima, with which Pericles must come to terms. He meets the Good Father in Simonides, the first such good father in all Shakespeare. Wise and balanced, Simonides has achieved that final integration psychologists have written about.[21] Recognizing his part in the cycle of human development, Simonides has overcome the desire to dominate or possess his daughter. No Lear, Brabantio, or stubborn Egeus, he releases her to the man she loves. With a wisdom beyond ego, he recognizes in Pericles a valiant young man worthy of his daughter and applauds her choice, unthreatened either by a younger rival for his daughter's affection or by her assertiveness:

> now to my daughter's letter:
> She tells me here, she'll wed the stranger knight,
> Or never more to view nor day nor light,
> 'Tis well, mistress; Your choice agrees with mine;
> I like that well: nay, how absolute she's in it,
> Not minding whether I dislike or no!
> Well, I do commend her choice;

And will no longer have it be delay'd,
Soft! here he comes: I must dissemble it.

[II.v.15-23]

As G. Wilson Knight observed, "Simonides enjoys not only his ruse but also his daughter's self-willed determination, expressed in a letter, to marry Pericles or no one, the long story of Shakespeare's tyrannic fathers from Capulet to Lear being most delightfully reversed."[22] Simonides takes upon himself the role of *senex iratus* to test his future son-in-law and strengthen the bond between the young lovers. This trial allows for the ritual transfer of his daughter's loyalty from father to husband.

Not all is resolved for Pericles, however. As Thaisa becomes pregnant, bringing him to the brink of paternity, everything suddenly goes awry. Antiochus is dead, and Pericles must return to his own kingdom in Tyre. On board ship his pregnant wife falls into labor, and Pericles finds himself in the grip of natural forces he cannot control. He cries out to the storm, to Lucina, goddess of childbirth, to all these mysterious forces beyond his comprehension.

Only in the romances is a female character represented as pregnant and going through childbirth. Both here and in *The Winter's Tale* the male protagonist is alienated from his queen, at least in part by the mystery of gestation, and loses both wife and child until a later "rebirth" and reunion.[23] Pericles errs in his imbalance, his fear of the irrational feminine mysteries to which he cannot relate.[24] He is courageous in combat, but in III.i.1-14 he walks the deck, crying out to the gods to allay the fierceness of the storm and his wife's labor, remaining far removed from the scene of childbirth. Apparently, he would rather confront the storm than comfort his wife. Beset by the throes of childbirth, Thaisa has become for him an alien "other," best left to Lychorida, another woman, to cope with these fleshly mysteries.

When Lychorida emerges with the infant, reporting his wife's death, she repeatedly counsels "patience" (19,26). But Pericles is hardly patient. He hastily accedes to the demands of the sailors for whom this woman on board is taboo, failing to realize that Thaisa is still sufficiently alive to be revived by Cerimon many hours later. Dominated by his fears, Pericles casts away his dearly loved wife, who has become for him a symbol of the fleshly mysteries of birth and death. Just as suddenly he casts his daughter from him at Tarsus. Initially the child needs a wet nurse, but he leaves her there as though there were no opportunities for her upbringing in his own country. Recoiling from the responsibilities of parenthood, Pericles casts aside these images of birth and death, renouncing his feminine side completely. He withdraws in self-imposed mourning, vowing not to cut his hair until his daughter marries, and once again affirms life. Years later, believing her dead, he retreats still further, going to sea, renouncing his emotions, and falling into catatonia. Tossed about by the sea, symbolic of the unconscious,[25] Pericles' physical condition mirrors his psychological state.

His daughter, Marina, represents the very virtue he lacks. She overcomes adversity patiently, in marked contrast to her despairing father. In her radiant innocence she reforms even the men in the brothel, by appealing to their higher nature, touching the benevolent anima in each of them. Reunited with Pericles, she offers beauty, renewal, and hope. She touches him with emotion, revives him, and restores his identity.

Her story sounds like a riddle, recalling the riddle he heard years ago in Antioch.[26] But the situation is now reversed. Attracted to this lovely girl, who resembles his lost wife, he responds as the Good Father, recognizing the attraction but loving within paternal bounds. Acknowledging his own anima, he can give his daughter in marriage, accepting the mysteries of birth and death from which he had retreated long ago:

> O, come hither,
> Thou that beget'st him that did thee beget;
> Thou that wast born at sea, buried at Tarsus,
> And found at sea again!   [V.i.196-99]

This time he sees beyond the flesh into a paradoxical pattern of birth and renewal, the irrational mysteries of human life illuminated with the radiant power of the spirit.

Pericles no longer fears his own emotions and the natural forces beyond his control. His suffering has prepared him for an enlargement of vision and an act of faith. The conclusion of this play, like those of the other romances, points to a greater harmony for those who find balance within themselves. Pericles' shattered world is finally restored to order. A vision of the goddess Diana leads him to Ephesus, where he finds his lost Thaisa. She has been revived by Cerimon, who anticipates the more complete portrayal of the magus in Prospero. The romances are filled with theophanies. Gods and goddesses touch this mortal world and reveal the workings of a benevolent providence beyond human understanding.[27] In *Pericles*, the deity is Diana; in *Cymbeline*, Jupiter. In *The Winter's Tale*, Apollo's prophecy indicates a supernatural power working behind the scenes, and *The Tempest* features a masque of benevolent goddesses as well as repeated references to grace and regeneration. Shakespeare's final plays are replete with visions of divine mercy. Their protagonists grow from inner division and alienation to a state of grace by integrating the opposing forces within into dynamic balance, becoming receptive to a greater harmony.

The Winter's Tale

Leontes' sudden attack of jealousy at the beginning of *The Winter's Tale* indicates that he, like Pericles, has not come to terms with his sexuality. His development has been arrested between youth and generativity, his intimacy with Hermione obscured by lingering fears and suspicions. As Coppélia Kahn noted, "though Leontes is a mature man—king, husband, father—the nine-month visit of his boyhood friend reveals that he is still split between two identities, the boy of the past and the father of the present."[28] Unlike Shakespeare's androgynous comic heroes, Leontes has not extended the lessons of friendship into mature commitment in marriage. Instead, he polarizes sexual love and friendship, looking back nostalgically to his boyhood with Polixenes as a state of innocence. In Polixenes' words, they had been "as twinn'd lambs . . . what we chang'd / Was innocence for innocence" (I.ii.67-69), until their attraction to their future wives awakened them to sexuality.

Leontes cannot respect Hermione as a friend because he knows her as a lover. She remains "other," epitomizing those disturbing erotic urges and mysteries of the flesh. Uncomfortable with his own flesh, he is uncomfortable with her. He fails to see her as a person, to recognize the strengths of character that transcend her flesh and her procreative function. Hermione is clever, witty, assertive, courageous, a queen in her own right. To Leontes, however, she is merely woman, feared because she brings out the irrational, the beast in man. In his marriage there is no trust, no faith. Their relationship stands in distinct contrast to the progressive marriages of the comedies, in which women are their husbands' friends and partners. To Leontes, "she is a possession who will betray her owner at the first opportunity and one which it is impossible to guard."[29]

Kahn attributes Leontes' jealousy to his attraction to Polixenes: "the hero's belief that his wife loves his best friend is his way of defending against the horrified realization that he too still loves that friend." For E.M.W. Tillyard, his jealousy springs from the sin of pride.[30] But Jungian psychology offers a new explanation for his jealousy. The many parallels between Leontes and Polixenes—they grew up together, are both now kings, husbands, and fathers of sons—indicate that they are "doubles." Two friends in the Renaissance sense, one soul in bodies twain, their similarity leads to a confusion of feelings and identities for Leontes. He sees Polixenes as his double or "dark shadow," projecting upon his friend his own lustful response to Hermione. His anima has become contaminated by his unintegrated emotions.[31] Having awakened in him the power of sexual desire, Hermione becomes a seductress, a dangerous woman, able to inflame the same desires in his friend.

Unable to respect and trust Hermione, Leontes sees her as simply a body, the incarnation of the flesh. His jealousy springs from his immature sexuality, his fear and loathing of the physical. In her state as a gestating woman, "swollen to the last stages of pregnancy," she has become even less of a person, more of a body, blamed for all the lustful desires he cannot admit in himself. "Her friendly courtesies to Polixenes he sees as lechery, the Bohemian King's nine-month visit an odious explanation for the Queen's conception."[32] It is the misfortune of more than one of Shakespeare's married women to be matched with a husband who sees her as a whore. Like Desdemona, Hermione accepts herself, body and soul, with a healthy awareness of her sexuality. Engaging in witty conversation with their guest, Hermione is confident of her charms despite the heaviness of advanced pregnancy. But Leontes sees none of her redeeming qualities. To him she is merely a body, the swollen symbol of lust, and seducer of his best friend.

Suddenly, their every action becomes suspect in Leontes' eyes:

> But to be paddling palms and pinching fingers,
> As now they are, and making practis'd smiles,
> As in a looking-glass, and then to sigh, as 'twere
> The mort o'th'deer; O, that is entertainment
> My bosom likes not, nor my brows. [I.ii.115-19]

Like Othello, he sees their courtesy as his cuckoldry, and animal images race through his mind: "the heifer and the calf" (I.ii.124). He leaves them alone in the garden, again endowing them with bestial motives:

> Go to! go to!
> How she holds up the neb, the bill to him!
> And arms her with the boldness of a wife
> To her allowing husband! [I.ii.182-85]

His misogyny grows as he generalizes that nymphomania is widespread: "it is a bawdy planet" (201) and provides a graphic description of woman as body, reduced to a voracious womb, vessel of unquenchable lust:

> be it concluded,
> No barricado for a belly; know't;
> It will let in and out the enemy
> With bag and baggage: many thousand on's
> Have the disease, and feel't not. [I.ii.203-7]

Two critics have recognized that Leontes' jealousy springs from unconscious fears and an infected imagination.[32] Neurotically unable to accept "the woman's part" in himself, he perceives Hermione as the lecherous malefic anima, lashing out with a hostility familiar in neurotics.[34] His frenzied misogyny recalls the witch-burning phobias that swept Europe throughout the Renaissance and seventeenth century. When Paulina brings the newborn princess to mollify her father, he calls her a "witch" and a "bawd" (II.iii.67,68), the infant a bastard, commanding all three women—Hermione, Paulina, and Perdita—to be burned at the stake.

A desolate Leontes recovers his senses in III.ii. His fury has caused the loss of his wife, his son, and his infant daughter. He is left alone with his remorse. Paulina, the only remaining woman, functions as a spiritual guide.[35] In her care, he slowly recovers what he has lost by enacting "the woman's part," for years of penance, patience, and passivity. "Unknowingly emulating Hermione,"[36] he prepares himself for the recovery of his anima, his daughter, and his lost wife.

Luminous in her youth, beauty, and innocence, the daughter provides a chaste alternative to the malefic anima, allaying her father's fears and suspicions of women. Shakespeare's daughters of romance conform to what Jung described as the "anima type," a woman whose "sphinx-like character . . . seems full of promises, like the speaking silence of a Mona Lisa."[37] We see them not as fully developed characters, but as their fathers' inspiration. Projecting the benevolent anima, their fathers recognize in their daughters their own potential for love, mercy, and renewal. Perdita, like Marina, redeems her father and restores him to emotional wholeness. "She reconciles virginity and erotic appeal . . . combines the qualities of the chaste preoedipal mother and the sexually desirable oedipal mother, symbolically uniting

Leontes' divided attitudes toward women."[38] For the first time in years, Leontes finds himself stirred by feelings of love, drawn to the endearing young couple seeking refuge at his court. Florizel reminds him of his childhood friend, and together the two recall his lost children. Leontes finds himself strongly attracted to Perdita. So Hermione had appeared before he lost her. Paulina tells him, "Your eye hath too much youth in't" (V.i.225). His concupiscent emotions redirected toward paternal care, he affirms a protective *caritas* for the young couple. After a flurry of rediscovery and reunion, Leontes and the others visit Paulina's chapel, where she tells them, "It is requir'd / You do awake your faith." (V.iii.95-96) There she reveals the statue that turns into the living Hermione, miraculously restored when her husband regains his faith and wholeness. Leontes has grown in his suffering to such a degree that he can accept his own feelings and even admit miracles. His violence has been slowly healed by years of penance, his misogyny by his acceptance of Perdita, and his jealousy and mistrust are finally overcome by a newfound faith in life's mysteries. The conclusion of this play is filled with deep spiritual significance. The statue coming to life is archetypal, reminiscent for some of the blessed mother, for others undeniably Hermetic.[39] It represents Leontes' own spiritual rebirth in the regeneration of the *anima*, his acceptance of the life-giving woman's part in himself.

Cymbeline

Cymbeline records the developmental journeys of two men, Cymbeline and Posthumus, the father and the husband of Imogen, each of whom must come to terms with the anima in himself. Like Leontes, Posthumus falls into violent jealousy. Although betrayed by the scheming Iachimo, his lack of trust in Imogen indicates an inner deficiency, an inability to trust those feelings that make him vulnerable. Like Othello, Posthumus is deceived because he doubts himself. His very name reveals his problem: he is Posthumus Leonatus, born after his father's death of a mother who died in childbirth. An orphan, he has known no family bonds. Although raised in the court of Cymbeline, he has been emotionally isolated. While excelling in external accomplishments, he has not yet learned basic trust, the earliest developmental lesson.[40] He cannot commit himself to another human being until he trusts his feelings and his world. His love for Imogen is necessarily flawed and immature. Her love, by contrast, is grounded in trust and commitment. As they are parted in I.i, she offers her ring, a ritualistic pledge of woman's fidelity in marriage:

> This diamond was my mother's: take it, heart;
> But keep it till you woo another wife,
> When Imogen is dead. [I.i.112-14]

Deprived of family bonds, Posthumus cannot value the ring for what it represents. Nor can he value Imogen's devotion and fidelity. Their gifts reveal their differences. She gives her ring in a ritual bond of love and commitment; he gives the bracelet as a "manacle of love" (I.i.122), a symbol of possession by force.[41]

Posthumus values Imogen, not as a marriage partner, but as a priceless possession, a thing that can easily be lost or stolen. It is impossible to trust a thing. In his mind Imogen and the ring are beautiful, valuable objects. Iachimo shrewdly advances the comparison. Using flattery and manipulation, he leads Posthumus to denigrate his love by wagering on Imogen's chastity as men wager on horses, cards, and dice, behavior not only distrustful, but disrespectful. Imogen is the beautiful and mysterious "other," of whom he boasts possession in the violent and competitive world of men. Robert Grams Hunter saw Cloten's headless body, clothed in the garments of Posthumus, as an ironic comment on Posthumus himself: "For he, too, has lost his head. By allowing himself to consider the love between him and Imogen to be a matter simply of things, he has reduced himself to the status of a thing—a mindless corpse."[42]

When the subtle Iachimo returns with the "ocular proof" of Imogen's infidelity, Posthumus, like Leontes and Othello, responds with jealous fury. His vision of sexual consummation, the brutal mounting of a "full-acorn'd boar" (II.v.16), recalls the ugly animal imagery of other jealous husbands. His violent soliloquy reveals his tormented psyche. In his subsequent denunciation of women, "What Posthumus is actually describing is the unconscious content of his own mind. The subject is Man, not Woman."[43]

Like Hamlet, his disillusionment with one woman turns to distrust of all, a misogyny that recoils upon himself, making him disdain his own fleshly origin:

> Is there no way for men to be but women
> Must be half-workers? We are all bastards;
> And that most venerable man which I

> Did call my father, was I know not where
> When I was stamp'd; some coiner with his tools
> Made me a counterfeit: yet my mother seem'd
> The Dian of that time: so doth my wife
> The nonpareil of this.   [II.v.1-7]

In blatant misogyny, he blames women for all vice and irrationality, constellating the malefic anima—woman as deceiver, bawd, and sorceress—repudiating "the woman's part" in himself, and slandering his own emotional nature.

>   Could I find out
> The woman's part in me! For there's no motion
> That tends to vice in man, but I affirm
> It is the woman's part: be it lying, note it,
> The woman's; flattering, hers; deceiving, hers;
> Lust and rank thoughts, hers, hers; revenges, hers;
> Ambitions, covetings, change of prides, disdain,
> Nice longings, slanders, mutability,
> All faults that may be nam'd, nay that hell knows.
>   [II.v.19-27]

Like Leontes, he succumbs to neurotic jealousy and violent misogyny, plotting his wife's death. Believing her dead, he begins a penitential journey, which teaches him to accept "the woman's part" in himself.

For Posthumus, this reconciliation involves the acknowledgment of family bonds. As Meredith Skura explained, "there is no way for him to find himself as husband until he finds himself as son, as part of the family he was torn from long ago."[44] He must learn basic trust from his parents before he can trust Imogen. He must accept the feminine feelings in himself before he can trust anyone. In V.i, holding a bloody cloth, he mourns Imogen, forgiving her and blaming himself for rushing to vengeance instead of showing mercy and understanding. With this expression of love and mercy, the benevolent anima begins to stir within him. To demonstrate his loyalty to Imogen, he determines to fight for her country and perhaps join her in death. Disguised in humble garments—another symbol of penance—he joins Belarius and the two young princes, saving the life of Cymbeline. With stoic detachment, he awaits his death in prison, receiving a mysterious vision of his family, who appeal to Jove in his behalf. He sees his mother, father, and brothers for the first time and witnesses their loving intercession. Here Posthumus finds a missing part of himself. Enclosed in the circle of familial love, he experiences basic trust, finding in their caring and compassion an affirmation of his own worth. Coming to terms with the powerful parent figures in his unconscious, he awakens with a promise of the future, a mysterious prophecy that becomes a vision of hope. In response to his family's prayers, Jupiter has descended in theophany, affirming the enduring quality of human bonds and promising redemption to all who strive for wisdom and personal growth.

In V.v, Posthumus is reunited with Imogen after she has symbolically died three times: in his supposed revenge, when she took the queen's potion, and as he struck her to the ground. He embraces her as his own with the words: "Hang there like fruit, my soul / Till the tree die" (V.v.263-64). These emblematic lines reveal an acceptance of Imogen on two levels: allegorically as the image of his soul, the anima or feminine principle within himself, which he later expresses in his mercy to the repentant Iachimo, and literally as the woman he has learned to love more deeply as his wife and partner.

Cymbeline, as well, gains greater vision and wholeness in the final act. After his queen's death, he learns of her deceptive, wicked character. She had plotted to murder both Imogen and himself to put Cloten on the throne. In her pride she had urged him to make war on Rome. Cymbeline had projected upon his evil queen an image of the benevolent anima, while misprizing his daughter as wicked and rebellious. His error reveals the extent to which he was out of touch with his own feminine nature. Now he admits his mistake and prays for grace:

> Mine eyes
> Were not in fault, for she was beautiful;
> Mine ears, that heard her flattery; nor my heart,
> That thought her like her seeming; it had been vicious
> To have mistrusted her: yet, O my daughter!
> That it was folly in me, thou mayst say,
> And prove it in thy feeling. Heaven mend all!
>
> [V.v.62-68]

Imogen reveals herself, receiving her husband's embrace and her father's blessing in lines 261-69. At this, Cymbeline weeps: "my tears that fall / Prove holy water on thee! Imogen" (V.v.268-69). His reunion with Imogen, now perceived as the benevolent anima, stirs his love and compassion. Acknowledging his feminine side, he describes the reunion with his daughter and two sons in maternal metaphor:

> O, what, am I
> A mother to the birth of three? Ne'er mother
> Rejoic'd deliverance more.   [V.v.368-70]

Affirming the influence of this merciful archetype, he embraces Belarius as a brother, extending the scope of family bonds. The underlying image concluding all of Shakespeare's romances is this benevolent anima, "maternal solicitude and sympathy . . . the wisdom and spiritual exaltation that transcends reason . . .[and] fosters growth and fertility."[45] Cymbeline's maternal imagery signals his birth into a higher consciousness, affirming the love within the human family. He upholds the values of care and cooperation that psychologically healthy and integrated men affirm at midlife.[46] Freed from the poisonous influence of his malefic queen, Cymbeline turns to Lucius, offering mercy to all the soldiers who fought against him, reaffirming his alliance with Rome in an external harmony that parallels his newfound harmony within.

The Wisdom of Prospero

In *The Tempest*, Shakespeare's final play, the themes of domination and defiance, integration and personal growth are brought to conclusion. The play opens with a storm, figuring the destructive power of unintegrated forces within the human psyche. This storm has been staged by Prospero, who has overcome his own violent tempests and will bring comic reconciliation out of potential tragedy. With grace and wisdom, Prospero overcomes two tragic situations in the plot: first his own usurpation, from which he had been miraculously preserved, and second, the temptation to turn the play into a revenger's tragedy by punishing his brother and Alonso. Able to overcome violent tendencies within himself, Prospero can meet the threat of violence from others, preventing the murder of Alonso and quenching the rebellion of Caliban, Stephano, and Trinculo, which offers a parodic parallel to the initial usurpation.

The usurpation contains the familiar tragic elements of greed and ambition that reap their fatal consequences in *Hamlet* and *Macbeth*. Preserved from drowning and brought to this island, Prospero sees his exile as both a trial and a blessing (I.ii.61). He recognizes that his own imbalance was partly responsible for his loss. Excessively contemplative, Prospero had retreated to his books, casting the cares of government upon his brother "and to my state grew stranger, being transported / And rapt in secret studies" (I.ii.76-77). He had forgotten the necessity of balance, the Aristotelian golden mean. Neglecting his duty, he "awak'd an evil nature" (93) in his brother, providing the occasion for Antonio's ambition. In his narration to Miranda, he acknowledges his error, a vital step in the process of regeneration, which leads him from the bitterness of revenge to wholeness, integration, and mercy.

As Harold Goddard observed, Prospero, "when expelled from his dukedom [was] a narrow and partial man."[47] His twelve years on the island have forced him to balance his retiring and contemplative nature with pragmatism, his excessive intellectualism with emotion, in the care of his daughter, Miranda. The consequences of Prospero's imbalance were also the cure. Alone on the island without servants, with a two-year-old child on his hands, Prospero was forced to become more responsible. This contemplative scholar had to provide for the daily needs of himself and his young daughter. The demands of daily existence have been, paradoxically, a spiritual exercise, developing the pragmatic, active side of his nature he had heretofore neglected. He has had his books as well, thanks to the kindness of Gonzalo, but has been forced by necessity to divide his labors between the active and the contemplative, moving toward internal balance.

Caring for Miranda has been more than an exercise in pragmatism. She has helped balance his excessive intellectualism with warmth and human caring, leading to the strength of mind and heart that constitutes a healthy human being. A helpless, loving child, Miranda has awakened the nurturing tendencies in Prospero, giving his life another level of meaning. In his words:

> a cherubin
> Thou wast that did preserve me. Thou didst smile,
> Infused with a fortitude from heaven,
> When I have deck'd the sea with drops full salt,
> Under my burthen groan'd; which rais'd in me
> An undergoing stomach, to bear up
> Against what should ensue.   [I.ii.152-58]

She has been a source of emotional sustenance. Responding to her goodness, love, and wonder, he has become deeper and wiser. While educating Miranda, he has educated his own emotional nature, developing the anima, which has made him a great magus.

We find Miranda at the beginning of the play in a familiar position for Shakespeare's daughters. A young woman "on the threshold of moral maturity,"[48] she is ready to leave behind her childhood obedience and strong filial bond for the adult commitment to love and intimacy. Lorie Jerrell Leininger sees Miranda as an innocent, obedient young woman dutifully married off by her father, a throwback to traditional womanhood and the dramatic counterpart of the Princess Elizabeth, for whose marriage this play was performed in 1613.[49] But Miranda is more than a beautiful pawn in the larger game of courtship and reconciliation. Although her character is barely sketched, there are touches of spirit, humor, and conflict. Miranda, for all her innocence, is warmly human, a young woman who thinks for herself. In her defense of Ferdinand, her unauthorized visit, and the revelation of her name, Miranda has the spark of Shakespeare's comic daughters who defy their fathers for love.[50] Although Prospero's domination is feigned, Miranda's loving defiance is very real.

Prospero's domination of Miranda has troubled some critics. Coleridge observed that his "interruption of the courtship has often seemed to me to have no sufficient motive."[51] But Shakespeare provides us with a motive in the text. Like Simonides, Prospero reveals the reason for his behavior in an aside:

At the first sight

They have chang'd eyes.
· · · · · · · · · · · · · · · · · · · ·
They are both in either's pow'rs; but this swift business
I must uneasy make, lest too light winning
Make the prize light.   [I.ii.440-41;449-51]

Prospero simulates the behavior of a *senex iratus*, placing obstacles between his daughter and her love. He calls Ferdinand a traitor, a spy, and a usurper, taking the young prince captive and subjecting him to the indignity of manual labor. In the role of *alazon*, he exerts a tyrannical authority against which the young couple will strengthen their love and commitment. Miranda disobeys her father, choosing romantic love over filial obedience. She offers to carry logs for Ferdinand, and in the tradition of Shakespeare's comic women, proposes to him. The young couple plight their troth, having achieved commitment and personal growth. Heretofore an obedient young woman, Miranda asserts herself to claim her love, and Ferdinand, a young prince accustomed to privilege, humbles himself to earn Miranda, realizing "for your sake / Am I this patient log-man" (III.i.66-67).

Forced to perform the labor of Caliban to earn his love, Ferdinand must also tame the Caliban, or unruly passions, within himself. Prospero's imposition of authority upon the young couple is an educational process that disciplines their passions, channeling them within the bonds of conjugal love. The father's tyrannical behavior provides the thesis, romantic passion the antithesis, synthesized in the commitment of marriage. Ferdinand finds in such love a greater liberty: "with a heart as willing / As bondage e'er of freedom: here's my hand" (III.ii.88-89).

Satisfied with Ferdinand's response, Prospero releases him from bondage and joins the couple in formal betrothal, telling the young prince that:

> all thy vexations
> Were but trials of thy love, and thou
> Hast strangely stood the test: here, afore Heaven,
> I ratify this my rich gift.   [IV.i.5-8]

Prospero acknowledges his love for Miranda, at the same time releasing her from his care. He tells Ferdinand:

> If I have too austerely punish'd you,
> Your compensation makes amends, for I
> Have given you here a third of my own life,
> Or that for which I live; who once again
> I tender to thy hand.   [IV.i.1-5]

Prospero warns Ferdinand repeatedly not to anticipate marriage by bedding Miranda "before / All sanctimonious ceremonies" (14-15). According to Wilson Knight, here "Prospero's paternal solicitude becomes a little too much for some of us."[52] Many have found his insistence excessive, indicative of unresolved passions and reluctance to release his much-loved daughter to the embraces of another man. Leslie Fiedler sees Prospero's warning as a reflection of the father's obsession with lust and the threat of rape of his daughter.[53] In Prospero's insistence, however, can be seen a strong belief in balance: the integration of reason and passion, the necessity of love within order. As Alan Hobson wrote, "No delicate and beautiful thing, whether in nature or in art can be received but by the humble and self-disciplined. The avid and the confident will devour, as Caliban would have devoured Miranda; the possessive will crush."[54] Prospero's advice reflects a deep metaphysical lesson: the necessity of discipline, faith, and humility in order to embrace a higher truth. Like the earlier romances, *The Tempest* portrays life as a spiritual exercise: the initiation of the individual into the higher order of love and grace.

In other plays, "a Desdemona must hurt her father in order to please her lover, an Ophelia must hurt her lover in order to please her father."[55] Only in two final romances is a daughter spared the tragic dilemma of domination or defiance. The father-daughter relationship is ordinarily permeated with possessiveness, pain, and difficult choices. It is Miranda's good fortune to have a father who transcends the desire to possess and dominate. He loves Miranda—she is a third of his life—and yet he releases her. Having attained a hermetic balance within himself, he acknowledges her need for growth and development as well.

The Tempest ends, as do many of Shakespeare's comedies, on a note of marriage and reconciliation. But the harmony of the romances springs from a deeper source than married love. As one critic pointed out, "in *The Tempest* happiness comes, not because Ferdinand and Miranda love each other, but because Prospero loves in a different and larger sense."[56] As Wilson Knight observed, "We see Miranda and Ferdinand through a father's eyes. . . . They appear to us as children, moving in a kind of subdued light of tenderness and compassion."[57] The core of the drama is not the struggles and raptures of young lovers as in Shakespeare's comedies and love tragedies. Paternal love informs the romances. We are led to see the world "through a father's eyes," following the struggles of the paternal protagonist as he faces the developmental challenges of middle life. He accepts his own sexuality and fatherhood, develops a nurturing love for his daughter and then releases her to seek her own commitments. In these final plays, Shakespeare's fathers discover a means of expressing care, reconciling the misdirected forces of eros into benevolent *caritas*.[58]

The reconciliation in this play has been called disturbing and incomplete, for unlike Leontes and Pericles, Prospero is not reunited with his wife. Kahn argued that "thus Prospero's final identity lacks the fullness of that achieved by the other heroes."[59] The difference is significant. In a developmental sense, Prospero is Shakespeare's oldest father, ready to face the final challenge of his life. His missing wife represents no deficiency, but an incorporation of the feminine element within himself. Having been "both father and mother to Miranda,"[60] he is in touch with his anima, which enables him to release his daughter to her destiny instead of possessively clinging to her. He has achieved individuation, a creative androgyny that makes his magic possible.

Many have recognized that Ariel and Caliban represent opposing forces within Prospero and the "twin potentialities of the human spirit." They can be seen as the mental and physical sides of his nature.[61] Earlier in his life, Prospero had been excessively intellectual, unable to express his feelings or recognize the negative passions growing in his brother. But caring for Miranda has actualized his benevolent emotions. Similarly, in contending with Caliban, he has recognized the reality of the shadow and the primitive urges he represents. In I.ii.311-13, he tells Miranda that Caliban must be controlled, but cannot be denied:

> We cannot miss him: he does make our fire,
> Fetch in our wood and serves in offices
> That profit us.

In Renaissance natural philosophy, Caliban corresponds to the vegetative and animal soul. He performs physical functions such as concoction, making the fire, and embodies the senses and passions. In contrast, Ariel, a spirit without a body, represents the rational soul.[62] In Milan, Prospero had buried himself in his books, denying his emotional and physical nature. At the end of the play, however, he claims Caliban as his own: "this thing of darkness I / Acknowledge mine" (V.i.275-76).

Prospero's reconciliation of the opposites within himself: body and soul, unconscious and conscious, masculine and feminine, produces a hermetic balance that gives him his power.[63] The integration of his anima has developed his compassion, enabling him to turn justice into mercy, rejecting the temptations of revenge. Prospero's compassion is evident as early as I.ii, when he commends Miranda for pitying the shipwrecked strangers and assures her that there's "no harm done" (16). When Ariel describes Alonso's repentance and the shipwreck victims' collective misery,

> Your charm so strongly works 'em
> That if you now beheld them, your affections
> Would become tender   [V.i.17-19]

Prospero answers that "mine shall" (20), proclaiming that "the rarer action is / In virtue than in vengeance" (26-27). He forgives them one and all, while recognizing the unregenerate state of Antonio and Sebastian. Keeping his eye on his reprobate brother, Prospero transcends any personal resentment, attaining the wisdom of detachment.

In the final scenes, Prospero renounces his magic, announcing that in Milan he will oversee the marriage of Ferdinand and Miranda and take up his duties as duke, while "every third thought shall be my grave" (V.i.311). Some people are troubled by this line, but the meaning is clear in the context of personal development. His magic has been a means to a greater end. It is spiritual alchemy, performed to produce the quintessence within the individual, the perfect balance that constitutes the integrated soul. Once this has been achieved, the means are no longer necessary. Prospero's hermetic magic has reconciled the conflicting forces within him and reunited Naples and Milan. His final challenge is to return to Milan, where he will reign as duke, balancing action and contemplation.

In *The Tempest*, all is not resolved into perfect harmony. The realities of the fallen world are still evident in those reprobate members of humankind who will not repent. This play does not offer the easy assurance and miraculous conversions of Shakespeare's festive comedies. Aware of political realities, Prospero will spend two-thirds of the time in strict vigilance, exercising his duties as duke. "Every third thought" will be devoted to a more personal responsibility. In the memento mori tradition, he will confront for himself the final crisis of integrity.

Prospero, like Lear, is an old man who faces the final developmental crisis, the confrontation with death. While Lear's internal conflicts reduce him to folly and impotence, Prospero faces this final challenge with wisdom and faith, "the detached and yet active concern with life itself in the face of death itself," which overcomes the temptation to despair and "the Dread of ultimate nonbeing."[64] He has managed to combine his conflicting tendencies into a vision which affirms his faith, worth, and the value of life itself. Having achieved the "state of grace" in personal integration, he can look beyond this life to the promise of heaven, his developmental journey and spiritual pilgrimage complete.

CHAPTER EIGHT

Beyond Domination and Defiance

Throughout his principal comedies, tragedies, and romances, Shakespeare examined the love between fathers and daughters from many points of view. The father-daughter bond reflects conflicts between progressive and traditional social norms, youth and age, male and female, self and other, and conflicting forces within the individual. In each play traditional stereotypes are rejected, affirming the need for a new synthesis, a resolution of conflict through cooperation.

In the double developmental crisis defined in chapter 1, Shakespeare's fathers and daughters face critical adult transitions. Leaving behind childhood security, the daughters reach out to embrace the challenge of romantic love, with new awareness of what it means to be a woman. The creative power of their love is reflected in the multiple marriages that conclude the comedies. At the same time, their fathers face the sobering challenge of middle life. Their loss of power, both physical and personal, is in marked contrast to their daughters' expansive new energy. These men feel diminished. Their masculine vigor in decline, they must face alone the specter of old age and death, looking for greater meaning in the crisis of integrity.[1]

Anticipating modern psychological research, Shakespeare's plays illustrate how profoundly a father influences his daughter's identity. He reinforces her for both competence and compliance, as she learns to please the first man in her life. His reactions define what it means to be a good daughter, the moral norm that will determine her self-concept and behavior in society.[2] Although Helena's physician father developed her medical competence in *All's Well*, and Simonides rejoices in his daughter's assertiveness in *Pericles*, the great majority of fathers in Shakespeare's plays, as in traditional societies, reinforce their daughters for compliance. Bound by the conventional stereotype, Hero,

Ophelia, and Desdemona find their identity, their happiness, in pleasing others.

Shakespeare's plays also reflect the epistemological crisis of the Renaissance, offering a redefinition of those values and commitments essential to human society. The fathers personify traditional values, demanding unconditional obedience from women and children, crushing their individuality with patriarchal authority. In chapter 2 I described the way daughters in the early Renaissance were commonly bartered by their fathers in marriage arrangements more economic than interpersonal. A woman was first her father's chattel, then her husband's, consigned to an eternal childhood of compliance. In such a world, those with power too easily victimize those without.

Shakespeare's comic daughters discussed in chapters 5 and 6 offer a new definition of responsible adulthood, affirming a concept of marriage drawn from Renaissance humanism and the Puritan emphasis on conscience and conjugal love. Refusing to be bartered like property, these young women assert their right to consent, to think for themselves and make adult commitments. While traditional compliance leads Ophelia and Desdemona to their deaths, their comic counterparts choose new lives. They defy their fathers and the patriarchal stereotypes that reduce them to unthinking children, daring to follow the authority of conscience. Moving courageously beyond childhood obedience, these young women reject traditional definitions of the good woman, speaking up in their own behalf and raising serious questions about the status quo. Daughters like Hermia, Katharina, and Ann Page affirm their integrity and individual rights, precipitating a generational crisis that leads to a more cooperative society. Their marriage commitments are more personal and more caring. The traditional marriage of Hero in *Much Ado* pales in comparison to the vibrant love matches of Rosalind, Viola, Beatrice, and Portia, which allow for dynamic interchange and personal growth. Combining the fidelity of friendship with the magic of romance, Shakespeare's comedies present a progressive view of marriage as partnership, moving beyond authoritarian coercion to the more personal bonds of love and trust as the basis for any enduring human relationship.

From Egeus to Lear to Prospero, all Shakespeare's fathers love their daughters dearly. Psychologically, the way we love reveals who we are—our vulnerabilities, our needs, our values. Shakespeare's fathers all too often love addictively, seeking to satisfy their needs for security, sensation, and power by dominating their daughters.[3] As explained in chapter 3, their paternal possessiveness points to deep insecurities and unresolved developmental issues.[4]

Nearly all these fathers demonstrate what Jung would call infantile love for their daughters. They have not resolved their own attachment to the mother imago, the unconscious anima figure who represents perfect love and primal security. Out of touch with their own feminine capacities, unintegrated men project their emotional needs on the women they love. When frustrated in marriage, fathers project these needs with remarkable frequency on their daughters, looking to them for beauty, purity, and maternal care.[5] Shakespeare's fathers love with a compulsiveness that approaches incest. Autocratic and possessive, they cherish their daughters and fear to lose them, for they have made them the basis of their security.[6]

A daughter's romantic love for another man nearly always comes as a shock to her father. Shakespeare's fathers respond to this threat to their security with outrage, anxiety, pain, and possessiveness. They refuse to release their daughters in marriage to the men they love, stubbornly clinging to their paternal prerogatives. Reactionary fathers like Egeus, Brabantio, and Cymbeline ignore their daughters' adulthood in an effort to deny time and change. Egocentric fathers like Leonato, Lear, and Shylock are so completely identified with their daughters that they can hardly discern them as separate individuals. A daughter's defiance or deviation from the anima ideal is experienced as a violent wrenching, a psychic revolution of their own flesh and blood, which leaves most of Shakespeare's fathers in agony.

Like Lear, many fathers couple their needs for security with sensation, in erotic attachments to their daughters. The most extreme example in Shakespeare is the incestuous Antiochus, but many of these fathers exhibit incestuous tendencies, their infantile emotions making them violently jealous. They subject potential suitors to ordeals, while locking their daughters away like valuable possessions.

Needs for security and sensation often mingle with the urge to power as fathers dominate their daughters, refusing to release them without a desperate struggle. Witness the vindictive frustration of Egeus as he tyrannizes over Hermia, feeling she has rejected him by loving Lysander. If he must lose her, she will at least marry someone she does not love and will acknowledge his power in the transaction. Shakespeare's mercenary fathers, like Baptista and Polonius, are more coldly calculating. They see their daughters merely as valuable objects and symbols of their power, using them to aggrandize themselves politically or economically.

Nearly all Shakespeare's fathers fail to respect their daughters' needs because of their own emotional imbalance. The festive comedies and romances present an important developmental lesson, requiring the father's blessing, the release of his daughter in marriage, as necessary for his own personal growth as well as hers. Duke Theseus requires Egeus's grudging release of Hermia to Lysander in the final act of *Midsummer*, and the Duke Senior ritualistically releases Rosalind at the end of *As You Like It*. The comedies end in weddings, feasts, and celebrations, incorporating the fathers and young couples into a synthesis that promises to renew society. The romances go a step further, requiring from the fathers an inner synthesis that allows them to release their daughters with loving detachment. Cymbeline and Prospero acknowledge their feminine capacity for care, seeing beyond the compulsive demands of ego in the continued growth in altruism that Shakespeare recognized as essential to adult development.

Anthropologists have offered a biologically based view of human society, in which "love and hate, passion and aggression [are] built into the very nature of the bonding process," with human societies behaving like primates: males controlling females "for sex and dominance, females using males" for impregnation and protection.[7] This is a graphic picture of behavior in most traditional societies: domination of the weak by the strong. But Shakespeare realized that what is common is not necessarily desirable. Enslaved by the biological imperative, reduced to polarized sex roles, individuals are denied their human dignity. Arrested in their emotional development, they remain incomplete as persons. When aggression is exalted as strength and care is denigrated as weakness, society inevitably erupts into violence.[8]

By exposing the limits of traditional sex roles, Shakespeare's plays look beyond domination and defiance. As we have seen in chapter 4, the traditional ideal reduces women to nonentities, exalting feminine weakness, passivity, and submission in order to perpetuate the patriarchy. Ophelia's fate demonstrates how excessive demands for compliance by authoritarian fathers can drive their daughters to insanity, and Desdemona's suicidal self-effacement reveals how closely woman's love has been linked to masochism.[9] Traditional norms subordinate individual women to their procreative function, prizing their chastity to ensure pure patrilineal succession. *Othello*, *Hamlet*, *Cymbeline*, and *Much Ado* illustrate how untenable and unhealthy this feminine ideal can be. So fragile is woman's identity in patriarchal society that when she fails to match men's dreams of perfection, she becomes a victim of their deepest fears and doubts. With a sudden shift in masculine perception, Desdemona, Ophelia, Imogen, and Hero change from the benevolent to the malefic anima, subject to vengeful diatribes, hatred, abuse, and even murder from the men

[167]

who love them. In plays from *Much Ado* to *Cymbeline*, Shakespeare demonstrates how men have traditionally idolized women's beauty, treating them like precious objects. This gilded ideal imprisons women just as surely as oppressive fashions have impeded them for centuries. Shakespeare liberates his spirited young women from artificial feminine standards, dressing seven of them in masculine attire, which allows them greater freedom of action. In judicial robes or doublets and hose, they enter man's world and develop their own masculine potential for assertiveness and accomplishment.

The logic of Shakespeare's plays denies the patriarchal norms that reduce adult women to anxious, submissive children and leave men emotionally immature, haunted by specters of incest and misogyny. By portraying the violence in a society that allocates aggressive action to men, care and compliance to women, Shakespeare's plays implicitly indict polarized sex roles as unhealthy for individuals and their society. In traditional male conditioning, the capacity for love, care, and nurturing remains unconscious, undeveloped. As we saw in chapter 7, a man out of touch with his own sexual feelings too readily projects these troublesome desires upon women.

Male behavior in the tragedies is polarized, ruthless, and aggressive. Lacking the feminine "quality of mercy," men like Macbeth, Lear, and Othello bring violence to their world. Even Romeo rejects his earlier efforts at peacemaking, the feminine principle he had wed in Juliet, to follow the aggressive model of Tybalt, his masculinity assaulted by Mercutio's death: "O sweet Juliet, / Thy beauty hath made me effeminate" (III.i.118-19). Some tragic women like Volumnia, Lady Macbeth, Goneril, and Regan attempt to outdo their men in aggression. Other women, excessively compliant, become tragic victims, like Ophelia and Desdemona symbols of the feminine principle sacrificed. For Carolyn Heilbrun, they represent "not only the feminine impulse in the tragic world, but the feminine part of the men themselves [which is] ruthlessly destroyed."[10]

Tragically polarized men love "not wisely, but too well" (*Othello* V.ii.344), prizing their women as beautiful objects, precious jewels, not human beings. Othello describes Desdemona as his "perfect chrysolite" (V.ii.145); Posthumus rates Imogen with the diamond she gave him. Such love turns quickly into jealousy because it is grounded in mistrust. These men love their wives as treasures, which may too easily be stolen from them. Their association of feminine virtue with numinous objects, in one instance a handkerchief, in the other a bracelet, reduces the women they love to objects in dramatic synecdoche. Judith Herman argues that patriarchal socialization produces adult males deficient in empathy and predisposed to violence. Heilbrun notes that in Shakespeare's problem plays, "men by the excessive exercise of their most virile attributes bring total disaster upon their world."[11]

Othello and Desdemona are a fatally matched, polarized pair. Early in the play he says of her: "She lov'd me for the dangers I had pass'd, / And I lov'd her that she did *pity* them" (I.iii.167-68, italics mine). Deficient in his own ability to pity, to feel compassion for another, Othello is drawn to Desdemona because she excels in what he lacks. A violent man, raised on the battlefield, Othello is used to solving problems with his sword. Had he more pity, he would not so rashly have murdered Desdemona. Shakespeare gives us another version of this lesson in *Cymbeline*, as the furious Posthumus plots to murder Imogen. This play redeems the jealous husband from the consequences of his wrath. But in both instances, Shakespeare exposes the heroic male norm as overaggressive. Men cannot "delegate" to women all their softer emotions of pity, care, and compassion, nor can women abdicate their strength and competence if there is to be health and balance in society.

Believing that women are biologically endowed with a capacity for nurturing, Erik Erikson urged them to affirm their values more actively to counteract male aggressiveness and reduce the violence in society.[12] But his well-meaning plea for peace overlooks the need for personal integration, perpetuating the dangers of sex-role polarization. Centuries earlier, Shakespeare apparently realized that unless *both* men and women seek individual balance while making a commitment to the greater human family, women's procreative function will only preordain their domination, and society will remain polarized into aggressive and nurturing factions. Shakespeare's plays offer a balanced alternative to continuing cycles of violence. His comic women develop their masculine capacity for decisive action. As lawyers, doctors, and social organizers, they heal the disorder around them, bringing greater harmony to their world. They temper the *alazons'* excessive justice with mercy, revealing the limits of morality "that has become principled at the expense of care."[13] Women like Portia and Rosalind win respect for their competence, bringing about a new definition of authority based on respect, care, and cooperation rather than irrational power and coercion. Marrying for love, Shakespeare's dynamic young women abandon enforced obedience to follow conscience. Rejecting conventional authority, they are developmentally adults, not good children. They move from what Gilligan called "a focus on goodness . . . to a reflective understanding of care," demonstrating the ability to care for themselves as well as others in a new spirit of cooperation that renews their society.[14]

In Jungian terms, Shakespeare's balanced characters bring the harmony of androgyny and individuation to their world. His androgynous daughters meet with courage the challenge to actualize their masculine potential, claiming their share of power and respect. Shakespeare's fathers face the equally difficult challenge of releasing their power and the need to dominate, learning lessons of humility, patience, love, and compassion that lead to inner growth. In the early plays, many fathers demonstrate the reluctance of the man at midlife to relinquish power.[15] In the romances, daughters like Perdita, Marina, and Miranda help their fathers develop their feminine potential, learning "maternal solicitude and sympathy . . . the wisdom and spiritual exaltation that transcends reason" and temporal power.[16] As explained in chapter 7, maternal images of nurturing and growth appear in Prospero's masque of Ceres and the language of Cymbeline in V.v.368-70. Cymbeline gives his children a mother's blessing, and Prospero can love Miranda, yet release her to another man, having achieved a hermetic *conjuntio*. Shakespeare's androgynous characters redeem their world from chaos to order because they find a balance within themselves.

Jung attributed most of society's problems to an "incapacity to love." A compulsive cycle of physical and psychological violence is the result of general mistrust: "where love stops, power begins, and violence, and terror."[17] Throughout his comedies, tragedies, and romances, Shakespeare presents a dramatic panorama of men and women who seek new ways of loving and relating. Shakespeare's successful fathers and daughters become paradigms of balance and integration. They learn to love with respect, without compulsiveness, fear, or domination, offering a hope that beckons like the light in Portia's window across the darkness of an often confused, competitive, and violent cosmos. Their love is informed with the strength of *caritas*, which binds together human society, promising peace to their world—and our own.

Notes

Chapter One: *A Psychological Perspective*

1. Michael E. Lamb, Margaret Tresch Owen, and Lindsay Chase-Lansdale, "The Father-Daughter Relationship," in *Becoming Female*, ed. Claire B. Kopp with Martha Kirkpatrick (New York: Plenum, 1979), p. 89; Sigmund Freud, *The Interpretation of Dreams*, trans. A.A. Brill (New York: Modern Library, 1950), p. 156; Signe Hammer, *Passionate Attachments* (New York: Rawson, 1982), p. 9.
2. Heilbrun, *Toward a Recognition of Androgyny* (New York: Alfred A. Knopf, 1973), p. 32; Boose, "The Father and the Bride in Shakespeare," *PMLA* 97 (1982): 325-47; Greer, *The Female Eunuch* (New York: McGraw Hill, 1971), pp. 204-6; Dash, *Wooing, Wedding, and Power* (New York: Columbia Univ. Press, 1981), p. 1 (Ms. Dash offers especially perceptive readings of women's roles in *Othello* and *The Taming of the Shrew*); Dusinberre, *Shakespeare and the Nature of Women* (New York: Barnes and Noble, 1975), p. 308; Pitt, *Shakespeare's Women* (London: David and Charles, 1981), pp. 75, 53.
3. *The Woman's Part: Feminist Criticism of Shakespeare*, Carolyn Ruth Swift Lenz, Gayle Greene, and Carol Thomas Neely, eds. (Urbana: Univ. of Illinois Press, 1980); *Representing Shakespeare: New Psychoanalytic Essays*, Murray Schwartz and Coppélia Kahn, eds. (Baltimore: Johns Hopkins Univ. Press, 1980); Kahn, *Man's Estate: Masculine Identity in Shakespeare* (Berkeley: Univ. of California Press, 1981); Sundelson, *Shakespeare's Restorations of the Father* (New Brunswick, N.J.: Rutgers Univ. Press, 1983); Bamber, *Comic Women, Tragic Men: A Study of Gender and Genre in Shakespeare* (Stanford, Calif.: Stanford Univ. Press, 1982); Garber, *Coming of Age in Shakespeare* (London: Methuen, 1981); Levinson, *The Seasons of a Man's Life* (New York: Alfred A. Knopf, 1978), pp. 227ff.
4. Gail Sheehy, *Passages: Predictable Crises of Adult Life* (New York: E.P. Dutton, 1976); Philip Aries, *Centuries of Childhood*, trans. Robert Baldick (New York: Alfred A. Knopf, 1962), p. 50; Diane Elizabeth Dreher, *The Fourfold Pilgrimage* (Washington, D.C.: Univ. Press of America, 1982), pp. 1-5; Stanley Stewart, *The Expanded Voice* (San Marino, Calif.: Huntington Library, 1970), pp. 14-15; Carl Gustav Jung, *Psychology and Alchemy*, trans. R.F.C. Hull, *Collected Works* (*CW*) 12 (New York: Pantheon Books, 1953), passim.
5. Joan Webber, *The Eloquent 'I'* (Madison: Univ. of Wisconsin Press, 1968), pp. 8-17.
6. See Lawrence Kohlberg, "Stages of Moral Development as a Basis for Moral Education," in *Moral Development, Moral Education, and Kohlberg*, ed. Brenda Munsey (Birmingham, Ala.: Religious Education Press, 1980), pp. 91-92.
7. Jung, "The Stages of Life," in *The Structure and Dynamics of the Psyche*, trans. R.F.C. Hull, *CW* 8 (New York: Pantheon Books, 1960): 390; Levinson, *Seasons*, pp. 18, 322, 227.
8. Erikson, *Childhood and Society*, 2d ed. (1950; reprint, New York: W.W. Norton, 1963), pp.

247-67; see also Erikson, "Reflections on Dr. Borg's Life Cycle," in *Adulthood*, ed. Erik H. Erikson (New York: W.W. Norton, 1978), pp. 25-27.

9. Harding, *The Parental Image* (New York: G.P. Putnam's Sons, 1965), p. 121.
10. Jung, "Stages of Life," 73-74.
11. Levinson, *Seasons*, p. 255.
12. Jung, "Conscious, Unconscious, and Individuation," in *The Essential Jung*, ed. Anthony Storr (Princeton: Princeton Univ. Press, 1983), p. 224.
13. Horney, *The Neurotic Personality of Our Time* (New York: W.W. Norton, 1937), p. 174.
14. Jung, *The Development of Personality*, trans. R.F.C. Hull, *CW* 17 (New York: Pantheon Books, 1954): 55.
15. Levinson, *Seasons*, pp. 249, 226.
16. Ibid., pp. 232-35.
17. Jung, "Marriage as a Psychological Relationship," in *Development of Personality*, 198.
18. William Shakespeare, *The Tempest*, in *The Complete Works of William Shakespeare*, ed. Hardin Craig and David Bevington (Glenview, Ill.: Scott, Foresman, 1973). All quotations from Shakespeare are from this edition and will hereafter be cited parenthetically in the text.
19. Jung, *The Integration of the Personality*, trans. Stanley Dell (New York: Farrar and Rinehart, 1939), p. 173.
20. Jung, "The Undiscovered Self, Past, Present and Future," in *The Essential Jung*, p. 381. See also Jung, *Psychology of the Unconscious*, trans. Beatrice M. Hinkle (London: Routledge and Kegan Paul, 1919), p. 175.
21. Horney, *New Ways in Psychoanalysis* (New York: W.W. Norton, 1939), p. 93.
22. Horney, *Our Inner Conflicts* (New York: W.W. Norton, 1945), p. 164; see also Horney, *New Ways*, p. 29.
23. deMause, "The Evolution of Childhood," in *The History of Childhood*, ed. Lloyd deMause (New York: Psychohistory Press, 1974), pp. 6-7.
24. Fromm, *Man for Himself* (New York: Rineholt, 1947), p. 101.
25. Jung, "The Significance of the Father in the Destiny of the Individual," in *Freud and Psychoanalysis*, trans. R.F.C. Hull, *CW* 4 (New York: Pantheon Books, 1961): 315-16.
26. Sullivan, *Personal Psychopathology* (New York: W.W. Norton, 1972), p. 249.
27. Suzanne Fields, *Like Father, Like Daughter* (Boston: Little, Brown and Co., 1983), p. 161.
28. Deutsch, *The Psychology of Women* (New York: Grune and Stratton, 1944), pp. 202, 249.
29. Judith Lewis Herman with Lisa Hirschman, *Father-Daughter Incest* (Cambridge: Harvard Univ. Press, 1981), p. 4.
30. A.S. Diamond, *The Evolution of Law and Order* (1951), pp. 21, 188-89, quoted in Herbert Maisch, *Incest*, trans. Colin Bearne (New York: Stein and Day, 1972), p. 219.
31. Herman, *Father-Daughter*, p. 2.
32. Maisch, *Incest*, p. 22.
33. Tiger and Fox, *The Imperial Animal* (New York: Holt, Rinehart and Winston, 1971), p. 116.
34. Jean Renvoize, *Incest* (London: Routledge and Kegan Paul, 1982), p. 4. Research done in 1979 indicates that within the United States alone approximately three quarters of a million women have experienced father-daughter incest, with another 16,000 cases occurring annually. Other studies suggest that the numbers are even higher, since many cases go unreported. As many as 20 million Americans may have been involved in incest, approximately one-tenth of the population. See Hammer, *Passionate Attachments*, p. 79; Herman, *Father-Daughter*, p. 12; Robert L. Geiser, *Hidden Victims* (Boston: Beacon Press, 1979), p. 45; and Fields, *Like Father*, p. 16.
35. Jeffrey Moussaieff Masson, *The Assault on Truth* (New York: Farrar, Straus, and Giroux, 1984), p. 15; Freud, *Totem and Taboo*, trans. A.A. Brill (London: Routledge, 1919), pp. 54, 205.
36. Maisch, *Incest*, pp. 102-3; Henry Giarretto, "The Treatment of Father-Daughter Incest," *Children Today* 5 (July-August 1976): 2; Geiser, *Hidden Victims*, pp. 48-51.

37. Maisch, *Incest*, p. 136.
38. Geiser, *Hidden Victims*, pp. 51-55.
39. Hammer, *Passionate Attachments*, p. 59; Renvoize, *Incest*, pp. 3, 77.
40. Herman, *Father-Daughter*, p. 87.
41. Jung, *Psychology of the Unconscious*, p. 2.
42. William H. Masters and Virginia E. Johnson, "Incest: The Ultimate Taboo," *Redbook*, April 1979, p. 6, quoted in Fields, *Like Father*, p. 98.
43. Judith Herman and Lisa Hirschman, "Father-Daughter Incest," *Signs* 2 (Summer 1977): 748.
44. Herman, *Father-Daughter*, pp. 120, 118.
45. Fields, *Like Father*, p. 29.
46. Hammer, *Passionate Attachments*, 131, citing the 1981 research of T. Berry Brazelton at Harvard.
47. Henry E. Biller, *Father, Child and Sex Role* (Lexington, Mass.: D.C. Heath, 1971), p. 103.
48. Lamb et al., "Father-Daughter Relationship," p. 107; see also Deutsch, *Psychology of Women*, p. 252.
49. Biller, *Father, Child*, p. 116.
50. Marilyn F. Graham and Beverly Birns, "Where Are the Women Geniuses?" in Kopp, *Becoming Female*, p. 303.
51. Fields, *Like Father*, p. 94.
52. Horney, *New Ways*, p. 91.
53. Biller, *Father, Child*, pp. 116-17.
54. Jung, "Marriage as a Psychological Relationship," 191.
55. Ibid., 190-91; Sullivan, *Personal Psychopathology*, p. 249.
56. E. Mavis Hetherington, "Effects of Father Absence on Personality Development in Adolescent Daughters," *Developmental Psychology* 7 (1972): 324, and "Girls without Fathers," *Psychology Today*, February 1973, p. 49.
57. Jung, "The Theory of Psychoanalysis," in *Freud and Psychoanalysis*, 168, 171-74, 154.
58. Jung, "The Family Constellation," in *Experimental Researches*, trans. Leopold Stein and Diana Riviere, *CW* 2 (Princeton: Princeton Univ. Press, 1973): 478.
59. Herman, *Father-Daughter*, p. 57.
60. Sullivan, *Personal Psychopathology*, p. 320; see also Deutsch, *Psychology of Women*, p. 199.
61. Karen Horney, *Neurosis and Human Growth* (New York: W.W. Norton, 1950), pp. 222, 218, 247.
62. Horney, *New Ways*, pp. 113, 251. See also idem, *Neurosis*, p. 236; Deutsch, *Psychology of Women*, pp. 273, 240.
63. Jung, "The Syzygy," in *The Essential Jung*, p. 113; see also Mary Ann Mattoon, *Jungian Psychology in Perspective* (New York: Free Press, 1981), pp. 84-87; M. Esther Harding, *The Way of All Women* (New York: Longmans, Green, 1933), p. 78.
64. T.W. Adorno et al., *The Authoritarian Personality* (New York: W.W. Norton, 1969), p. 343.

Chapter Two. *The Renaissance Background*

1. Juan Luis Vives, *The Instruction of a Christen Woman*, trans. Rychard Hyrde (1524; London: n.p., 1557), sig. 68v.
2. Henrie Smith, *A Preparative to Mariage* (London: Thomas Orwin for Thomas Man, 1591), pp. 54-55.
3. Elizabeth I, quoted in Alison Plowden, *Tudor Women* (London: Weidenfeld and Nicolson, 1979), p. 154; Pitt, *Shakespeare's Women*, p. 27, notes that Elizabeth was proficient in history, geography, mathematics, music, architecture, astronomy, Latin, Greek, French, Italian, Spanish, Flemish, and probably Welsh.
4. Plowden, *Tudor Women*, pp. 164-65.

5. Gervase Markham, *The English Hous-Wife*, in *A Way to Get Wealth* (1623; London: William Wilson, 1660), pp. 3-4.
6. William Gouge, *Of Domesticall Duties* (London: John Haviland for William Bladen, 1622; facsimile reprint, Amsterdam: Theatrum Orbis Terrarum, 1976), p. 279.
7. Lawrence Stone, "The Rise of the Nuclear Family in Early Modern England," in *The Family in History*, ed. Charles E. Rosenberg (Philadelphia: Univ. of Pennsylvania Press, 1975), p. 53.
8. Thomas Heywood, *A Curtaine Lecture* (London: Robert Young, 1637), p. 143.
9. John Knox, *The First Blast of the Trumpet against the Monstrous Regiment of Women* (n.p.: n.p., 1558), pp. 9-14.
10. Heywood, *Curtaine Lecture*, p. 171.
11. Gouge, *Of Domesticall Duties*, pp. 18, 30; see also Thomas Gataker, *Marriage Duties* (London: William Jones for William Bladen, 1620), p. 9.
12. Myles Coverdale, *The Christen State of Matrimonye* (London; n.p. 1541), sig H2; Gouge, *Of Domesticall Duties*, p. 16.
13. Gouge, *Of Domesticall Duties*, pp. 272-73.
14. Ibid., sig. Alv; Gataker, *Marriage Duties*, pp. 12-13.
15. Markham, *English Hous-Wife*, p. 3; Gataker, *Marriage Duties*, pp. 14-15; Heywood, *Curtaine Lecture*, pp. 263-64.
16. Gataker, *Marriage Duties*, p. 2; Robert Pricke, *The Doctrine of Superioritie, and of Subjection* (London: Ephraim Dawson and Thomas Downe, 1609), sig. B2.
17. John Stockwood, *A Bartholomew Fairing for Parentes* (London: John Wolfe, 1589), pp. 21-22, 24; Gataker, *Marriage Duties*, p. 32.
18. Stockwood, *Bartholomew Fairing*, p. 19; Gouge, *Of Domesticall Duties*, pp. 439, 451, 458-61; Richarde Whitforde, *A Werke for Housholders* (London: Roberte Redman, 1537), sig D3.
19. Stockwood, *Bartholomew Fairing*, pp. 82-83.
20. Bartholomew Batty, *The Christian Man's Closet*, trans. William Lowth (London: Thomas Dawson and Gregorie Seton, 1581), p. 64v.
21. Derek Wright, *The Psychology of Moral Behaviour* (Harmondsworth, Middlesex: Penguin, 1971), p. 216; Roger Ascham, *The Scholemaster* (London: John Dare, 1570), p. 11v.
22. Lawrence Stone, *The Family, Sex and Marriage in England 1500-1800* (New York: Harper and Row, 1977), p. 162; Batty, *Christian Man's Closet*, pp. 25v; 24-24v.
23. Batty, *Christian Man's Closet*, pp. 55v, 75-75v.
24. Gataker, *Marriage Duties*, p. 19; Coverdale, *Christen State*, sig. K2, K4-K4v.
25. Stone, *The Family*, p. 5.
26. Stockwood, *Bartholomew Fairing*, p. 71; see also Chilton Latham Powell, *English Domestic Relations, 1487-1653* (New York: Columbia Univ. Press, 1917), p. 14.
27. Batty, *Christian Man's Closet*, p. 100v; Smith, *Preparative to Mariage*, pp. 43-44; Gouge, *Of Domesticall Duties*, pp. 446-47.
28. Rev. Charles Wheatley, *A Rational Illustration of the Book of Common Prayer* (London: George Bell, 1875), pp. 412-13.
29. Plutarch, *The Education or bringinge up of Children*, trans. Thomas Elyot (London: n.p., n.d. [c.1535]), sig. F3v; Heywood, *Curtaine Lecture*, pp. 97-98.
30. Vives, *Instruction*, p. 54; Stockwood, *Bartholomew Fairing*, pp. 18, 11; Stone, *The Family*, p. 5.
31. Coverdale, *Christen State*, sig. B3; Bullinger, *The Golden Boke of Christen Matrimonye* (London, 1543), quoted in Carroll Camden, *The Elizabethan Woman* (New York: Elsevier, 1952), p. 85; Stockwood, *Bartholomew Fairing*, p. 34; Pierre Ayrault, *A Discourse for Parents Honour and Authoritie*, trans. John Budden (London: E. Griffin for W. Harper, 1614), quoted in Powell, *English Domestic Relations*, p. 135.
32. Vives, *Instruction*, p. 54, sig. P2v.
33. Plowden, *Tudor Women*, pp. 130-31.

34. Batty, *Christian Man's Closet*, p. 100v; Stockwood, *Bartholomew Fairing*, pp. 77-78.
35. Stone, *The Family*, p. 193.
36. Stone, "Rise of the Nuclear Family," p. 45.
37. Stone, *The Family*, p. 182.
38. Elmer Edgar Stoll, *Shakespeare Studies* (New York: Macmillan, 1927), p. 61.
39. Coverdale, *Christen State*, sig. B6; Gouge, *Of Domesticall Duties*, p. 181.
40. Phillip Stubbes, *The Anatomie of Abuses* (London: Richard Jones, 1583), p. 55.
41. Frederick J. Furnivall, ed., *Child-Marriages, Divorces, and Ratifications, &C In the Diocese of Chester, A.D. 1561-6* (London: Kegan Paul, 1897), p. XV.
42. Batty, *Christian Man's Closet*, p. 78v.
43. V.G. Kiernan, "Human Relationships in Shakespeare," in *Shakespeare in a Changing World*, ed. Arnold Kettle (New York: International Publishers, 1964), pp. 43, 50.
44. Gouge, *Of Domesticall Duties*, pp. 465, 467-68; Pricke, *Doctrine of Superioritie*, sig. J2v; Gataker, *Marriage Duties*, p. 30.
45. Camden, *Elizabethan Woman*, pp. 9, 148.
46. Samuel Schoenbaum, *William Shakespeare* (New York: Oxford Univ. Press, 1977), p. 286.
47. Lodowik Lloid, *The Choyce of Jewels* (London: Thomas Purfoot, 1607), pp. 37-38.
48. Frederick, Duke of Württemburg, quoted in Camden, *Elizabethan Woman*, p. 17.
49. Violet A. Wilson, *Society Women of Shakespeare's Time* (New York: Dutton, 1925), p. vii; Plowden, *Tudor Women*, pp. 168, 3-4.
50. Van Meteran, quoted in Plowden, *Tudor Women*, pp. 1-2; Platter, *Thomas Platters Travels in England, 1599*, trans. Clare Williams (London: Jonathan Cape, 1937), pp. 181-82.
51. Alfred Harbage, *Shakespeare's Audience* (New York: Columbia Univ. Press, 1941), pp. 77-78. He lists four contemporary references from Stephen Gosson's and Robert Anton's complaints about women in the theatres in 1579 and 1617 to Philip Julius's and Father Busino's comments in 1602 and 1614 that respectable ladies frequented plays.
52. Stubbes, *Anatomie of Abuses*, p. 37v.
53. Juliet Dusinberre, *Shakespeare and the Nature of Women* pp. 7-8.
54. Gouge, *Of Domesticall Duties*, pp. 25-26, 285, sig. A2.
55. Cornelius Agrippa, *The Commendation of Matrimony*, trans. David Clapam (London: n.p., 1534), sig. C2v-C3.
56. Christopher Hill, *Milton and the English Revolution* (New York: Viking, 1977), p. 119; see also Bernard I. Murstein, *Love, Sex, and Marriage through the Ages* (New York: Springer, 1974), p. 200.
57. Stone, *The Family*, p. 137; Powell, *English Domestic Relations*, pp. 120-21.
58. Whately, quoted in Jean-Louis Flandrin, *Families in Former Times*, trans. Richard Southern (London: Cambridge Univ. Press, 1979), p. 166; Smith, *Preparative to Marriage*, pp. 33-34; 71-73, 56.
59. Flandrin, *Families in Former Times*, p. 167.
60. Smith, *Preparative to Mariage*, pp. 25-26; Agrippa, *Commendation of Matrimony*, sig. C2-C2v.
61. Heywood, *Curtaine Lecture*, pp. 98-100; Martin Luther, *Letters of Spiritual Counsel* (Philadelphia: Westminster, 1955), p. 264, quoted in Murstein, *Love, Sex, and Marriage*, p. 180.
62. Gataker, *A Good Wife Gods Gift* (London: John Haviland, 1624), pp. 11-12.
63. Flandrin, *Families in Former Times*, p. 167.
64. Dusinberre, *Shakespeare and the Nature of Women*, p. 96.
65. Keith Wrightson, *English Society, 1580-1630* (London: Hutchinson, 1982), pp. 44-45, 106-15, 70-72, 92-93.
66. Stone, *The Family*, pp. 92, 103, 104.
67. Batty, *Christian Man's Closet*, p. 99; Stockwood, *Bartholomew Fairing*, pp. 76-77, sig. A4v.
68. *The Dictionary of National Biography*, ed. Sir. Leslie Stephen and Sir Sidney Lee (1917; London: Oxford Univ. Press, 1938), 12: 1283-84.

69. Stone, *The Family*, pp. 30-31, 32. Note that the traditional wedding ceremony, even today, incorporates both sets of vows.
70. Ibid., pp. 31-32, 35.
71. Dusinberre, *Shakespeare and the Nature of Women*, pp. 5, 7-8.
72. Stone, *The Family*, pp. 180-81, 87.
73. Powell, *English Domestic Relations*, pp. 194-202; see also Camden, *Elizabethan Woman*, p. 85.
74. Kiernan, "Human Relationships," p. 57.
75. Kiernan, in "Human Relationships," p. 62, argues that "it has been often enough or too often said that Shakespeare had a horror of anarchy, of social disorder; what really horrified him was not any breakdown of 'order' in the policeman's understanding of the word, but something more fundamental, the destruction of men's faith in one another."

Chapter Three. *The Paternal Role in Transition*

1. Stone, *The Family*, p. 7; see also Kahn, *Man's Estate*, pp. 14-15.
2. See Arnold Van Gennep, *The Rites of Passage*, trans. Monika B. Vizedom and Gabrielle L. Caffee (London: Routledge and Kegan Paul, 1960), pp. 3, 10-11.
3. Erikson, *Childhood*, pp. 247-67; Jung, "Stages of Life," 390; Levinson, *Seasons*, p. 18.
4. Stockwood, *Bartholomew Fairing*, pp. 79, 76. See also Heywood, *Curtaine Lecture*, p. 100; Agrippa, *Commendation of Matrimony*, sigs. B8-B8v; Gibbon, *A Work Worth the Reading* (London: Thomas Orwin, 1591), pp. 1-16; Swinburne, *A Treatise of Spousals* (London: S. Roycroft, 1686), p. 4; Whetstone, *An Heptameron of Civill Discourses*, sig. F1, quoted in Camden, *Elizabethan Woman*, p. 86; Gouge, *Of Domesticall Duties*, p. 113; *William Hay's Lectures on Marriage* (1542) ed. and trans. John C. Barry (Edinburgh: Stair Society, 1967), p. 9.
5. Charles Frey, "'O Sacred, shadowy, cold and constant queen,'" in Lenz, Greene, and Neely, *Woman's Part*, p. 297.
6. F.L. Lucas, "On King Lear," in *The Design Within*, ed. M.D. Faber (New York: Science House, 1970), p. 211.
7. Ibid., p. 212; see also Horney, *Neurotic Personality*, p. 174; Jung, *Development of Personality*, p. 55; Levinson, *Seasons*, p. 249.
8. Boose, "Father and the Bride," 18; see also Jung, "Significance of the Father," 315-16.
9. See William J. Stover and Jawad Adra, "Models of International Crisis Bargaining and Middle East Conflict," *International Review of History and Political Science* 18 (August 1981): 20-21; Richard Nisbett and Lee Ross, *Human Inference* (Englewood Cliffs, N.J.: Prentice-Hall, 1980), pp. 178-86.
10. Gouge, *Of Domesticall Duties*, p. 113; Hay, *Lectures on Marriage*, p. 9.
11. As Edward A. Snow noted in "Sexual Anxiety and the Male Order of Things in *Othello*," *English Literary Renaissance* 10 (1980): 386n, "Othello's sense of Desdemona as a *pearl* he threw away is in contrast to Brabantio's sense of his daughter as a jewel that was *stolen* from him," reflecting "a common male attitude about women as objects either of value or adornment."
12. Dash, *Wooing, Wedding*, p. 74; see also Kahn, *Man's Estate*, p. 94.
13. Margaret Loftus Ranald, "'As Marriage Binds, and Blood Breaks': English Marriage and Shakespeare," *Shakespeare Quarterly* 30 (1979): 70.
14. Tony Manocchio and William Petitt, *Families under Stress* (London: Routledge and Kegan Paul, 1975), p. 69.
15. Craig and Bevington, *Complete Works of Shakespeare*, p. 915n; Eric Partridge, *Shakespeare's Bawdy* (New York: E.P. Dutton, 1960), p. 113.
16. Calvin S. Hall and Vernon J. Nordby, *A Primer of Jungian Psychology* (New York: Mentor, 1973), p. 45; see also Diane E. Papalia and Sally Wendkos Olds, *Human Development* (New

York: McGraw Hill, 1981), p. 196; and Alan Hobson, *Full Circle: Shakespeare and Moral Development* (London: Chatto and Windus, 1972), p. 15.

17. Erikson, *Childhood*, pp. 260-67.
18. The incestuous feelings of Shakespeare's fathers for their daughters have been noted by Norman N. Holland, in *Psychoanalysis and Shakespeare* (New York: McGraw Hill, 1966), pp. 118-19, and by Boose, in "Father and the Bride," 334, 339-41.
19. Boose, "Father and the Bride," 331.
20. See Renvoize, *Incest*, p. 4; Hammer, *Passionate Attachments*, p. 79; Herman, *Father-Daughter*, p. 12; Geiser, *Hidden Victims*, p. 45; Fields, *Like Father*, p. 16; Christine A. Dietz and John L. Craft, "Family Dynamics of Incest," *Social Casework* 61 (1980): 602-9.
21. Vives, *Instruction*, p. xvi verso.
22. Gouge, *Of Domesticall Duties*, p. 500.
23. Boose, "Father and the Bride," 338-39.
24. George Elliott Howard, *A History of Matrimonial Institutions* 1 (Chicago: Univ. of Chicago Press, 1904): 173-74.
25. Howard, 1: 166, 259, 266.
26. Howard, 1: 305-6; Boose, "Father and the Bride," 326; *The Book of Common Prayer*, ed. John E. Booty (Charlottesville: Univ. of Virginia Press, 1976), pp. 291-92.
27. Van Gennep, *Rites of Passage*, pp. 10-11; Boose, "Father and the Bride," 326.
28. Gouge, *Of Domesticall Duties*, p. 449; Agrippa, *Commendation of Matrimony*, sig. Bl.
29. Boose, "Father and the Bride," 327-28.
30. Ibid., p. 332.
31. Ibid., pp. 329-30.
32. Northrop Frye, *Anatomy of Criticism* (Princeton: Princeton Univ. Press, 1957), pp. 163, 172; see also Sir Arthur Quiller-Couch, *Paternity in Shakespeare* (1932; London: Folcroft Press, 1970), p. 11.
33. Boose, "Father and the Bride," 328.
34. Barber, *Shakespeare's Festive Comedy* (New York: World, 1963), pp. 2-15.
35. Freud, "The Theme of the Three Caskets," in Faber, *Design Within*, pp. 204-5.
36. Richard P. Wheeler, "'Since first we were dissevered,'" in Schwartz and Kahn, *Representing Shakespeare*, p. 152.
37. Freud, "Three Caskets," pp. 204-5.
38. Ibid.
39. Erikson, in "Reflections," p. 5, notes, "One cannot help thinking of Cordelia, driving Lear's despair to the surface."
40. John Donnelly in "Incest, Ingratitude, and Insanity," in *The King Lear Perplex*, ed. Helmut Bonheim (San Francisco: Wadsworth, 1960), p. 142, observes that "Filial gratitude is demanded in less healthy relationships, particularly when the parent is abnormal in one or two emotional spheres."
41. Jung, "Theory of Psychoanalysis," in *Freud and Psychoanalysis*, 197.
42. Boose, "Father and the Bride," 334.
43. Lear falls into the childish preconventional level of moral development. See Kohlberg, "Stages of Moral Development," pp. 91-92.
44. Lucas, "On King Lear," p. 210; Donnelly, "Incest, Ingratitude," p. 143.
45. Jung, *Psychology of the Unconscious*, p. 2; Fields, *Like Father*, p. 98.
46. Gouge, *Of Domesticall Duties*, p. 579.
47. Barber, "The Family in Shakespeare's Development," in Schwartz and Kahn, *Representing Shakespeare*, p. 197.
48. As Papalia and Olds, in *Human Development*, p. 480, have pointed out, generativity is not merely having children but reaching out to others in altruistic care and nurturing.
49. Holland, *Psychoanalysis and Shakespeare*, pp. 111-14; Hobson, *Full Circle*, p. 15. For a discussion of moral development, see Erikson, *Childhood*, pp. 247-67; Kohlberg, "Stages of

Moral Development," pp. 15-98; Jung, "Stages of Life," 390; Levinson, *Seasons*, p. 18; and William G. Perry, Jr., *Forms of Intellectual and Ethical Development in the College Years* (New York: Holt, Rinehart and Winston, 1968), pp. 134-38.

50. See Wheeler, "Since First," pp. 52-53.
51. See William R. Elton, *King Lear and the Gods* (San Marino, Calif.: Huntington Library Press, 1968), pp. 173-74.
52. Erikson, *Childhood*, pp. 247-50.
53. Wheeler, "Since First," p. 163.
54. Gouge, *Of Domesticall Duties*, p. 548.
55. See Phyllis Rackin, *Shakespeare's Tragedies* (New York: Ungar, 1978), pp. 91-103, for a detailed discussion of the clothing symbolism in *Lear*.
56. For this reading of Lear's final lines, I am grateful to Paul Shelley, of the Royal Shakespeare Company, in an interview on *King Lear* in performance, Richmond, England, June 2, 1982.

Chapter Four. *Dominated Daughters*

1. In "Images of Women in Shakespeare's Plays," *Southern Humanities Review* 11 (1977): 145-50, Barbara A. Mowat describes the double image of Shakespeare's women, contrasting the way they are seen by their men with the way the audience perceives them.
2. Carol Jones Carlisle, *Shakespeare from the Greenroom* (Chapel Hill: Univ. of North Carolina Press, 1969), pp. 143-44.
3. Bradley, *Shakespearean Tragedy* (New York: St. Martin's Press, 1969), pp. 135-36.
4. Agnes Mure MacKenzie, *The Women in Shakespeare's Plays* (Garden City, N.Y.: Doubleday, 1924), p. 218.
5. Norman N. Holland, *The Shakespearean Imagination* (New York: Macmillan, 1964), p. 167; Bernard McElroy, *Shakespeare's Mature Tragedies* (Princeton: Princeton Univ. Press, 1973), p. 75; E.K. Chambers, *Shakespeare: A Survey* (New York: Hill and Wang, 1958), p. 187. Like Kenneth Muir, in *Shakespeare's Tragic Sequence* (London: Hutchinson Univ. Library, 1972), p. 83, I reject the view that Ophelia is "sophisticated and Hamlet's cast-off mistress." This view has been expounded by Jan Kott in *Shakespeare Our Contemporary*, trans. Boleslaw Taborski (Garden City, N.Y.: Anchor, 1966), p. 86.
6. G.B. Harrison, *Shakespeare's Tragedies* (London: Routledge and Kegan Paul, 1951), p. 101; Rosalie L. Colie, *Shakespeare's Living Art* (Princeton: Princeton Univ. Press, 1974), p. 219; John Masefield, quoted in *Shakespeare's Critics*, ed. A.M. Eastman and G.B. Harrison (Ann Arbor: Univ. of Michigan Press, 1964), p. 180.
7. Carlisle, *Shakespeare from the Greenroom*, pp. 136-37.
8. George Gordon, *Shakespearian Comedy* (Oxford: Oxford Univ. Press, 1944), p. 56.
9. Anna Jameson, *Shakespeare's Heroines* (New York: Burt, 1948), p. 139.
10. Gilligan, *In a Different Voice* (Cambridge: Harvard Univ. Press, 1982), p. 8. Erikson, in *Identity, Youth and Crisis* (New York: W.W. Norton, 1968), p. 87, explains that in adolescent role confusion "the young person counterpoints rather than synthesizes his sexual, ethnic, occupational, and typological alternatives and is often driven to decide definitely and totally for one side or the other."
11. See Gilligan, *Different Voice*, p. 17.
12. Lynda Boose noted that Laertes poisons Ophelia's mind with a "quite obscene picture of sex presented through images of military bombardment and young flowers being stroked to death," in "The Fashionable Poloniuses," *Hamlet Studies* 1 (1980): 77.
13. Gilligan, *Different Voice*, p. 105.
14. Her symptoms parallel those described by Horney in *New Ways*, p. 84. Irving Ribner in *Patterns in Shakespearean Tragedy* (New York: Barnes and Noble, 1960), p. 88, believes that Ophelia's "obedience to her father causes her to see love as madness and lust, to reject her

fellow man in Hamlet," while I would reverse the cause and effect: her terror at the picture of sexuality Polonius presents causes her to retreat into conventionality.

15. Laing, *The Divided Self* (London: Tavistock, 1960), p. 195.
16. Thomas McFarland, *Tragic Meanings in Shakespeare* (New York: Random House, 1966), p. 47.
17. Gilligan, *Different Voice*, p. 16.
18. Granville-Barker, *Prefaces to Shakespeare* (London: Batsford, 1947), 1: 212.
19. Boose, "Fashionable Poloniuses," pp. 75-76.
20. As Granville-Barker has noted in *Prefaces* 1: 215, she seeks to deal politely with his public humiliation of her.
21. Herman Harrell Horne, *Shakespeare's Philosophy of Love* (Raleigh, N.C.: Edwards and Broughton, 1945), p. 104.
22. Craig and Bevington, *Complete Works of Shakespeare*, p. 933n. See also Bridget Gellert Lyons, "The Iconography of Ophelia," *ELH* 44 (1977): 69.
23. According to Dr. Ira S. Wile, in "Some Shakespearean Characters in the Light of Present Day Psychologies," *Psychological Quarterly* 16 (1942): 62-90, quoted in Holland, *Psychoanalysis and Shakespeare*, p. 198, "her obscene language is not unknown in wards of mental hospitals—she is a victim of mania."
24. Charlotte Otten, in "Ophelia's 'Long Purples,'" *Shakespeare Quarterly* 30 (1979): 397-402, presents evidence from Renaissance herbals identifying the "long purples" as Orchis Serapias or Satyrion Royall, both associated with the male sex organ by their names, legends, and physical descriptions.
25. M. Esther Harding, *The 'I' and the 'Not-I'* (Princeton: Princeton Univ. Press, 1965), p. 171.
26. William Hazlitt (1817), Georg Brandes (1895), and B.A. Young (1965), quoted in *Shakespeare: "Much Ado About Nothing" and "As You Like It": A Casebook*, ed. John Russell Brown (London: Macmillan, 1979), pp. 30-31, 42, and 228.
27. Donald Stauffer, "Words and Actions," in Brown, *Casebook*, p. 87; and Paul and Miriam Mueschke, "Illusion and Metamorphosis," in Brown, *Casebook*, p. 130.
28. Mueschke and Mueschke, "Illusion," p. 135; see also Arthur Kirsch, *Shakespeare and the Experience of Love* (Cambridge: Cambridge Univ. Press, 1981), p. 54.
29. Alexander Leggatt, *Shakespeare's Comedy of Love* (London: Methuen, 1974), p. 155.
30. Jung, "Marriage as a Psychological Relationship," 198.
31. Vives, *Instruction*, p. 54.
32. Mueschke and Mueschke, "Illusion," p. 135.
33. Erikson, as described by Gilligan in *Different Voice*, p. 98; see Erikson, *Identity*, p. 266.
34. Elmer Edgar Stoll in *Othello* (1915; New York: Gordian Press, 1967), p. 9, paralleled Othello's sudden loss of faith in Desdemona with the behavior of Leonato, who acts "as if he cherished a grudge against" his daughter. Barbara Mowat, in "Images," provides a more specific definition of this "grudge": "the fathers of Hero and Desdemona must listen as their daughters—seemingly so chaste, so perfect—are described in animalistic sexual terms: . . . Both fathers, confronted with the vision of the sweet girl-child turned lecherous animal, lash out at their own daughters and at the treachery, the terrible lust of all women" (p. 152).
35. Sexton, *The Slandered Woman in Shakespeare* (Victoria, B.C.: English Literary Studies, 1978), pp. 39-44. In 1613 Shakespeare himself had some direct experience with the question of slander when his daughter Susannah brought action for defamation against John Lane, who had accused her of lewd conduct and adultery, as W. Nicholas Knight pointed out in "Patrimony and Shakespeare's Daughters," *Hartford Studies in Literature* 9 (1977): 181-82.
36. Gilligan, *Different Voice*, p. 132.
37. Ribner, *Patterns*, p. 94; Knight, *The Wheel of Fire* (New York: Meridian Books, 1930), p. 249.

38. Auden, *The Dyer's Hand* (New York: Random House, 1962), p. 269; Kott, *Shakespeare Our Contemporary*, p. 118.

39. S.N. Garner, "Shakespeare's Desdemona," *Shakespeare Studies* 9 (1976): 235; R.N. Hallstead, "Idolatrous Love," *Shakespeare Quarterly* 19 (1968): 107; Marvin Rosenberg, *The Masks of Othello* (Berkeley: Univ. of California Press, 1961), p. 209; Kirsch, *Experience of Love*, p. 15; W.D. Adamson, "Unpinned or Undone?: Desdemona's Critics and the Problem of Sexual Innocence," *Shakespeare Studies* 13 (1980): 179-80.

40. Garner, "Shakespeare's Desdemona," 243; Auden, *Dyer's Hand*, p. 268; Rymer, quoted in Eastman and Harrison, *Shakespeare's Critics*, p. 13.

41. Harrison, *Shakespeare's Tragedies*, p. 143; Robert Dickes, "Desdemona: An Innocent Victim," *American Imago* 27 (1970): 286.

42. Kirsch, *Experience of Love*, p. 17; Auden, *Dyer's Hand*, p. 269; Bradley, *Shakespearean Tragedy*, p. 150; McElroy, *Mature Tragedies*, p. 135; Neely, "Women and Men in *Othello*: 'what should such a fool / Do with so good a woman?' " *Shakespeare Studies* 10 (1977): 133.

43. Rosenberg, *Masks*, pp. 135-37, 139.

44. Harold C. Goddard, *The Meaning of Shakespeare* (Chicago: Univ. of Chicago Press, 1951), pp. 469-70.

45. See Garner, "Shakespeare's Desdemona," pp. 239, 236.

46. Kirsch, *Experience of Love*, p. 14. See Jung, "Theory of Psychoanalysis," pp. 168-74.

47. Goddard, *Meaning of Shakespeare*, p. 457.

48. As Nancy Friday observed in *My Mother/My Self* (New York: Dell, 1977), pp. 22–23, many women unconsciously imitate their mothers in their marriages, no matter how independent and assertive they have been.

49. Vives, *Instruction*, sig. 68v.

50. Gilligan, pp. 105, 87. See also Gayle Greene, " 'This That You Call Love': Sexual and Social Tragedy in *Othello*," *Journal of Women's Studies in Literature* 1 (1979): 25; and MacKenzie, *Women*, p. 253, both of whom note her filial deference to him as expressed in her addressing him as "my lord." See also Harding, *Way of All Women*, p. 153, for a psychological discussion of father transference.

51. MacFarland, *Tragic Meanings*, pp. 64-65; Kirsch, *Experience of Love*, p. 14; Stephen Reid, "Desdemona's Guilt," *American Imago* 27 (1970): 259.

52. See Dickes, "Desdemona," pp. 281-96; Reid, "Desdemona's Guilt," pp. 259, 281.

53. Carlisle, in *Shakespeare from the Greenroom*, p. 248, notes "a certain Joan-of-Arc quality in her nature." Horney, in *New Ways*, p. 113, and Deutsch, in *Psychology of Women*, p. 273, explained how traditional cultural norms predispose virtuous women to masochism.

54. Horney, *Neurosis*, p. 221.

55. Both Pitt, in *Shakespeare's Women*, pp. 50-51, and Harold Skulsky, in *Spirits Finely Touched* (Athens: Univ. of Georgia Press, 1976), pp. 240-41, find Desdemona excessively willful, while I see her behavior as a slavish attempt to conform to the contemporary image of the good wife.

56. Both Leonora Leet Brodwin, *Elizabethan Love Tragedy* (New York: New York Univ. Press, 1971), p. 213, and Martha Andreson-Thom, "Thinking about Women and Their Prosperous Art," *Shakespeare Studies* 11 (1978): 264, see Desdemona's conformity to tradition beginning when she feels she has lost Othello's love. I see it originating in her very definition of marriage.

57. Gouge, *Of Domesticall Duties*, sig. Alv.

58. Bradley, *Shakespearean Tragedy*, p. 171. See Horney, *Inner Conflicts*, pp. 58-59, and *The Neurotic Personality of Our Time* (New York: W.W. Norton, 1937), p. 140.

59. See Horney, *Inner Conflicts*, pp. 121-22, for a discussion of compulsive compliance.

60. Gilligan, *Different Voice*, p. 132.

61. Inga-Stina Ewbank, "Shakespeare's Portrayal of Women," in *Shakespeare: Pattern of Excel-*

ling Nature, ed. David Bevington and Jay L. Halio (Newark: Univ. of Delaware Press, 1978), p. 224.

62. Gilligan, *Different Voice*, p. 65. See also Lynda Elizabeth Boose, "Othello's Handkerchief," *English Literary Renaissance* 5 (1975): 360-74, for a discussion of its symbolic significance. Desdemona's motives in concealing the handkerchief's loss have been variously interpreted as fear by Garner, "Shakespeare's Desdemona," p. 246, and MacKenzie, *Women*, p. 258. Robert B. Heilman, in *Magic in the Web* (1956; Westport, Conn.: Greenwood Press, 1977), p. 200, argues that Desdemona "knows" the handkerchief is missing but does not really believe this, hoping for some miracle to recover it in an irrational combination of belief and hope.

63. See Horney, *New Ways*, pp. 271-72; and Garner, pp. 246-47.

64. M.D. Faber, "Two Studies in Self-Aggression in Shakespearean Tragedy," *Literature and Psychology* 14 (1964): 85-87; see also Gilligan, *Different Voice*, p. 87.

65. As Edward Snow, "Sexual Anxiety," pp. 407-8, maintains, "the tragedy of the play . . . is the inability of Desdemona to escape or triumph over restraints and Oedipal prohibitions that domesticate women to the conventional male order of things." See also Deutsch, *Psychology of Women*, p. 240; Horney, *New Ways*, p. 113.

Chapter Five. *Defiant Daughters*

1. Erikson, *Identity*, p. 265; see also Jung, "Theory of Psychoanalysis," pp. 171-74.

2. Gilligan, *Different Voice*, pp. 105, 149.

3. Erikson, *Identity*, p. 16; see also Harding, *Parental Image*, p. 121; and Frey, "O Sacred," p. 299.

4. Erikson, *Identity*, p. 37.

5. Milton, *Areopagitica*, in *John Milton: Complete Poems and Major Prose*, ed. Merritt Y. Hughes (New York: Odyssey, 1957), p. 728.

6. See Gilligan, *Different Voice*, p. 149.

7. Ibid.; see also John C. Bean, "Comic Structure and the Humanizing of Kate in *The Taming of the Shrew*," in Lenz, Greene, and Neely, *Woman's Part*, p. 66; Richard Levin, "Shakespeare or the Ideas of His Time," *Mosaic* 10 (1977): 132-33; and Flandrin, *Families in Former Times*, pp. 166-67; as well as such Renaissance sources as Gataker, *Good Wife*, pp. 11-12; Smith, *Preparative to Mariage*, pp. 25-26; Agrippa, *Commendation of Matrimony*, sig. C2-C2v; and Heywood, *Curtaine Lecture*, pp. 98-100.

8. See Hugh M. Richmond, *Shakespeare's Sexual Comedy* (New York: Bobbs Merrill, 1971), p. 107, and Ralph Berry, *Shakespeare's Comedies* (Princeton: Princeton Univ. Press, 1972), p. 95, for further discussion.

9. Granville-Barker, *Prefaces*, 2: 344; Dash, *Wooing, Wedding*, pp. 85-86.

10. See Kahn, *Man's Estate*, p. 97; and Dash, *Wooing, Wedding*, p. 74.

11. Gouge, *Of Domesticall Duties*, pp. 467-68; Pricke, *Doctrine of Superioritie*, sig. J2v; Gataker, *Good Wife*, p. 30.

12. Milton, *Areopagitica*, pp. 720, 746-48.

13. Jameson, *Shakespeare's Heroines*, p. 29; Austin C. Dobbins and Roy W. Battenhouse, "Jessica's Morals," *Shakespeare Studies* 9 (1976): 107; Holmes, *Shakespeare's Public* (London: Murray, 1960), p. 65.

14. Gouge, *Of Domesticall Duties*, pp. 454-55.

15. Quiller-Couch, "Introduction," *The Merchant of Venice* by William Shakespeare, ed. Sir Arthur Quiller-Couch and John Dover Wilson (Cambridge: Cambridge Univ. Press, 1953), p. xx; Charlton, *Shakespearean Comedy* (New York: Macmillan, 1940), pp. 157-58.

16. MacKenzie, *Women*, p. 93.

17. Haim G. Ginott, *Between Parent and Child: New Solutions to Old Problems* (London: Staples, 1965), p. 64.
18. Dobbins and Battenhouse, "Jessica's Morals," pp. 116-17.
19. Boose, in "Father and the Bride," p. 336, argues that her mother's "ring" and her father's "stones" represent female and male genitalia, that in selling these items and buying a monkey she has cast away "the symbol of her parents' procreative act," figuratively delegitimizing herself in exchange for "a grotesque imitation of the infant human form."
20. Dobbins and Battenhouse, "Jessica's Morals," pp. 113-14.
21. See Milton, *Areopagitica*, p. 739.
22. Sigurd Burkhardt, *Shakespearean Meanings* (Princeton: Princeton Univ. Press, 1968), pp. 223-24; Richmond, *Sexual Comedies*, p. 128.
23. Gordon, *Shakespearean Comedy*, pp. 122-23, sees in Goneril and Regan a "barbarous and primitive inability to look on Age without contempt."
24. Maynard Mack points out this historical parallel in *King Lear in Our Time* (Berkeley: Univ. of California Press, 1965), p. 45.
25. Stephen Reid, "In Defense of Goneril and Regan," *American Imago* 27 (1970): 239-40.
26. Ginott, *Between Parent and Child*, pp. 138-39, writes of such "children whose . . . destructiveness is not accompanied by visible guilt. Some of these children are capable of extreme cruelty without apparent anxiety or repentance."
27. Coleridge, *Lectures and Notes on Shakespeare and Other English Poets*, ed. T. Ashe (Freeport, N.Y.: Books for Libraries Press, 1972), p. 334; Mowat, "Images," p. 153.
28. John J. McLaughlin, "The Dynamics of Power in *King Lear*," *Shakespeare Quarterly* 29 (1978): 41.
29. John Holloway, "Lear," in *Essays in Shakespearean Criticism*, ed. James L. Calderwood and Harold E. Toliver (Englewood Cliffs, N.J.: Prentice-Hall, 1970), pp. 494-96.
30. Reid, "In Defense," pp. 243-44.
31. Dowden, *Shakspere: His Mind and Art* (1872; New York: Capricorn Books, 1962), p. 259; Rackin, *Shakespeare's Tragedies* (New York: Ungar, 1978), p. 90.
32. Thomas Hobbes, *Leviathan*, Intro. Herbert W. Schneider (New York: Bobbs-Merrill, 1958), p. 107.
33. Early critics idealized her. To A.C. Bradley, she was "a thing enskied and sainted," *Shakespearean Tragedy*, pp. 262-63. Anna Jameson described her as "a saint prepared for heaven" in Carlisle, *Shakespeare from the Greenroom*, p. 309. Edward Dowden, in "Shakespeare's Portraiture of Women," *Shakespeariana* 2 (1885): 217, called her "the martyr and patron saint of filial truth and devotion." As recently as 1977, she has been seen as a Christ figure—by James P. Driscoll, in "The Vision of King Lear," *Shakespeare Studies* 10 (1977): 159-63. Her inability to articulate her love has been variously explained. Harold Goddard, in *Meaning of Shakespeare*, p. 524, proposed that she fears marriage to the mercenary Burgundy rather than France, whom she loves. G.B. Harrison, in *Shakespeare's Tragedies*, p. 165, believed she suffers from shyness, "that devastating paralysis of the will which not uncommonly grips a young and emotional girl when commanded to exhibit in public her secret loyalties." Others argue that she is unable to speak when deeply moved. Bradley, in *Shakespearean Tragedy*, pp. 264-65, cited her repetition of words or phrases and her own admission that her love is more ponderous than her tongue. See also Pitt, *Shakespeare's Women*, p. 63. Cordelia may have a slight speech impediment, an involuntary repetition of words or phrases known as palilalia; see Oliver Sachs, *Awakenings* (New York: Vintage Books, 1976), p. 340, for the definition.
34. Carlisle, *Shakespeare from the Greenroom*, p. 310; Roy Battenhouse, *Shakespearean Tragedy* (Bloomington: Indiana Univ. Press, 1969), p. 283; MacKenzie, *Women*, pp. 286-87. See also Robert B. Heilman, *This Great Stage: Image and Structure in King Lear* (Baton Rouge: Louisiana State Univ. Press, 1948), p. 36.

35. Jorgensen, *Lear's Self-Discovery* (Berkeley: Univ. of California Press, 1967), p. 85.
36. See Gilligan, *Different Voice*, p. 132.
37. Gouge, *Of Domesticall Duties*, pp. 113, 111.
38. Gilligan, *Different Voice*, p. 16, wrote that "women's moral weakness, manifest in an apparent diffusion and confusion of judgment, is . . . inseparable from women's moral strength, an overriding concern with relationships and responsibilities." In her concern for her father and desire to be the "good child," Cordelia neglects her responsibilities to her husband and herself. See also Jung, "Theory of Psychoanalysis," p. 154; and idem, "Family Constellation," p. 478.
39. See, for example, George R. Hibbard, "*The Taming of the Shrew*," in *Shakespearean Essays*, ed. Alwin Thaler and Norman Sanders (Knoxville: Univ. of Tennessee Press, 1964), pp. 19-25; Kahn, *Man's Estate*, p. 104; and Berry, *Shakespeare's Comedies*, pp. 54-55.
40. Pitt, *Shakespeare's Women*, p. 96.
41. See Jung, "Marriage as a Psychological Relationship," p. 198.
42. See Hibbard, "*Taming*," p. 25.
43. Craig and Bevington, *Complete Works of Shakespeare*, p. 169n.
44. Richmond, *Sexual Comedy* p. 100; and Wolfgang Weilgart, *Shakespeare's Psychognostic* (Tokyo: Hokuseido Press, 1952), pp. 128-29. See also Dash, *Wooing, Wedding*, p. 41; Kahn, *Man's Estate*, p. 104; and Greer, *Female Eunuch*, p. 220, all of whom emphasize her protest against convention. Nevill Coghill, in "The Basis of Shakespearean Comedy," in Eastman and Harrison, *Shakespeare's Critics*, p. 303, emphasizes her neglect by her father.
45. See Hibbard, "*Taming*," p. 24; Peter G. Phialas, *Shakespeare's Romantic Comedies* (Chapel Hill: Univ. of North Carolina Press, 1966), p. 34.
46. Kahn, *Man's Estate*, p. 104; Leggatt, *Comedy of Love*, p. 51.
47. Kahn, *Man's Estate*, p. 109.
48. Ranald, in "As Marriage Binds," p. 69, argues that Petruchio is not a fortune hunter, that his approach to Bassanio follows established Elizabethan custom. So it does, but what are we to make of his earlier boast to "wive it wealthily in Padua" (I.ii.75)? H.B. Charlton, in *Shakespearean Comedy* (New York: Macmillan, 1940), pp. 97-98, sees Petruchio as purely pragmatic. To him, the courtship is merely a means for Petruchio to tame Katharina and provide himself with a means to domestic ease.
49. Kahn, in *Man's Estate*, p. 110, sees this speech as hyperbolic and parodic: "It is impossible that Shakespeare meant us to accept Petruchio's speech uncritically: it is the most shamelessly blunt statement of the relationship between men, women, and property, to be found in the literature of this period."
50. See John Masefield's complaint, in Phialas, *Shakespeare's Romantic Comedies*, p. 33, that he is "a boor who cares only for his own will, her flesh, and her money"; and Marilyn French, *Shakespeare's Division of Experience* (New York: Summit, 1981), p. 83, who accuses him of total oppression, imprisonment, and brainwashing.
51. J. Dennis Huston, in *Shakespeare's Comedies of Play* (New York: Columbia Univ. Press, 1981), p. 60; Hibbard, "*Taming*," p. 27; and Dash, *Wooing, Wedding*, p. 59, have all pointed to Petruchio's restraint as evidence of his respect for her.
52. See Coghill, "Shakespearean Comedy," pp. 303-4; Huston, *Comedies of Play*, p. 7; and Kahn, *Man's Estate*, p. 113, who note the creative role of humor and play in resolving the power battle of the sexes.
53. See Kahn, *Man's Estate*, p. 115; Huston, *Comedies of Play*, p. 64; Berry, *Shakespeare's Comedies*, p. 67.
54. See S.C. Sen Gupta, *Shakespearian Comedy* (London: Oxford Univ. Press, 1950), p. 115; Ruth Nevo, *Comic Transformations in Shakespeare* (London: Methuen, 1980), p. 49; and Greer, *Female Eunuch*, p. 221, all of whom emphasize the love and partnership between the two.

Chapter Six. *Androgynous Daughters*

1. Bradley, *Shakespearean Tragedy*, p. 26.
2. See Rhona Rapoport and Robert Rapoport, *Growing through Life* (New York: Harper and Row, 1980), p. 15.
3. Eric W. Stockton, "The Adulthood of Shakespeare's Heroines," in Thaler and Sanders, *Shakespearean Essays*, p. 162; see also Robert Speaight, "Shakespeare's Heroines," *Essays by Divers Hands* n.s. 39 (1977): 149.
4. Speaight, "Shakespeare's Heroines," pp. 150-51.
5. Dusinberre, *Shakespeare and the Nature of Women*, p. 233; although Heilbrun, in *Androgyny*, p. 37, argues that *Twelfth Night* was drawn from the Italian *commedia dell'arte* tradition, in which girls' parts were played by girls, who often disguised themselves as boys.
6. Although Erikson, in *Identity*, pp. 282-83, upholds a more traditional concept of female development, which exalts "the inner space" of their procreative capacity, maintaining that "something in the young woman's identity must keep itself open" for her future husband and children, even he sees in adolescence "a psychosocial moratorium" in which a young girl is "relatively freer of the tyranny of the inner space." She may venture out "with a bearing and a curiosity which often appears hermaphroditic if not outright 'masculine,' . . . trying out "a variety of possible identifications with the phallic-ambulatory male even as she experiments with the experience of being his counterpart."
7. Heilbrun, *Androgyny*, pp. x-xi. For a discussion of the anima and animus, see Harding, *I and Not-I*, pp. 108-9; and Jung, *Alchemical Studies*, *CW* 13 (Princeton: Princeton Univ. Press, 1967): 38-43.
8. Heilbrun, *Androgyny*, p. 30.
9. Kahn, *Man's Estate*, p. 12.
10. Carole McKewin, "Shakespeare Liberata: Shakespeare, the Nature of Women, and the New Feminist Criticism," *Mosaic* 10 (1977): 158.
11. Harding, *Way of All Women*, p. 78; see also Jung, "Psychological Types," in *The Essential Jung*, p. 102.
12. Dusinberre, *Shakespeare and the Nature of Women*, p. 95.
13. Stone, *The Family*, p. 58.
14. See Holmes, *Shakespeare's Public*, pp. 27-28.
15. Clara Claiborne Park, "As We Like It: How a Girl Can Be Smart and Still Popular," in Lenz, Greene, and Neely, *Woman's Part*, p. 108. As Dusinberre noted in *Shakespeare and the Nature of Women*, p. 233, "disguise makes a woman not a man but a more developed woman."
16. Like Rosalind, Julia functions almost as a fatherless daughter. All we hear of her father is the single line in I.ii.130: "Dinner is ready, and your father stays."
17. Goddard, *Meaning of Shakespeare*, pp. 41-42.
18. Hobson, in *Full Circle*, pp. 174-75, has noted the similarity between Julia and Viola, criticizing Julia for her lack of altruism, her "cold" suit, while overlooking the essential difference: Julia and Proteus are betrothed while Viola only loves Orsino from afar.
19. Erikson, "Youth: Fidelity and Diversity," in *Youth*, ed. Erik H. Erikson (New York: Basic Books, 1963), p. 3. In *Identity*, p. 283, Erikson emphasizes the adolescent quest for identity as a predominantly male concern, with girls waiting to fill their "inner space." I would expand his concept of fidelity to include women, finding same-sex friendships equally important in developing both male and female identity in adolescence.
20. Coleridge, *Lectures*, p. 294.
21. For a discussion of the way the father-daughter relationship unconsciously influences a young woman's choice of husband, see Jung, "Marriage as a Psychological Relationship," pp. 190-91, and Sullivan, *Personal Psychopathology*, p. 249; see also Boose, "Father and the Bride," p. 327.

22. For a discussion of the importance of this "trial by ordeal" in the transition to adulthood, see Jung, "Theory of Psychoanalysis," p. 155, and *Psychology of the Unconscious*, p. 251; see also Harding, *Parental Image*, p. 121.
23. Roberto Assagioli points this out in *The Act of Will* (Baltimore: Penguin, 1973), pp. 52-53; see also Larry S. Champion, *The Evolution of Shakespeare's Comedy* (Cambridge: Harvard Univ. Press, 1970), p. 66; and Pitt, *Shakespeare's Women*, p. 116.
24. See D.J. Palmer, "*As You Like It* and the Idea of Play," in Brown, *Casebook*, pp. 194-95; Leggatt, *Comedy of Love*, p. 202; and Robert Kimbrough, "Androgyny Seen through Shakespeare's Disguise," *Shakespeare Quarterly* 33 (1982): 23-24.
25. Jung in "Undiscovered Self," p. 399, emphasized the importance of acknowledging "the shadow," or one's imperfections, for any lasting relationship.
26. See Nancy K. Hayles, "Sexual Disguise in *As You Like It* and *Twelfth Night*," *Shakespeare Survey* 32 (1979): 65; and John Russell Brown, "The Presentation of Comedy," in Brown, *Casebook*, pp. 80-81.
27. See David Young, *The Heart's Forest* (New Haven: Yale Univ. Press, 1972), p. 67; and Champion, *Evolution*, p. 66.
28. Stone, *The Family*, pp. 30-32.
29. Jung, *Man and His Symbols* (Garden City, N.Y.: Doubleday, 1979), pp. 177-207; Harding, *I and Not-I*, pp. 108-9, 216-18; Jung, *Mysterium Coniunctionis*, *CW* 14 (New York: Pantheon Books, 1963): 457-553; see also Hugh Richmond, *Sexual Comedy*, p. 140; Heilbrun, *Androgyny*, p. 29; and Mattoon, *Jungian Psychology*, pp. 84-85.
30. Hobson, *Full Circle*, pp. 175-76; Sen Gupta, *Shakespearian Comedy*, pp. 165-66.
31. Goddard, *Meaning of Shakespeare*, p. 304.
32. Speaight, "Shakespeare's Heroines," pp. 152-55; see also Richard A. Levin, "Viola," *Durham University Journal* 71 (1979): 213-22, who emphasizes Viola's pragmatic realism, seeing her as a clever manipulator.
33. Kahn, *Man's Estate*, p. 206.
34. See Fields, *Like Father*, p. 62; Hetherington, "Father Absence," p. 324, and "Girls without Fathers," p. 49.
35. R. Chris Hassel, *Faith and Folly in Shakespeare's Romantic Comedies* (Athens: Univ. of Georgia Press, 1980), p. 157.
36. Dusinberre, *Shakespeare and the Nature of Women*, p. 256.
37. Dash, *Wooing, Wedding*, p. 252.
38. G.K. Hunter, *William Shakespeare* (London: Longmans, 1962), p. 22; Sen Gupta, *Shakespearian Comedy*, p. 149.
39. Huston, *Comedies of Play*, p. 30.
40. Pitt, *Shakespeare's Women*, pp. 108-9.
41. See Hetherington, "Father Absence," p. 324, and "Girls Without Fathers," p. 49; Fields, *Like Father*, p. 62.
42. A.P. Riemer, *Antic Fables* (New York: St. Martin's, 1980), p. 95.
43. Berry, *Shakespeare's Comedies*, p. 162.
44. Dowden, "Shakespeare's Portraiture," pp. 212-13.
45. Vera M. Jiji, "Portia Revisited," *Literature and Psychology* 26 (1976): 8.
46. As Leslie A. Fiedler suggests in *The Stranger in Shakespeare* (New York: Stein and Day, 1972), p. 213.
47. See Alexander Schmidt, *Shakespeare Lexicon* 2 (New York: Dover, 1971): 1370, which cites *will* as "carnal desire," listing twenty-four uses by Shakespeare of the word in this sense. See also Eric Partridge, *Shakespeare's Bawdy*, p. 221.
48. Quiller-Couch, "Introduction," p. xxv; Champion, *Evolution*, p. 63.
49. Berry, *Shakespeare's Comedies*, p. 141; see also Goddard, *Meaning of Shakespeare*, p. 102.
50. For example, Boose, "Father and the Bride," 337-38.

51. "A Valediction: Forbidding Mourning," ll. 13-14, from *John Donne*, ed. Helen Gardner (Oxford: Clarendon Press, 1965), p. 63.

52. J. Leeds Barroll, *Artificial Persons* (Columbia: Univ. of South Carolina Press, 1974), p. 119; Ruth Leila Anderson, *Elizabethan Psychology and Shakespeare's Plays* (New York: Russell, 1966), p. 123.

53. See Dusinberre, *Shakespeare and the Nature of Women*, p. 85.

54. Actualizing the animus apparently frees her from what Hetherington, in "Father Absence," p. 324, and others have seen as the relationship problems of fatherless daughters.

55. See Stone, *The Family*, pp. 30-32.

56. See Charles Wheatley, *Rational Illustration*, p. 416; I am grateful to a former graduate student, Elyse Tomlinson, for this insight from her seminar paper, "Androgyny in *The Merchant of Venice*," Santa Clara University, Spring 1980, pp. 17-18.

57. Pitt, *Shakespeare's Women*, p. 92.

58. Ibid., pp. 92-93.

59. Gilligan, *Different Voice*, pp. 105 and 65ff.

60. Burckhardt, *Shakespearean Meanings*, p. 210; see also Jung, *Man and His Symbols*, pp. 246ff., and *Mysterium Coniunctionis*, p. 463; Jose and Miriam Argüelles, *Mandala* (Berkeley: Shambala, 1972), pp. 12-20, 46-49, and illustrations passim.

61. *The Book of Common Prayer, 1559*, ed. John E. Booty (Charlottesville: Univ. Press of Virginia, 1976), p. 291. See also Wheatley, *Rational Illustration*, p. 417; Agrippa, *Commendation of Matrimony*, sig. B1; Whately, quoted in Flandrin, *Families in Former Times*, p. 166; Gouge, *Of Domesticall Duties*, p. 449.

62. Marilyn L. Williamson, "The Ring Episode in *The Merchant of Venice*," *South Atlantic Quarterly* 71 (1972): 588-89.

63. Sen Gupta, *Shakespearian Comedy*, p. 59; Champion, *Evolution*, p. 120.

64. Shaw reference in Speaight, "Shakespeare's Heroines," p. 156; William Witherle Lawrence, *Shakespeare's Problem Comedies* (New York: Macmillan, 1931), p. 38; Champion, *Evolution*, p. 125; and Goddard, *Meaning of Shakespeare*, p. 426.

65. Lawrence, *Problem Comedies*, p. 38.

66. Chambers, *Shakespeare*, pp. 202-3.

67. See Hetherington, "Father Absence," p. 324, and "Girls without Fathers," p. 49; also see Fields, *Like Father*, p. 62.

68. Fields, in *Like Father*, p. 94, discusses at length the problems faced by such daughters in relating to men.

69. R.G. Hunter, "*All's Well That Ends Well*," in Calderwood and Toliver, *Essays*, p. 341, has found Helena "something of an oddity among the usual heroines of romance. It is the function of the lady, ordinarily, to appear, at least, to be pursued rather than the pursuer." Helena is not a heroine, however, but a hero who demonstrates virtuous action in a trial by ordeal.

70. Spencer, "*All's Well That Ends Well*" in *Discussion of Shakespeare's Problem Comedies*, ed. Robert Ornstein (Boston: D.C. Heath, 1961), p. 43.

71. Pitt, *Shakespeare's Women*, p. 98.

72. Richmond, *Sexual Comedy*, p. 148.

73. Ranald, in "As Marriage Binds," pp. 79-80, notes that Bertram's forced marriage constituted "defective consent," which could be used to dissolve the union. Furthermore, the marriage is unconsummated and Bertram leaves the country. In English law, absence for three years outside the country or two years inside it would annul an unconsummated marriage.

74. See Erikson, *Childhood*, pp. 247-67.

Chapter Seven. *Redemptive Love and Wisdom*

1. See Jung, "Conscious, Unconscious," p. 224; Erikson, *Childhood*, pp. 265-67, and "Reflections," pp. 25-27; and Derek Traversi, *Shakespeare* (Stanford, Calif.: Stanford Univ. Press, 1953), p. 263.
2. D.S. Brewer, "The Ideal of Feminine Beauty in Medieval Literature," *Modern Language Review* 50 (1955): 269, quoted in Hallett Smith, *Shakespeare's Romances* (San Marino, Calif.: Huntington Library Press, 1972), p. 24.
3. Mowat, "Images," p. 154.
4. Cyrus Hoy, "Fathers and Daughters in Shakespeare's Romances," in *Shakespeare's Romances Reconsidered*, ed. Carol McGinnis Kay and Henry E. Jacobs (Lincoln: Univ. of Nebraska Press, 1978), p. 84.
5. Goddard, *Meaning of Shakespeare*, p. 629; Frey, "O Sacred," p. 302.
6. Harris, *The Women of Shakespeare* (London: Methuen, 1911), pp. 228-29; Sachs, quoted in Holland, *Psychoanalysis and Shakespeare*, pp. 104-5.
7. Harding, *I and Not-I*, pp. 206-7.
8. Jung, *Man and His Symbols*, p. 178.
9. Levinson, *Seasons*, pp. 234-35.
10. Harding, *I and Not-I*, p. 206.
11. Heilbrun, *Androgyny*, p. 33.
12. Paula Berggren, "The Woman's Part: Female Sexuality as Power in Shakespeare's Plays," in Lenz, Greene, and Neely, *Woman's Part*, p. 23.
13. Francis Gies and Joseph Gies, *Women in the Middle Ages* (New York: Barnes and Noble, 1978), p. 9; Greer, *Female Eunuch*, p. 268.
14. Berggren, "Woman's Part," p. 21; see also Madelon Gohlke, "'I wooed thee with my sword,': Shakespeare's Tragic Paradigms," in Schwartz and Kahn, *Representing Shakespeare*, pp. 179-80; Kimbrough, "Androgyny," p. 19.
15. Barber, "The Family," pp. 195-96.
16. Jung, *Psychology and Alchemy*, pp. 217-93; idem, *Alchemical Studies*, pp. 204-37; see also Titus Burckhardt, *Alchemy: Science of the Cosmos, Science of the Soul*, trans. William Stoddart (Baltimore: Penguin, 1971), pp. 144-46, 149-51. Frances Yates has written extensively of the influence of hermeticism upon Renaissance literature. See her *Giordano Bruno and the Hermetic Tradition* (Chicago: Univ. of Chicago Press, 1964), passim; *Shakespeare's Last Plays* (London: Routledge and Kegan Paul, 1975), pp. 87, 12-13, and *The Occult Philosophy in the Elizabethan Age* (London: Routledge and Kegan Paul, 1979), passim, especially pp. 75-159.
17. Yates, *Shakespeare's Last Plays*, pp. 12-13.
18. Berggren, "Woman's Part," p. 26.
19. Robert W. Uphaus, *Beyond Tragedy: Structure and Experience in Shakespeare's Romances* (Lexington: Univ. Press of Kentucky, 1981), p. 8.
20. See Jung, "The Relations between the Ego and the Unconscious," in *The Essential Jung*, pp. 94-95.
21. Erikson, "Reflections," pp. 5-6; Horney, *Neurotic Personality*, p. 174; Jung, *Development of Personality*, p. 55; Levinson, *Seasons*, pp. 249, 226.
22. Knight, *The Crown of Life* (London: Methuen, 1965), p. 50.
23. Kahn, *Man's Estate*, p. 198, pointed out how these two plays "mirror anxiety and even disgust about desire, female sexuality, and procreation."
24. He shrinks from what Levinson, in *Seasons*, pp. 197, 232, sees as two major lessons of midlife male development: coming to terms with what is "feminine" in himself as well as confronting the issue of human mortality.
25. See Harding, *I and Not-I*, p. 171.

26. Andrew Welsh points out the parallel in "Heritage in *Pericles*," in *Shakespeare's Late Plays*, ed. Richard C. Tobias and Paul G. Zolbrod (Athens: Ohio Univ. Press, 1974), p. 101.

27. Welsh, "Heritage in *Pericles*," p. 32.

28. Kahn, *Man's Estate*, pp. 214-15.

29. D.R.C. Marsh, *The Recurring Miracle* (Lincoln: Univ. of Nebraska Press, 1962), p. 130.

30. Kahn, *Man's Estate*, p. 215; E.M.W. Tillyard, "The Tragic Pattern," in *Shakespeare: The Winter's Tale: A Casebook*, ed. Kenneth Muir (London: Macmillan, 1968), p. 83.

31. Jung, *Man and His Symbols*, pp. 168-76; idem, *Integration of the Personality*, p. 173.

32. Champion, *Evolution*, p. 157.

33. Goddard, *Meaning of Shakespeare*, p. 652; and Donald A. Stauffer, "The Winter's Tale," in Muir, *Casebook*, p. 71.

34. See Jung, *Man and His Symbols*, p. 178; Harding, *I and Not-I*, pp. 206-7; and Horney, *New Ways*, p. 200.

35. See Carolyn Asp, "Shakespeare's Paulina and the *Consolatio* Tradition," *Shakespeare Studies* 11 (1978): 153.

36. Berggren, "Woman's Part," p. 30.

37. Jung, "Marriage as a Psychological Relationship," pp. 199; see also Harding, *Way of all Women*, p. 18.

38. Kahn, *Man's Estate*, p. 219.

39. Asp, "Shakespeare's Paulina," p. 156; Barber, "The Family," p. 196; Riemer, *Antic Fables*, pp. 149-51.

40. Erikson, *Childhood*, pp. 247-52.

41. Marsh, *Recurring Miracle*, p. 28.

42. Hunter, *Shakespeare and the Comedy of Forgiveness* (New York: Columbia Univ. Press, 1965), p. 158; see also Marsh, *Recurring Miracle*, p. 34.

43. Goddard, *Meaning of Shakespeare*, p. 637.

44. Meredith Skura, "Interpreting Posthumus' Dream from Above and Below: Families, Psychoanalysis, and Literary Critics," in Schwartz and Kahn, *Representing Shakespeare*, pp. 207, 210-12; see also Jung, *Freud and Psychoanalysis*, pp. 133-34; and Harding, *Parental Image*, pp. 12-14, for the importance of consciously reconciling oneself with the parent imagos.

45. Jung, *The Archetypes and the Collective Unconscious*, trans. R.F.C. Hull, *CW* 9 (New York: Pantheon Books, 1959): 82; see also Berggren, "Woman's Part," p. 27.

46. Gilligan, in *Different Voice*, p. 17, notes the tendency of men in midlife to discover for themselves the value of care, which "women have known from the beginning." See also Erikson, *Identity*, pp. 285-86; and Levinson, *Seasons*, p. 329.

47. Goddard, *Meaning of Shakespeare*, p. 676.

48. Traversi, *Shakespeare*, p. 196.

49. Leininger, "The Miranda Trap: Sexism and Racism in Shakespeare's *Tempest*," in Lenz, Greene, and Neely, *Woman's Part*, pp. 285-86.

50. See Alex Aronson, *Psyche and Symbol in Shakespeare* (Bloomington: Indiana Univ. Press, 1972), pp. 189-90, who holds that "her love for Ferdinand is in no way different from that known at first sight by Rosalind for Orlando and by Viola for Orsino."

51. Coleridge, *Lectures*, p. 279.

52. Knight, *Myth and Miracle: An Essay on the Mystic Symbolism of Shakespeare* (London: J. Burrows, 1974), p. 402.

53. Fiedler, *Stranger*, p. 243; see also Boose, "Father and the Bride," pp. 340-41.

54. Hobson, *Full Circle*, pp. 58-59.

55. Thomas McFarland, *Shakespeare's Pastoral Comedy* (Chapel Hill: Univ. of North Carolina Press, 1972), p. 166.

56. Hobson, *Full Circle*, p. 210.

57. Knight, *Myth and Miracle*, pp. 401-2.

58. See Gilligan, *Different Voice*, p. 17; Levinson, *Seasons*, p. 329; Erikson, *Identity*, pp. 285-86.

59. Kahn, *Man's Estate*, p. 220.
60. Gordon, *Shakespearian Comedy*, p. 81.
61. Knight, *Crown of Life*, p. 24; see also Frank Davidson, "*The Tempest*," in *Shakespeare: The Tempest: A Casebook*, ed. D.J. Palmer (London: Macmillan, 1968), p. 218; and David William, "*The Tempest* on the Stage," in *Shakespeare's Later Comedies*, ed. D.J. Palmer (Harmondsworth, Middlesex: Penguin, 1971), p. 457.
62. For these insights I am indebted to the late Professor James Emerson Phillips of UCLA.
63. See Jung, *Mysterium Coniunctionis*, pp. 457-553; Mattoon, *Jungian Psychology*, p. 84; and Heilbrun, *Androgyny*, p. 30.
64. Erikson, "Reflections," p. 26.

Chapter Eight. *Beyond Domination and Defiance*

1. Erikson, "Reflections," pp. 25-27.
2. See Fields, *Like Father*, p. 29; Biller, *Father, Child*, p. 103; Lamb et al., "Father-Daughter Relationship," p. 94; Hammer, *Passionate Attachments*, p. 137.
3. Ken Keyes, Jr., *Handbook to Higher Consciousness*, 5th ed. (Berkeley: Living Love Center, 1975), pp. 19-22, 59.
4. Horney, *Neurotic Personality*, p. 115.
5. Jung, *Psychology of the Unconscious*, pp. 108, 184-85; idem, *Archetypes and Collective Unconscious*, 60-61.
6. See Horney, *New Ways*, p. 57.
7. Tiger and Fox, *Imperial Animal*, pp. 60, 84.
8. See Gilligan, *Different Voice*, p. 17; and Heilbrun, *Androgyny*, pp. 33-34.
9. Biller, *Father, Child*, p. 117; Horney, *Neurosis*, p. 252; Deutsch, *Psychology of Women*, p. 240.
10. Heilbrun, *Androgyny*, p. 32.
11. Herman, *Father-Daughter*, p. 56; Heilbrun, *Androgyny*, p. 33.
12. Erikson, *Identity*, pp. 261-66.
13. Gilligan, *Different Voice*, p. 105.
14. See Kohlberg, "Stages of Moral Development," pp. 91-92; Gilligan, *Different Voice*, p. 105.
15. See Erikson, *Identity*, p. 264; Levinson, *Seasons*, p. 226; Jung, *Development of Personality*, p. 55; Horney, *Neurotic Personality*, p. 174.
16. Jung, *Archetypes and Collective Unconscious*, p. 82.
17. Jung, *Psychology of the Unconscious*, p. 107; idem, "Undiscovered Self," p. 400.

Bibliographical Note

Although the father-daughter relationship is a principal theme in Shakespeare's comedies, tragedies, and romances, no book on the subject has hitherto appeared. This study reflects three significant themes in recent Shakespeare scholarship: a concern with his women characters, marriage and the family, and psychological development. Acknowledged classics by such authors as C.L. Barber, Roy Battenhouse, A.C. Bradley, Lily Bess Campbell, Harley Granville-Barker, Edward Dowden, G. Wilson Knight, and L.C. Knights are, of course, relevant to all work in the field, but will not be listed here. References to Shakespeare's plays are taken from *The Complete Works*, ed. Hardin Craig and David Bevington (Glenview, Ill.: Scott, Foresman, 1973). In the three specialized areas cited above, I found the following works most illuminating.

Among studies of Shakespeare's women, Agnes Mure Mackenzie's *The Women in Shakespeare's Plays* (Garden City: Doubleday, 1924) and Anna Jameson's *Shakespeare's Heroines* (New York: A.L. Burt, 1948) are informative early works. Juliet Dusinberre's *Shakespeare and the Nature of Women* (New York: Barnes and Noble, 1975) describes a wave of feminism that swept England from the late 1590s onward. Angela Pitt takes a more traditional view in *Shakespeare's Women* (London: David and Charles, 1981), while Irene Dash concentrates on the importance of Elizabethan marriage customs in her excellent study *Wooing, Wedding, and Power* (New York: Columbia Univ. Press, 1981). Recent articles have shed additional light on Shakespeare's women. Inga-Stina Ewbank's "Shakespeare's Portrayal of Women: A 1970's View," in *Shakespeare: Patterns of Excelling Nature*, ed. David Bevington and Jay L. Halio (Newark: Univ. of Delaware Press, 1978), pp. 222-29; Barbara Mowat's "Images of Women in Shakespeare's Plays," *Southern Humanities Review* 11 (1977): 145-57; and Velma Bourgeois Richmond's "Shakespeare's Women," *Midwest Quarterly* 19 (1978): 330-42, provide helpful overviews.

Feminist critics have brought new perspectives to Shakespeare studies. *The Woman's Part: Feminist Criticism of Shakespeare*, ed. Carolyn Ruth Swift Lenz, Gayle Greene, and Carol Thomas Neely (Urbana: Univ. of Illinois Press, 1980), and *The Authority of Experience: Essays in Feminist Criticism*, ed. Arlyn Diamond and Lee R. Edwards (Amherst: Univ. of Massachusetts Press, 1977), are lively and innovative crit-

Bibliographical Note

ical collections. Marcia Landry's "The Silent Woman: Towards a Feminist Critique," in *Authority of Experience*, ed. Diamond and Edwards, pp. 16-27, repudiates the traditional stereotype. Carole McKewin's "Shakespeare Liberata: Shakespeare, the Nature of Women, and the New Feminist Criticism," *Mosaic* 10 (1977): 157-64, offers a useful critical summary. McKewin sheds new light on women's loyalties in "Counsels of Gall and Grace: Intimate Conversations between Women in Shakespeare's Plays," in *Woman's Part*, ed. Lenz, Greene, and Neely, pp. 117-32. Joyce Sexton's *The Slandered Woman in Shakespeare* (Victoria, B.C.: English Literary Series, 1978) emphasizes the helplessness and vulnerability of women who conform to tradition. Eric W. Stockton's "The Adulthood of Shakespeare's Heroines," in *Shakespearean Essays*, ed. Alwin Thaler and Norman Sanders (Knoxville: Univ. of Tennessee Press, 1964), pp. 161-80, is a useful reevaluation of women's roles.

One especially fascinating topic in recent years, marriage and the family in Shakespeare, has produced a series of lively critical debates in MLA panels and scholarly articles. C.L. Barber's fine study "The Family in Shakespeare's Development: Tragedy and Sacredness" in *Representing Shakespeare: New Psychoanalytic Essays*, ed. Murray M. Schwartz and Coppélia Kahn (Baltimore: Johns Hopkins Univ. Press, 1980), pp. 188-202, explores the spiritual significance of family bonds. Meredith Skura's excellent "Interpreting Posthumus' Dream from Above and Below: Families, Psychoanalysis, and Literary Critics," in *Representing Shakespeare*, ed. Schwartz and Kahn, pp. 203-16, describes the importance of these bonds in forming an integrated sense of self. Lynda Boose's outstanding "The Father and the Bride in Shakespeare," *PMLA* 97 (1982): 325-47, examines the ritualistic significance of the marriage ceremony. Carol Thomas Neely's "Women and Men in *Othello*: 'What should such a fool / Do with so good a woman?'" *Shakespeare Studies* 10 (1977): 133-58, is a useful critique of traditional male and female roles. Margaret Loftus Ranald offers a valuable overview in "'As Marriage Binds, and Blood Breaks': English Marriage in Shakespeare," *Shakespeare Quarterly* 30 (1979): 68-81.

Critical responses to developmental psychology have produced such excellent works as Marjorie Garber's *Coming of Age in Shakespeare* (London: Methuen, 1981) and Alan Hobson's *Full Circle: Shakespeare and Moral Development* (London: Chatto and Windus, 1972). Daniel J. Levinson describes the developmental conflict of King Lear along with contemporary case studies in *The Seasons of a Man's Life* (New York: Alfred A. Knopf, 1978). *Representing Shakespeare*, ed. Schwartz and Kahn, offers some fascinating psychological perspectives, such as the intriguing essay by Richard P. Wheeler, "'Since first we were dissevered': Trust and Autonomy in Shakespearean Tragedy and Romance," pp. 150-69.

The developmental crisis of Shakespeare's fathers has been explored by a number of critics. Paul A. Jorgensen offers a sensitive examination in *Lear's Self Discovery* (Berkeley: Univ. of California Press, 1967). Lear's turbulent conflicts even attracted the attention of Sigmund Freud, whose article "The Theme of the Three Caskets" in *The Design Within*, ed. M.D. Faber (New York: Science House, 1970), pp. 195-206, examines his tormented psyche and the symbolic significance of his daughters. Sir Arthur Quiller-Couch treated *Paternity in Shakespeare* in an early but still useful study

Bibliographical Note

(1932; reprint, London: Folcroft, 1970). David Sundelson has contributed his excellent "'So Rare a Wonder'd Father: Prospero's *Tempest*," in *Representing Shakespeare*, ed. Schwartz and Kahn, pp. 33-53, and *Shakespeare's Restorations of the Father* (New Brunswick, N.J.: Rutgers Univ. Press, 1983). Coppélia Kahn's creative and innovative *Man's Estate: Masculine Identity in Shakespeare* (Berkeley: Univ. of California Press, 1981) is a treasury of insights on masculine development.

On the father-daughter relationship itself, there have been some fine articles, including Boose, "The Father and the Bride," cited above; Cyrus Hoy, "Fathers and Daughters in Shakespeare's Romances," in *Shakespeare's Romances Reconsidered*, ed. Carol McGinnis Kay and Henry E. Jacobs (Lincoln: Univ. of Nebraska Press, 1978), pp. 77-90; Richard Jaarsma, "The 'Lear Complex' in *The Two Gentlemen of Verona*," *Literature and Psychology* 22 (1972): 199-202; and W. Nicholas Knight, "Patrimony and Shakespeare's Daughters," *Hartford Studies in Literature* 9 (1977): 175-85.

There have been a number of sensitive psychological studies of Shakespeare's daughters. Among the most interesting for my purposes were Robert Dickes, "Desdemona: An Innocent Victim," *American Imago* 27 (1970): 279-97; Charles Frey, "'O Sacred, shadowy, cold and constant queen': Shakespeare's Imperiled and Chastening Daughters of Romance," in *Woman's Part*, ed. Lenz, Greene, and Neely, pp. 295-313; Gayle Greene, "'This That You Call Love': Sexual and Social Tragedy in *Othello*," *Journal of Women's Studies in Literature* 1 (1979): 16-32; and Vera Jiji, "Portia Revisited: The Influence of Unconscious Factors upon Theme and Characterization in *The Merchant of Venice*," *Literature and Psychology* 26 (1976): 5-15. Also interesting is David Leverenz, "The Women in Hamlet: An Interpersonal View," in *Representing Shakespeare*, ed. Schwartz and Kahn, pp. 110-28. Richard Levin emphasizes Viola's crafty assertiveness in "Viola: Dr. Johnson's 'Excellent Schemer,' " *Durham University Journal* 71 (1979): 213-22. Charlotte Otten combines psychology and iconography in her study of "Ophelia's 'Long Purples,' " *Shakespeare Quarterly* 30 (1979): 397-402. Stephen Reid casts exciting new light on motivation in "Desdemona's Guilt" and "In Defense of Goneril and Regan," *American Imago* 27 (1970): 245-62 and 226-44, respectively.

In a number of works the implications of male and female sex roles in Shakespeare have been explored. Linda Bamber offers some interesting theories in *Comic Women, Tragic Men: A Study of Gender and Genre in Shakespeare* (Stanford, Calif.: Stanford Univ. Press, 1982). Edward A. Snow, in his excellent article "Sexual Anxiety and the Male Order of Things in *Othello*," *English Literary Renaissance* 10 (1980): 384-412, emphasizes the violence underlying traditional stereotypes. Janice Hays, in "Those 'soft and delicate desires': *Much Ado* and the Distrust of Women," in *Woman's Part*, ed. Lenz, Greene, and Neely, pp. 79-99, points to men's underlying suspicion of female sexuality. Mary Williamson explores similar tensions in "The Ring Episode in *The Merchant of Venice*," *South Atlantic Quarterly* 71 (1972): 587-94. Madelon Gohlke's "'I wooed thee with my sword': Shakespeare's Tragic Paradigms," in *Representing Shakespeare*, ed. Schwartz and Kahn, pp. 170-87, offers some stunning parallels between sex-role polarization and violence. Robert Kimbrough affirms an alternative in "Androgyny Seen Through Shakespeare's Disguise," *Shakespeare Quarterly* 33 (1982): 17-

33. V.G. Kiernan argues that Shakespeare upheld a new paradigm for human commitments in "Human Relationships in Shakespeare," *Shakespeare in a Changing World*, ed. Arnold Kettle (New York: International Publishers, 1964), pp. 43-64.

I have also benefited from a number of works on the plays in performance: Carol Jones Carlisle's *Shakespeare from the Greenroom: Actors' Criticisms of Four Major Tragedies* (Chapel Hill: Univ. of North Carolina Press, 1969); Helena Faucit Martin's *Shakespeare's Female Characters* (New York: AMS, 1970); Marvin Rosenberg's *The Masks of Othello: The Search for the Identity of Othello, Iago, and Desdemona by Three Centuries of Actors and Critics* (Berkeley: Univ. of California Press, 1961); and David William's "*The Tempest* on the Stage" in *Shakespeare's Later Comedies*, ed. D.J. Palmer (Harmondsworth: Penguin, 1971), pp. 432-59.

For this book I have drawn upon an extensive historical and psychological background. Of the many primary works on marriage and the family during Shakespeare's time, I found the following most helpful: Cornelius Agrippa, *The Commendation of Matrimony* (London: n.p., 1534); Heinrich Bullinger, *The Golden Boke of Christen Matrimonye* (London: n.p., 1543); Myles Coverdale, *The Christen State of Matrimonye* (London: n.p., 1541); and Thomas Gataker, *Marriage Duties* (London: William Jones for William Bladen, 1620) and *A Good Wife Gods Gift* (London: John Haviland for Fulke Clifton, 1624). William Gouge, *Of Domesticall Duties* (London: John Haviland for William Bladen, 1622; reprint, Amsterdam: *Theatrum Orbis Terrarum*, 1976) is a compendium of traditional family mores. Other important works are: Gervase Markham, *The English Hous-Wife* (London: William Wilson, 1660); Henrie Smith, *A Preparative to Mariage* (London: Thomas Orwin for Thomas Man, 1591); John Stockwood, *A Bartholomew Fairing for Parentes* (London: John Wolfe, 1589); Henry Swinburne, *A Treatise of Spousals* (London: S. Roycroft, 1686); and Juan Luis Vives, *Instruction of a christen woman* (London: n.p., 1557). References to other primary works are found in chapter two.

Among secondary studies, Chilton Latham Powell, *English Domestic Relations, 1487-1653* (New York: Columbia Univ. Press, 1917) is an early but still valuable source. Another helpful work is Jean-Louis Flandrin, *Families in Former Times* (London: Cambridge Univ. Press, 1979). Lawrence Stone's monumental *The Family, Sex, and Marriage in England, 1500-1800* (New York: Harper and Row, 1977) is a treasury of information. Arnold Van Gennep's *The Rites of Passage* (London: Routledge and Kegan Paul, 1960) reveals the profound significance of ritual in family bonds. Philip Aries's *Centuries of Childhood* (New York: Alfred A. Knopf, 1962) and *The History of Childhood* (New York: Psychohistory Press, 1974), ed. Lloyd deMause, provide valuable insights into the conditions of children during Shakespeare's time.

The emphasis on women's studies during the past few decades has generated many histories and reexaminations of women's roles. Among the valuable works in this area, I found the following most helpful: Frances and Joseph Gies, *Women in the Middle Ages* (New York: Barnes and Noble, 1978); three earlier studies, Carroll Camden, *The Elizabethan Woman* (New York: Elsevier, 1952), Ruth Kelso, *Doctrine for the Lady of the Renaissance* (Urbana: Univ. of Illinois Press, 1956), and Violet A. Wilson, *Society Women of Shakespeare's Time* (New York: E.P. Dutton, 1925); and the more recent Alison Plowden, *Tudor Women: Queens and Commoners* (London: Weidenfeld and

Nicolson, 1979). I also recommend Antonia Fraser's fascinating study *The Weaker Vessel* (New York: Alfred A. Knopf, 1984), which appeared just as this book was going to press. Suzanne Hull's *Chaste, Silent, and Obedient: English Books for Women, 1475-1640* (San Marino, Calif.: Huntington Library, 1982) records what Renaissance women were reading. Germaine Greer's *The Female Eunuch* (New York: McGraw Hill, 1971) is an important general study.

The psychological background required for this book was, understandably, extensive. A more complete account can be found in the notes to chapter one. As classics on neurosis and personal development, I recommend: Sigmund Freud's *Totem and Taboo* (London: Routledge, 1919) and *The Interpretation of Dreams* (New York: Modern Library, 1950); Karen Horney's *New Ways in Psychoanalysis* (New York: W.W. Norton, 1939), *Neurosis and Human Growth* (New York: W.W. Norton, 1950), *The Neurotic Personality of Our Time* (New York: W.W. Norton, 1937), and *Our Inner Conflicts* (New York: W.W. Norton, 1945); and Harry Stack Sullivan's *Personal Psychopathology* (New York: W.W. Norton, 1972). R.D. Laing offers intriguing insights about schizophrenia in *The Divided Self* (London: Tavistock, 1960).

Studies of women's psychology reveal dramatically different definitions of healthy feminine development. Helene Deutsch's early study *The Psychology of Women* (New York: Grune and Stratton, 1944) emphasizes traditional conditioning for compliance. M. Esther Harding approaches feminine identity from a Jungian perspective in *The Way of All Women* (New York: Longmans, Green, 1933). A more recent work, *Becoming Female: Perspectives on Development*, ed. Claire B. Kopp with Martha Kirkpatrick (New York: Plenum, 1979), offers exciting new perspectives on women's role conflicts. Arguing that moral development in women differs from that in men, Carol Gilligan's *In a Different Voice: Psychological Theory and Women's Development* (Cambridge, Mass.: Harvard Univ. Press, 1982) is a sensitive and revealing study.

Psychologists lament the lack of any substantive literature on the father-daughter relationship. In recent research and popular studies, however, this primal bond has been given close attention. An excellent article by Michael E. Lamb, Margaret Tresch Owen, and Lindsay Chase-Lansdale, "The Father-Daughter Relationship: Past, Present, and Future," in *Becoming Female*, ed. Kopp, pp. 89-112, provides a valuable overview. Carl Gustav Jung's insights into the masculine and feminine unconscious are most enlightening, especially his studies of the anima and the animus. I have made ample use of *The Collected Works of C.G. Jung* (*CW*), published jointly by Routledge and Kegan Paul in London and in this country by the Bollingen Foundation through Pantheon Books in New York from 1953 to 1967, and from 1967 to 1978 by the Princeton University Press. See *The Archetypes and the Collective Unconscious*, *CW* 9 (Princeton: Princeton Univ. Press, 1968) and "The Family Constellation," *CW* 2 (Princeton: Princeton Univ. Press, 1973) as well as "The Significance of the Father in the Destiny of the Individual," *CW* 4 (New York: Pantheon Books, 1961). The father's profound effect on his daughter's identity is apparent in two studies by E. Mavis Hetherington, "Effects of Father Absence on Personality Development in Adolescent Daughters," *Developmental Psychology* 7 (1972): 313-26, and "Girls without Fathers," *Psychology Today* 6 (February 1973): 47-52. Two recent popular works are Suzanne Fields, *Like Father, Like Daughter: How Father Shapes the Woman His Daughter Becomes* (Boston: Little,

Bibliographical Note

Brown and Co., 1983), and Signe Hammer, *Passionate Attachments: Fathers and Daughters in America Today* (New York: Rawson, 1982).

The father-daughter relationship invariably brings up the question of incest, dramatically explored in the following studies: Robert L. Geiser, *Hidden Victims: The Sexual Abuse of Children* (Boston: Beacon Press, 1979); Henry Giaretto, "The Treatment of Father-Daughter Incest: A Psycho-Social Approach," *Children Today* 5 (July-August 1976): 2-5, 34-35; Judith Lewis Herman and Lisa Hirschman, "Father-Daughter Incest," *Signs* 2 (1977): 735-56; Herman with Hirschman, *Father-Daughter Incest* (Cambridge, Mass.: Harvard Univ. Press, 1981); Herbert Maisch, *Incest* (New York: Stein and Day, 1972); and Jean Renvoize, *Incest: A Family Pattern* (London: Routledge and Kegan Paul, 1982).

I have also drawn upon many excellent sources in developmental psychology from early classics to modern studies. Among the most helpful were Erik H. Erikson's *Childhood and Society*, 2d ed. (New York: W.W. Norton, 1963); *Identity: Youth and Crisis* (New York: W.W. Norton, 1968); "Reflections on Dr. Borg's Life Cycle," in *Adulthood*, ed. Erik H. Erikson (New York: W.W. Norton, 1978), pp. 1-31; and *Youth: Change and Challenge* (New York: Basic Books, 1963); as well as the following works by Carl Jung: *The Development of Personality*, CW 17 (New York: Pantheon Books, 1954); *Freud and Psychoanalysis*, CW 4 (New York: Pantheon Books, 1961); *The Integration of the Personality* (New York: Farrar and Rinehart, 1939); *Psychology of the Unconscious* (London: Routledge and Kegan Paul, 1919); and "The Stages of Life," CW 8 (New York: Pantheon Books, 1960). M. Esther Harding offers excellent insights in *The 'I' and the 'Not-I'* (New York: Pantheon Books, 1965) and *The Parental Image* (New York: G.P. Putnam's Sons, 1965). Two pioneers in moral development are Lawrence Kohlberg, "Stages of Moral Development as a Basis for Moral Education," in *Moral Development, Moral Education, and Kohlberg*, ed. Brenda Munsey (Birmingham: Religious Education Press, 1980), pp. 15-98; and William G. Perry, Jr., *Forms of Intellectual and Ethical Development in the College Years* (New York: Holt, Rinehart and Winston, 1968). Interesting recent works on adult development are Daniel J. Levinson, *The Seasons of a Man's Life* (New York: Alfred A. Knopf, 1978); and the popular *Passages: Predictable Crises of Adult Life* by Gail Sheehy (New York: E.P. Dutton, 1976).

Finally, I have drawn upon selected works on alchemy and androgyny to convey the changing concepts of male and female identity during Shakespeare's time. Two valuable modern works are: Carolyn G. Heilbrun, *Toward a Recognition of Androgyny* (New York: Alfred A. Knopf, 1973); and June Singer, *Androgyny: Toward a New Theory of Sexuality* (New York: Doubleday, 1976). For an understanding of Renaissance alchemy, I have drawn upon Titus Burckhardt, *Alchemy: Science of the Cosmos, Science of the Soul*, (Baltimore: Penguin, 1971); and two books by Frances Yates: *Giordano Bruno and the Hermetic Tradition* (Chicago: Univ. of Chicago Press, 1964) and *The Occult Philosophy in the Elizabethan Age* (London: Routledge and Kegan Paul, 1979). For a description of alchemy as the androgynous balance of masculine and feminine potentialities within the human soul, Carl Jung's *Alchemical Studies*, CW 13 (Princeton: Princeton Univ. Press, 1967); *Mysterium Coniunctionis*, CW 14 (New York: Pantheon Books, 1963); and *Psychology and Alchemy*, CW 12 (New York: Pantheon Books, 1953) are invaluable.

Index

Adam (*As You Like It*), 39, 123
Against Disobedient and Wilful Rebellion, 106
Agrippa, Cornelius, 32–33, 60
alazons, 62–63, 99, 123, 159, 169
alchemy, 3, 74, 116, 134, 146, 162–63
Alexander VI, Pope (Roderigo Borgia), 9
All's Well That Ends Well, 12–13, 19, 122, 136–42, 164. *See also* Bertram; Helena
Alonso, 157, 162
Amoretti, The (Spenser), 36
androgyny, 116, 127, 143–46, 170; in women, 89, 115–17, 127, 143–44, 150, 164–70; in men, 127, 143–46, 161, 170
anima, 7, 143–46; projection of, 8, 9, 85, 109, 137–38, 144–45, 151, 153, 155, 166–68; integration of, 116, 143–44, 153, 158, 161–62
animus, 7, 143–46; integration of, 14, 116–17, 123–24, 144; projection of, 14, 137–38
Annesley, Cordell, 105
Annesley, Sir Brian, 105
Antiochus, 10, 147–48, 166
Antonio (*Much Ado*), 85
Antonio (*The Merchant*), 130, 133–35
Antonio (*The Tempest*), 158, 162
Ariel, 56, 161–62
Arragon, Prince of, 130–31
Ascham, Roger, 30
As You Like It, 119–23; personal growth in, 14, 16–17, 62–63, 116–17, 120–24, 135, 169–70; courtship in, 37, 119–23, 137, 165; friendship in, 39, 62, 81, 103, 120, 122–23, 165. *See also* Rosalind
Auden, W.H., 88

Bamber, Linda, 2
Baptista Minola, 51–52, 110, 111; mercenary motives of, 9, 51–52, 166; arranges daughters' marriages, 25, 48, 111
Barber, C.L., 63, 72, 145–46
Bassanio, 62, 111–12, 130–33, 135, 140
Battenhouse, Roy, 103
Batty, Bartholomew, 22, 23, 25, 27–28, 29, 35
Baxter, Richard, 33
Beatrice, 127–29; defensiveness of, 13, 127–28; wit of, 27, 127–29, 137; friendship with Hero, 86–87, 128; as fatherless daughter, 116, 128; love for Benedick, 127, 129, 165
Belarius, 155, 157
Benedick, 13, 84–86, 127–29
Berggren, Paula, 146
Berry, Ralph, 129
Bertram, 12, 19, 136–42
Bianca, 52, 109–11
Boose, Lynda, 2, 60–61
Borachio, 87
Borgia, Cesare, 10
Borgia, Lucretia, 10
Borgia, Roderigo. *See* Alexander VI, Pope
Botticelli, Sandro, 116
boy actors, 116–17
Brabantio, 44–46, 56–58; grief at daughter's elopement, 15, 42; developmental crisis of, 40; sees daughter as a child, 44–46, 48, 90, 166; believes his daughter bewitched, 56–58; parodic "giving" of daughter, 61, 99, 147
Bradley, A.C., 76, 88–89, 115
Budden, John, 26–27

Bullinger, Heinrich, 26
Burgundy, Duke of, 43, 69–71

Caliban, 7, 157, 159–62
Cambio. *See* Lucentio
"Canonization, The" (Donne), 36
Capulet, 50–51; arranges daughter's marriage, 25, 48; as a loving father, 26, 40, 50, 56; treats daughter like property, 51, 148
Cassio, 88, 94–95
Castiglione, Baldassare, 30, 116, 131
Cecil, Sir Robert, 105
Celia, 119–22; friendship with Rosalind, 39, 103, 119–21; defies father, 81, 103, 120–21
Cenci, Beatrice, 10
Cerimon, 148–49
Cesario. *See* Viola
Chambers, E.K., 136
Champion, Larry, 130
Charlemagne, 43
Charlton, H.B., 102
chastity: men's perceptions of, 2, 23, 55, 58, 76, 86, 93–94, 95, 167; as the Renaissance ideal, 24, 76, 78, 80, 84–87, 89, 95
children, 21–30, 34–35; obedience of, 16, 20–22, 39, 47–48, 90, 98, 101, 165; as property, 21, 29, 79, 100; education of, 22–24; and conscience, 30, 47, 103; parental love for, 34. *See also* daughters
Claudio, 84, 86–87, 128, 140
Claudius, 53–54, 80
Cloten, 8, 43, 46–48, 100–101, 154, 156
Coke, Sir Edward, 28
Coleridge, Samuel Taylor, 119, 159
conscience, 30, 165. *See also* children; women
Cordelia, 64–75, 107–8; Lear's love for, 8–9, 64–65, 69–75; arrested development of, 11, 14, 108; as redeemer, 22, 108; inability to flatter, 22, 61, 65–67, 71, 107; links father and husband, 67, 120
Coriolanus, 93, 117
Coriolanus, 93, 106, 117, 168
Courtier, The (Castiglione), 30, 116
courtship: traditional, 84, 109–10, 135; unconventional, 90–91, 99–100, 112–14, 121–22, 127–28, 137–40; significance of, 140, 159–60. *See also* love: as personal growth; love: romantic
Coverdale, Miles, 19, 24, 26, 28
Cymbeline, 46–48, 156–57; imbalance of, 6, 156; paternal domination by, 8, 44, 46–

48, 156; sees daughter as child, 46–47, 56, 100, 166; regeneration of, 59, 146, 155–57, 167; gives paternal blessing, 63, 101, 156–59
Cymbeline, 46–48, 100–101, 153–57; paternal domination in, 8, 46–48, 166; reconciliation in, 59, 63, 149, 156–57, 170; misogyny in, 145, 154–55, 167–69

Dante Alighieri, 7, 88, 138, 143
Dash, Irene, 2, 50, 99–100
daughters, 4–6, 11–15, 23–27, 76–142; defiant, 4, 6, 21, 24, 45–47, 51, 55, 68, 81, 89–91, 93, 96–114, 120–21, 147–48, 159, 165, 168; tragic, 4, 6–9, 11–14, 20–23, 26–27, 42, 44–47, 49–51, 55, 57–58, 60–61, 64–86, 88–100, 102, 104–10, 116, 120–22, 145, 151, 160, 165, 167–69; dominated, 6, 11, 62, 76–95, 129, 164–66; in romances, 7–8, 15, 46–48, 56, 59, 63, 96, 100–101, 129, 140, 143–44, 146–49, 152–54, 156–62, 167–70; comic, 12–14, 17, 19, 31, 37–39, 49, 52, 55, 62–63, 76, 84–87, 94–99, 102–3, 109–25, 127–42, 144, 165–67, 169–70; link fathers and husbands, 12, 45, 67, 90–91, 93, 119–20, 124, 136; raised as sons, 12, 138, 164; fatherless, 13, 116–17, 119, 124–25, 128, 137; as redeemers, 15, 22, 59, 108, 115, 143, 145–47, 149, 152–53, 156–58, 161, 170; obedience of, 24, 44, 53, 61, 120–21, 159. *See also* Beatrice; Bianca; Celia; Cordelia; Desdemona; Goneril; Helena (*All's Well*); Helena (*Midsummer*); Hermia; Hero; Imogen; Jessica; Julia; Juliet; Katharina; Marina; Miranda; Olivia; Ophelia; Perdita; Portia; Regan; Rosalind; Silvia; Thaisa; Viola; women: obedience of
Dekker, Thomas, 38
DeMause, Lloyd, 8
Demetrius, 43, 49–50, 58, 97–98, 119
Desdemona, 13–14, 87–95, 167–69; defiance of, 2, 4, 21, 45, 89–91, 93, 96, 98, 99, 160; elopement of, 6, 42, 44–45, 58, 61, 88, 90–91, 99; neurotic self-effacement of, 11, 13–14, 76, 88–96, 99, 109, 121, 165, 167–69; links father and husband, 45, 66, 90–91, 93, 120; on the stage, 89, 116; Othello's perception of, 145, 167–69
Deutsch, Helene, 9
Diana Capilet, 140–41
Disobedient Child, The, 38
Dobbins, Austin, 103

Don John, 128
Donne, John, 4, 7, 17, 36, 74, 131
Donnelly, John, 69
Don Pedro, 84, 86, 128, 140
Dowden, Edward, 106, 129
Drake, Sir Francis, 3
Drayton, Michael, 38
Duke (*Two Gentlemen*), 49, 51, 56, 62–63, 99
Duke Senior, 39, 63, 120, 123, 167
Dusinberre, Juliet, 2, 37–38, 116, 126
Dympha, Saint, 9

Edgar, 108
Edmund, 22, 65, 104, 106
Education of a Christian Prince (Erasmus), 30
Education or Bringing Up of Children, The (Plutarch), 25
Egeus, 49–50, 56–58; as domineering father, 24, 25, 48, 147, 165–66; sees daughter as property, 49–50, 51; gives paternal blessing, 63, 167
Elizabeth, Princess (daughter of James I), 159
Elizabeth I (queen of England), 3, 17, 30–31, 35, 146, 173 n. 3
Elyot, Thomas, 25, 30
Emilia, 88, 92–95
Englishman for My Money (Houghton), 38
Epithalamion, The (Spenser), 36
Erasmus, Desiderius, 30, 126
Erikson, Erik H., 1, 5, 85, 96, 169. *See also* generativity; identity; integrity; intimacy

Faerie Queene, The (Spenser), 36, 116
fathers, 4–11, 24–26, 40–75, 143–63; tragic, 2, 14–15, 22, 42, 44–46, 48–58, 61, 63–75, 78–82, 90, 99, 104–5, 107, 145, 147, 163, 165–66; domination of daughters by, 6, 8, 10–11, 24, 42, 48, 62, 129, 156, 159, 165–67; authoritarian, 7, 10, 12, 22, 39, 42, 54, 97, 167; egocentric, 7–9, 42–43, 51, 54–56, 64, 68, 72, 166; mercenary, 8–9, 43, 48–54, 64, 66, 148, 166; incest of, 9–11, 58–59, 146–47, 166, 168; jealous, 9–10, 43–44, 49, 56–63, 64, 69–71, 166; incestuous tendencies of, 11, 49, 56, 59, 67, 74–75, 144, 146, 149, 153, 166; surrogate, 11, 13, 91, 120; comic, 14–15, 24, 25, 39, 40, 42–43, 48–52, 55–58, 62–63, 110–11, 120, 165–67; in romances, 15, 44,

46–48, 56, 59, 140, 143–44, 146–53, 155–64, 167, 170; wise, 15, 147, 157–59, 161–64, 170; reactionary, 26, 40, 43–48, 50, 56–58, 63–64, 70. *See also* Baptista Minola; Brabantio; Capulet; Cymbeline; Duke (*Two Gentlemen*); Duke Senior; Egeus; Lear; Leonato; Leontes; Pericles; Polonius; Prospero; Shylock; Simonides
Faucit, Helena, 77, 89
Faust, 6
feminism, 32, 37, 77, 115
Fenton, 101
Ferdinand, 140, 159–62
Fiedler, Leslie, 160
Fields, Suzanne, 9
Florizel, 153
Fox, Robin, 10
France, King of (*All's Well*), 137, 139, 141
France, King of (*King Lear*), 43, 69–71
France, Princess of, 118
Frederick, Duke (*As You Like It*), 123
Frederick, Duke of Württemberg, 31
Freud, Anna, 12
Freud, Sigmund, 1, 10, 13, 52, 65
friar (in *Romeo and Juliet*), 81
friendship, 39, 118–19; developmental lessons in, 5, 54, 62, 81, 99, 118, 120–22, 128, 141, 150, 165, 184 n. 19; in love relationships, 62–63, 114, 119, 123, 125–27, 134–35; Renaissance ideal of, 119, 133, 151
Fromm, Erich, 8
Frye, Northrop, 61
Furnivall, Frederick, 29

Ganymede. *See* Rosalind
Garber, Marjorie, 2
Gataker, Thomas, 18, 20–21, 24, 30, 34, 101
gender stereotypes, 115, 134, 138–39. *See also* sex roles
generativity, crisis of, 5, 56, 72, 74, 150, 177 n. 48
Gertrude, 61, 81
Gilligan, Carol: on excessive altruism in women, 77, 87, 90, 94, 183 n. 38; on healthy development in women, 80, 96, 98, 134, 169–70
Glendower, 64
Gloucester, 22, 104
Goddard, Harold, 90, 117, 124, 158
Goeppert-Mayer, Maria, 12
Goneril, 104–6; defiant revenge of, 6, 55, 96, 102, 168; flattery of, 22, 66–68, 104;

sibling rivalry of, 65, 105, 107; sadism of, 104–6

Gonzalo, 158

Gouge, William: on submission of children, 18, 102; on marriage, 18, 20, 25, 32, 47, 60, 92–93, 108; on conscience, 30, 101–2; on unnatural love of children, 58–59, 70, 73

Governour, The (Elyot), 30

Granville-Barker, Harley, 80

Gratiano, 62

great chain of being, 21, 29

Greer, Germaine, 2, 145

Grey, Lady Jane, 22, 30

Griselda, 20, 124, 136, 142

Hamlet, 52–54, 77–83, 89; relationship with Ophelia, 9, 52–54, 61, 77–83; friendship with Horatio, 54, 81, 89; relationship with father, 90, 117; misogyny of, 145, 154

Hamlet, 52–54, 76–84; paternal domination in, 6, 9, 11–14, 48, 52–54, 76–83, 95, 109, 160, 166; criticism on, 76–77, 80, 83; on the stage, 77, 116

Harding, M. Esther, 5

Harris, Frank, 143–44

Hay, William, 47

Hazlitt, William, 84

Heilbrun, Carolyn, 2, 116, 168–69

Helena (*All's Well*), 136–42; raised as son, 12, 138, 164; as fatherless daughter, 13, 137; courtship of Bertram, 19, 122, 137–40; androgyny of, 136–37, 139, 142; as traditional wife, 142

Helena (*Midsummer*), 81, 98, 118–19

Henry IV, Part 1, 64

Henry VIII (king of England), 20, 30, 35

Herbert, George, 17

Herbert, Magdalen, 17

Herman, Judith Lewis, 11, 169

hermeticism, 146, 153, 161–63, 170

Hermia, 97–100; defiance of, 4, 6, 96–100; arranged marriage of, 25, 49; love for Lysander, 58, 62–63, 96–100, 166–67; friendship with Helena, 81, 118–19

Hermione, 146, 150–53

Hero, 84–87, 127–29; passivity of, 13, 84–87, 94–95, 96, 109, 116, 121, 127, 165; as traditional daughter, 27, 76, 84–87, 116; men's perceptions of, 55, 85–87, 140, 167

heroes: tragic, 41, 93, 115; comic, 115–16, 144, 169–70; of romance, 144

Heywood, Thomas, 18, 20, 25–26, 34

Hippolyta, 63

Hirschman, Lisa, 11

Hobbes, Thomas, 104, 107

Hobson, Alan, 160

Holmes, Martin, 102

Holt, Sir Thomas, 28

Horatio, 54, 81

Horney, Karen, 6–7

Hortensio, 109–10, 112

Hotspur, 64

humanism, 4, 29–30, 38–39; effect on women, 30–32, 98, 138; effect on relationships, 38–39, 165

Hunter, Robert Grams, 154

Iachimo, 47, 101, 153–54, 156

Iago, 49, 79, 88, 92, 94–95, 99

identity, crisis of, 5, 11, 72–74, 77, 91, 108, 118, 128, 140

Imogen, 46–48, 100–101, 153–57; fidelity of, 6, 48, 101, 129, 154; defiance by, 46–47, 96, 100; men's perceptions of, 46–47, 56, 100, 154–56, 166–69; as redeeming force, 146, 156–57

incest, 9–11; history of, 9, 58–60; fathers' motivation, 10–11, 58, 146–47, 166; Freudian theory, 10, 91; in *Pericles*, 10, 59, 146–47, 166; statistical profiles of, 10, 172 n. 34. *See also* fathers: incestuous tendencies of

individualism, 4, 29–30, 35, 101, 107, 138

individuation, 3, 41, 134, 146; in men, 4, 6–7, 143, 161, 170; in women, 14, 77, 123, 170

integrity, crisis of, 5; fathers' anxiety in, 40–42, 64–65, 71–72; wisdom of, 74, 143, 161–64

intimacy, crisis of, 5, 96; adjustment problems in, 11, 13, 72–74, 76–77, 108, 140, 150. *See also* love: romantic

Isabella, 107

James I (king of England), 32

Jaques, 3, 122

Jessica, 101–4; defiance by, 4, 6, 12, 49, 55, 96, 102–4; motivated by Christianity, 81, 102–3

Jiji, Vera, 129

John XXII, Pope, 10

Johnson, Virginia, 11

Jonson, Ben, 17

Jorgensen, Paul, 107

Julia, 62, 96, 99, 117–18, 129

Juliet, 50–51, 60–61, 99–100; as Romeo's anima, 7, 168; as Capulet's child, 26, 27, 50–51; courage of, 47, 81, 100; awakened by love, 99–100, 122

Jung, Carl Gustav: on alchemy, 3, 134, 146; on feminine development, 1, 4, 11, 13, 123, 144, 170; on masculine development, 1, 4, 8, 144, 151–52, 170; on possessive fathers, 8, 11, 54, 166; on violence in society, 170. *See also* anima; animus; individuation; shadow

Juventas Pater Uxor, 38

Kahn, Coppelia, 2, 111, 150, 161

Katharina, 108–14; defiance by, 96, 110, 165; sibling rivalry of, 110–11; frustration of, 110–12; wit of, 112–14

Katharine of Aragon (queen of England), 20, 30

Kemble, Fanny, 89

Kent, 22, 72, 75

Kiernan, V.G., 39

King Lear, 63–75, 104–8; developmental crisis in, 2, 6–7, 14, 64–67, 72–75, 120, 163; neurotic love in, 12, 22, 51, 61, 63–75, 165–66; affirmation in, 41, 65, 75; criticism on, 65, 69, 72–73. *See also* Lear

Kirsch, Arthur, 88

Knight, G. Wilson, 88, 148, 160–61

Knox, John, 3, 18

Kott, Jan, 88

Lady Macbeth, 106, 168

Laertes, 77–79

Laing, R.D., 80

Lear, 63–75, 104–8; egocentricity of, 7, 9, 51, 55, 64, 68, 72, 166; infantilism of, 7–8, 64–68, 71–73, 104–5; grief of, at daughters' betrayal, 15, 69, 71; as reactionary father, 22, 63–64; possessiveness of, 63–75, 147–48, 165; as mercenary father, 64, 66–69; jealousy of, 64, 69–71; faces death, 64–68, 73–75, 163; final affirmation of, 65, 75; seeks reassurance, 65–67, 69, 107; incestuous tendencies of, 67, 74–75, 166; madness of, 73–74, 109

"Lear complex," 43

Leicester, Earl of (Robert Dudley), 3

Leininger, Lorie Jerrell, 159

Leonato, 42–43, 55, 85, 87; identification with daughter, 8, 55, 72, 166; grief at Hero's dishonor, 15, 42–43, 55; arranges daughter's marriage, 25, 127–28

Leontes, 150–53; misogyny of, 7, 152–53; regeneration of, 59, 146, 153, 161; jealousy of, 150–52, 154–55

Levinson, Daniel, 2, 4, 6

Lloid, Lodowik, 30

Lorenzo, 63, 103, 133

Louis XII (king of France), 35

love: possessive, 2, 5–9, 10–11, 42–58, 60–62, 63–75, 165–66; romantic, 3, 7, 26, 34, 35–36, 38–39, 58, 62, 81, 83, 96–101, 118, 121–22, 126–27, 131–32, 135, 159–60, 164, 165, 166, 169; nurturing, 7, 153, 158, 161–62, 167, 169–70; as filial duty, 16, 44–45; sexual, 26, 33–34, 126–27, 150; conjugal, 33–36, 38–39, 135, 160, 165; as divine mystery, 34, 39, 101, 131; as harmonizing force, 38–39, 81, 103–4, 107, 123, 135, 157, 167, 170; as appetite, 53–54, 79–83, 104–6, 131, 141, 151–52; as personal growth, 62–63, 96–97, 99–100, 121–23, 126–27, 130–32, 135, 159–61, 165, 167; as idolatry, 125, 127, 137–40; neoplatonic, 131–32. *See also* friendship; marriage: personal choice in

love melancholy, 26, 53, 81–83, 125–26

Love's Labour's Lost, 118

Lucas, F.L., 69

Lucentio, 109–10

Luther, Martin, 34

Lychorida, 148

Lyly, John, 38

Lysander, 57–58, 62–63, 98–99; as threat to Egeus, 43, 49–50, 58, 166–67; loved by Hermia, 57–58, 62–63, 97–98, 166–67

Macbeth, 168

Macbeth, 106, 157, 168

McElroy, Bernard, 89

MacKenzie, Agnes Mure, 102

Macready, William Charles, 89

Mariana, 19, 137, 141–42

Marina, 59, 144, 146–47, 149, 152, 170

Markham, Gervase, 18, 20

marriage, 17–21, 24–29, 32–38, 40–41; companionship in, 2, 32–34, 38–39, 100–101; rituals, 2, 25, 41, 59–60, 67, 133, 135; traditional, 13, 17–20, 24, 25, 28, 33, 85, 90–95, 98, 113, 165; dowry and jointure, 26, 36–37, 60, 135; personal choice in, 27–28, 35, 38–39, 46, 97–101, 122, 165, 169; child, 28–29, 34; forced, 28, 34, 42–43,

58, 141, 166, 186 n. 73; as partnership, 32–34, 37–39, 100–101, 110, 112–14, 119, 121, 123, 126–27, 132, 135, 150, 156, 165; love as divine mystery in, 34, 101; laws, 36–37, 48, 58, 122, 186 n. 73; secret, 36–37, 46–47, 110; as rite of passage, 40–41, 60. *See also* Puritans; spousals

Mary I (queen of England), 30

Mary Tudor (sister of Henry VIII), 35

Masters, William H., 11

Measure for Measure, 19, 107, 137, 141–42

men: suspicious of women, 7, 78, 81, 86, 88, 135, 144–45, 147, 153–54, 167–69; violence of, 7, 80, 93–95, 111, 123, 128, 134, 144, 152, 154–56, 167–69; tragic, 87–95, 115, 151, 153–54, 157, 165–69. *See also* fathers; misogyny; psychology

Merchant of Venice, The, 102–4, 129–35; mercenary values in, 12, 49, 103, 130–31; personal growth in, 62–63, 111–12, 116–17, 124, 129–32, 135, 140, 165; humanistic values in, 81, 103–4, 116, 130–35, 169–70; criticism on, 102–3, 129–31, 134. *See also* Portia; Shylock

Mercutio, 168

Merry Devil of Edmonton, The (Drayton), 38

Merry Wives of Windsor, The, 96, 101, 165

Midas (Lyly), 38

middle life. *See* generativity; integrity

Midsummer Night's Dream, A, 48–49, 56–58, 97–99; young love in, 6, 39, 56–58, 62, 96–100; paternal domination in, 24, 25, 48–51, 58, 165–66; friendship in, 81, 118–19. *See also* Egeus

Milton, John, 33, 97, 101

Miranda, 158–62; as anima figure, 7, 144, 158, 162; love for Ferdinand, 140, 159–61; redeems Prospero, 146, 158, 161, 170

misogyny, 7, 144–46, 152–55, 167–68, 179 n. 34

More, Margaret (Roper), 30

More, Sir Thomas, 30

Morocco, prince of, 130–31

Much Ado About Nothing, 55, 84–87, 127–29; courtship in, 25, 27, 84–87, 118, 127–29, 140; male perception of women in, 42–43, 55, 84–87, 128, 166–68; criticism on, 84, 87, 128–29. *See also* Beatrice; Hero

Navarre, King of, 118

Neely, Carol Thomas, 89

Nerissa, 81, 130, 133, 135

Nurse (*Romeo and Juliet*), 100

obedience, 16, 44–45, 47, 62. *See also* children; daughters; women

Oliver, 39, 123

Olivia, 13, 122–25

Ophelia, 52–54, 76–84; criticism on, 2, 76–77, 80, 83; role confusion of, 11, 13, 61, 77, 80–84, 95; madness of, 12, 77–78, 83–84, 167; passivity of, 14, 80, 83, 90, 109, 116, 160, 165, 168; intelligence of, 77, 79; love for Hamlet, 77–83, 96; on the stage, 77, 116

Orlando, 37, 39, 62–63, 119–23

Orsino, 124–26, 137

Othello, 87–95, 167–69; misogyny of, 7, 145, 167–68; courtship and elopement of, 44, 49, 57, 88–91, 99; jealousy of, 79–80, 94, 145, 151, 154; violence of, 93, 95, 168–69

Othello, 56–58, 87–95, 167–69; violence in, 7, 95, 154, 167–69; male perception of women in, 42, 44–46, 49, 56–58, 61, 76, 78–79, 88, 94–95, 145, 167–69; criticism on, 88–89, 91; on the stage, 89, 116. *See also* Brabantio; Desdemona

Page, Ann, 96, 101, 165

Paris (*Romeo and Juliet*), 50–51, 100

Parolles, 141

patriarchy, 5–6, 40, 81, 96, 134; domination of women by, 6, 11–12, 76–78, 80, 87, 95, 109, 112, 114, 142, 145, 165, 167; values of, 54, 89, 107, 123, 134, 142, 145, 167–69

Paulina, 152–53

Pembroke, Countess of (Mary Sidney), 17, 24, 30

Perdita, 144, 146, 152–53, 170

Pericles, 7, 59, 146–50, 161, 170

Pericles, 146–50; fear of women in, 7, 147–49; incest in, 10, 59, 146–47, 166; personal growth in, 59, 147, 149–50, 152, 170. *See also* Marina; Simonides

Petrarch (Francesco Petrarca), 7, 138, 143

Petruchio, 35, 110–14

Phoebe, 122, 124, 137

Piaget, Jean, 3

Pitt, Angela, 2, 128, 134

Plato, 30–31

Platter, Thomas, 31

Plutarch, 9, 25

Polixines, 150–51, 153

Polonius, 52–54, 78–83; as authoritarian personality, 6, 12, 48; economic motives of, 9, 52–54, 166; as manipulator, 52–54, 61

Portia, 115–17, 129–35; androgyny of, 14, 115–17, 129, 132–35, 144, 169–70; wisdom of, 31, 81, 103, 134–35; as fatherless daughter, 116–17, 124; and her father's will, 129–30; in the casket scene, 130–32; plays the male role, 132–35, 137; as doctor of law, 133–35, 137; and the ring trick, 135

Posthumus Leonatus, 153–56; relationship with Cymbeline, 43, 46, 63, 100; regeneration of, 101, 146, 155–56; misogyny of, 145, 154–55; jealousy of, 153–55, 168–69

Powell, Chilton Latham, 38

Pricke, Robert, 21, 30, 101

Prospero, 157–63; integration of, 7, 146, 158, 161–63; loving release of Miranda by, 15, 56, 161, 165, 167, 170; wisdom of, 15, 157–58, 161–63, 170; imbalance of, 56, 157–58, 161–62; as *senex iratus*, 140; regeneration of, 158, 161–62, 167; confrontation with death by, 162–63

Proteus, 62, 99, 117–18

Prothalamion, The (Spenser), 36

psychology: developmental, 2–9, 11–15, 41–42, 72–75, 77, 90, 96–97, 107–8, 119–20, 128, 134, 136, 140–41, 144, 147, 150, 153, 155–57, 161–63, 164–70, 178 n. 10, 184 nn. 6, 21, 187 n. 24, 188 n. 46; of men, 6–11, 42–44, 54–56, 58–59, 64–66, 69, 111, 116, 118, 125–28, 139–41, 144–45, 147, 149–57, 159–63, 166–70, 187 n. 24, 188 n. 46; of women, 11–14, 16, 19, 77, 80, 83–84, 87, 90–91, 94–95, 105, 109–12, 116–17, 119–20, 124–25, 127–28, 136, 138, 142, 164–65, 167, 169–70, 183 n. 38, 184 n. 6. *See also* love: as personal growth

Puritans: on personal choice in marriage, 29, 98; on conjugal love, 34, 39, 101, 165; on marriage as partnership, 34, 37–38

Quiller-Couch, Sir Arthur, 102, 130

Rackin, Phyllis, 106

Regan, 104–6; defiant revenge of, 6, 55, 96, 102, 168; flattery of, 22, 66–68, 104; sibling rivalry of, 65, 105, 107; sadism of, 104–6

Reid, Stephen, 105

Representing Shakespeare (Schwartz and Kahn), 2

Reynaldo, 52

Ribner, Irving, 88

Rich, Lady Penelope (Devereux), 31

Richmond, Hugh, 139

rites of passage, 41, 63. *See also* marriage

Romeo, 7, 23, 27, 81, 100, 168

Romeo and Juliet, 50–51, 99–100; young love in, 7, 38, 99–100, 122; paternal love in, 26, 50–51, 56, 148; marriage ritual in, 60–61. *See also* Capulet; Juliet; Romeo

Rosalind, 115–17, 119–23; balance of, 14, 122–23, 124; as Ganymede, 37, 117, 121–23; friendship with Celia, 39, 103, 119–22; love for Orlando, 39, 62–63, 119–23, 165; androgyny of, 115–17, 123, 129, 135, 144, 169–70; relationship with father, 117, 119, 167; links father and husband, 119–20

Rymer, Thomas, 88

Sachs, Hans, 144

"Satyre III (On Religion)" (Donne), 4

Scholemaster, The (Ascham), 30

Seasons of a Man's Life, The (Levinson), 4

Sebastian (*The Tempest*), 162

Sebastian (*Twelfth Night*), 124–25

senex iratus: domineering father as, 8, 14, 62–63, 97, 130; wise father as, 62, 140, 148, 159

sex roles: changing, 2, 129, 137–39; polarized, 17, 76–80, 84–87, 89–95, 109, 116, 165, 167–69; reversed, 125, 137–39. *See also* androgyny; gender stereotypes

Sexton, Joyce, 87

shadow, 7, 151, 162

Shakespeare, Judith (Quiney), 144

Shakespeare, Susanna (Hall), 30, 144

Shakespeare, William: midlife crisis of, 4; career of, 17; as a feminist, 115; androgyny of, 116; relationship with daughters, 143–44, 179 n. 35

Shaw, George Bernard, 136

Shoemakers' Holiday, The (Dekker), 38

Shylock, 55, 102–3, 134; mercenary motives of, 12, 49, 63; grief at daughter's betrayal, 15, 49, 103; identification with daughter, 55, 72, 166

Sidney, Lady Barbara (Gamage), 31

Sidney, Mary. *See* Pembroke, Countess of

Sidney, Sir Philip, 17, 24

Silvia, 49, 62–63, 96, 99, 117–18

Silvius, 123, 125, 137

Simonides, 147–48, 159, 164

Skura, Meredith, 155

Slandered Woman in Shakespeare, The (Sexton), 87

Smith, Henrie, 17, 25, 33

Spencer, Hazelton, 139

Spenser, Edmund, 36, 116, 138
spousals, 36–37, 48, 60, 122, 132
Stephano, 157
Stockwood, John, 21, 24–28, 35, 42
Stoll, E.E., 28
Stone, Lawrence, 28, 37–38
Stubbes, Phillip, 28–29, 31–32
Suffolk, Duke of (Charles Brandon), 36
Sullivan, Harry Stack, 9, 13
Sundelson, David, 2

Taming of the Shrew, The, 108–14; comic
  irony in, 23, 108–9, 114; traditional femi-
  nine behavior in, 109–10; rejection of con-
  vention in, 110–14, 165. *See also* Baptista
  Minola; Petruchio
Tempest, The, 157–63; personal growth in, 7,
  15, 56, 146, 150, 157–63; paternal love in,
  15, 56, 140, 158–61; young love in, 140,
  158–60. *See also* Miranda; Prospero
Terry, Ellen, 89
Thaisa, 59, 146–49
theatre, 29, 31, 37–39, 41
Theobald, Lewis, 119
theophany, 146, 149–50, 156
Theseus, 25, 63, 81, 97–98, 167
Thurio, 43
Tiger, Lionel, 10
Tillyard, E.M.W., 150–51
Timon of Athens, 145
Touchstone, 122
Traherne, Thomas, 3
Tranio, 109–10
trial by ordeal, 14, 43, 129–30, 148, 159–60;
  strengthens young love, 39, 62–63, 97–
  99, 121, 130–32, 140, 148, 159–60
Trinculo, 157
Tutin, Dorothy, 124
Twelfth Night, 124–27; androgyny in, 14,
  116–17, 124, 126–27; melancholy in, 124–
  26; friendship in, 125–27, 165. *See also*
  Olivia; Orsino; Viola
Two Gentlemen of Verona, 62–63, 117–18;
  courtship in, 35, 43, 62–63, 99, 117–18;
  paternal domination in, 49, 51; friendship
  in, 62, 99, 117–18
Tybalt, 50, 168
Tyndale, William, 33

"Valediction, Forbidding Mourning, A"
  (Donne), 36, 131
Valentine, 35, 43, 51, 62–63, 99, 118
Van Meteran, Emanuel, 31
Viola, 115–17, 124–27; androgyny of, 14, 115–
  17, 124, 129, 165; as fatherless daughter,
  116–17, 124; as Cesario, 117, 124–26, 137;
  effect on Olivia, 124–26; effect on Orsino,
  124–27; empathy of, 124, 126; links father
  and husband, 124
violence, 167–70. *See also* men; women
virginity, 20, 78, 86, 152. *See also* chastity
Virgin Mary, 145–46, 153
Vives, Juan Luis, 16, 26, 27, 58, 85, 90
Volumnia, 106, 168

Warwick, Lady Ann (Dudley), 31
Whately, William, 33
Winter's Tale, The, 7, 59, 146, 148–55, 161,
  170
Woman's Part, The (Lenz, Greene, and
  Neely), 2
women, 4–6, 11–14, 16–21, 23–27, 30–35;
  passivity of, 13, 18, 20, 76–95, 98–99,
  164–65, 167; obedience of, 16, 18–19, 20,
  39, 44–45, 76, 80, 84–85, 87, 90, 92, 94,
  98–100, 132, 136, 165; patience of, 16, 20,
  93–94, 99; silence of, 16, 20, 27, 84–87,
  95, 98, 110; as wives, 17–20, 31–36, 38–
  39, 90–95, 99, 113–14, 123, 132–33, 135,
  141–42, 150–52, 154, 156; traditional role
  of, 17–28, 76–80, 84–87, 89–95, 98–99,
  109–10, 121, 169; modesty of, 20, 24, 76,
  85, 92, 109, 121, 136; as property, 22, 29–
  30, 49–53, 79, 85, 98, 113, 150, 154, 165–
  66, 168–69, 176 n. 11; and conscience, 30,
  47, 98, 101, 165, 169; emancipation of,
  30–32; in men's clothes, 31–32, 37, 101,
  103, 116–18, 121–26, 129, 133–35, 137, 144,
  168; in public theatres, 31, 175 n. 51; as
  shrews, 32, 108–13, 121, 127; assertiveness
  of, 32–33, 114; victimized, 76–95,
  116, 121, 142, 148, 150–52, 165, 167–69;
  violent, 104–6, 168; tragic, 106, 120, 168;
  as redeemers, 115, 141–42, 146, 152–53,
  156–57; pregnancy of, 142, 148, 151, 169.
  See also chastity; daughters; marriage; psychology